Managing People at Work

John Hunt is Plowden Professor of Human Relations at the London Business School. His previous work experience has been varied and has included jobs with the UK Ministry of Education, with Peter Jones, the London department store, and management consultancy experience in America, Asia, Australia, and the UK. Before joining the academic world he was Director of Management Studies with the Australian Institute of Management. His career has since taken him to the University of New South Wales and Carnegie-Mellon University, Pittsburgh. Most recently he was Professor of Management at Macquarie University, Sydney, Visiting Professor at the London Business School and Visiting Professor of Organizational Behaviour at the Centre d'Etudes Industrielles, Geneva.

John Hunt

Managing People at Work

A manager's guide to behaviour in organizations

Pan Books London, Sydney and Auckland

First published 1979 by McGraw-Hill Book Company (UK) Ltd
This edition published 1981 by Pan Books Ltd,
Cavaye Place, London SW10 9PG
19 18 17 16 15 14 13 12 11
© McGraw-Hill Book Company (UK) Ltd 1979
ISBN 0 330 26259 9
Printed and bound in Great Britain by
Cox & Wyman Ltd, Reading

Contents

Preface

My prime objective in writing this book was to provide a summary of my ideas on the major subject areas of organizational behaviour – motivation, perception, communication, groups, roles, power, organizations, structures, managers, leaders, participation, and change. Second, I wanted to distil from a vast literature on the subject those theories or models which have endured because they seemed to be useful to managers. That distilling comes from over ten years of teaching managers on executive programmes and from being concerned that so many had not been given the behavioural tools to manage.

I have not attempted a theoretical or research summary of other people's work, as there are numerous books available for that purpose. I wanted to clarify, not confuse. Moreover, I have presented a summary in my earlier book, *The Restless Organisation*.

My third objective was to present the material in a form which made it easy to read, especially for practising managers. For this reason I have left out referencing and tried to control my use of academic jargon. References are given at the end of chapters, but only as guides for further reading.

My fourth objective was to publish in a readable form some results of my own research, and especially conclusions drawn from consulting experiences. Where I have done this I have endeavoured to link that research into the practical world of managers. In some cases my arguments are based on extensive research data. In other cases I suggest conclusions on the basis of having seen the phenomenon so often that I believe it to be true.

My fifth objective was to provide a book which might find its way into applied courses in institutes, colleges, and universities, but was more likely to find use in management development programmes of government and business organizations. It is in many of these programmes that the really first-class training of managers is done. What seemed to be lacking was a book which did not involve the practising manager in a whole range of academic theories and arguments. His job in complex organizations is difficult enough without inflicting on him academic controversies.

It is important to me and would be useful for the reader if, when reading this book, these objectives were kept in mind. This book was not designed for my academic friends – although I hope some of them will read it and get excited or angry with it. For some readers I will have been too prescriptive and too willing to classify, but I believe that if the behavioural sciences are to be useful to the manager then prescriptions, classifications, and models are what he desperately wants. If we, the academics, have something useful for him, then I think we should let him have it straight so that he can get on with the job of managing.

Because of the objectives I set myself, I found this book difficult to write. Difficult in the sense of knowing where to establish the level of discourse, because I wanted to free managers for a further deluge of expert advice by talking to them in their language about situations they confronted.

Over the past five years of writing, many people have helped me keep my feet on the organizational ground. In Australia, Robert Spillane, Roger Collins, Georgie McNamara, Peter Saul, Murray Ainsworth, and Bob Clark reviewed most chapters and made very useful suggestions. At the London Business School, where the book was finished in 1978 and 1979, David Chambers provided me with superb conditions for writing and many of my colleagues, especially Denis Pym, Will McQuillan, Jean Millar, Eric Walton, and Dennis Bumstead either reviewed chapters or willingly debated issues of organizational behaviour. My Canadian friend Cam Mackie, on study leave in London, read much of the manuscript and reminded me, in numerous discussions, to write for the public sector. Diana Jackson, Joan Bloomfield, and Eileen Field in Sydney, and Carmel Gradenwitz and Kay Schraer in London tolerated my changing views and retyped chapters with enthusiasm.

To all these people I am particularly grateful. But to the thousands of managers with whom I have spoken on three continents I am hopeful that they found our discussions as stimulating as I did. This book was written for them. If it clarifies the world of work for managers than I will be delighted.

John W. Hunt
London 1979

1 Individuals and organizations (I)

This chapter discusses influences on the behaviour of individuals at work. It concentrates, as far as it is possible to isolate them, on *personal* influences, in particular *abilities* and *motives*. Subsequent chapters examine the influence of other people, groups, structure, technology, and bosses.

Why do people behave the way they do in organizations? Why do some work so very hard, while others appear to do the minimum required? Why do some like structured jobs, while others like freedom and autonomy? Why do some seem satisfied, while others appear to be unhappy in their jobs? Why are some money-hungry, while others are almost unaffected by monetary rewards? Why do some like to work on their own? Why do some seek power and status, while others like to follow their leaders?

The factors or variables which affect behaviour in organizations fall into three broad groups: first, there are *individual* variables – age, sex, educational level, experience, goals, perceptions, motives, abilities, values, etc.; second, there are the *organizational* or situational variables – structure, jobs, technologies, roles, markets, work groups, etc.; and third, there are the *outcomes* of putting individuals into situations in organizations – productivity, satisfaction, love, hate, power, alienation, identification, market share, etc.

This chapter concentrates on individual variables affecting people's performance in organizations. Employers collect a great deal of data on individual variables – because they have found that a particular combination of these biographic variables and experience is more likely to match an individual with a specific job. And in the absence of any other data we all develop commonsense theories about selecting people for jobs. Through trial and error we establish stereotypes of what is wanted for a job. Before long, stereotypes of biographic data become 'types' and 'personalities' and, while it is easy to criticize the commonsense theories of selectors, the behavioural sciences have so far provided little scientific evidence to lift common sense onto an objective plane.

The first really scientific attempts to predict performance in organizations concentrated on abilities and aptitudes. Selectors of new employees added information from ability and aptitude tests to their commonsense stereotypes. However, the improvement in matching recruit with job was marginal for most jobs. The reader who is interested in a more detailed discussion of abilities than follows here will find suggestions for further reading at the end of this chapter.

More recently, another variable of individual performance – motives – has attracted attention. Common sense told us decades ago that motives were important for predicting behaviour, but common sense does not always dictate research, and there has been an abysmal lack of research on motives and particular jobs. The research that has been done (see Additional reading) suggests that motive is the most important variable in predicting behaviour in organizations. So, after a quick look at ability as a variable, chapters 1 and 2 move on to discuss motives and motivation.

Abilities

More research has been conducted on abilities than on any other individual variable. In schools, universities, and work organizations, abilities are measured religiously and predictions made from the results. Where the testing is not formalized, it is carried out unofficially by parents, teachers, relatives, and friends; and there is much to commend this analysis. Some children are undeniably better at maths than others; some are better at verbal exercises than others; some are better at running than others.

When the teenager applies for a job, data on his/her school record, and some further ability tests, may be used to assess the applicant's potential value to the employer. If the employer wants a clerk, then the information that he/she has perceptual speed and accuracy will be useful. Similarly, if the employer is seeking a journalist, it would be useful to have data on the applicant's verbal and writing skills.

However, the practice of jumping to conclusions based on ability tests is fraught with dangers. For example, even in predicting performance for manual work, manual *ability* has only a moderate correlation with *performance*. What is clear is that knowing something about a person's abilities gives only a glimpse of what to expect in career performance. Perhaps more anxious parents, concerned about their children's abilities, should be told the facts about performance at work – there is much more to performance than ability.

Abilities and aptitudes

There have been numerous attempts to isolate and measure abilities (believed to be inherited) and aptitudes (the capacity to learn and develop abilities). A major issue has been whether aptitudes or abilities are unitary or complex. Can we even talk about *an* ability and measure it separately?

The most frequently cited ability groups are:

- Reasoning ability
- Spatial-visual ability
- Perceptual speed and accuracy ability
- Manual ability

From these general groups a variety of additional categories have been identified:

- Reasoning
  verbal
  numerical
  abstract
- Spatial
  practical intelligence
  non-verbal ability
  creative ability
- Perceptual
  clerical ability
- Manual
  mechanical ability
  manual ability
  musical ability
  athletic ability

However, most of these subcategories are mixtures of ability, interest, and motives. For example, mechanical ability (or aptitude) is a complex of other aptitudes and characteristics. It

11

consists of spatial visualization, reasoning, and experience. Despite its complexity, it can be treated as a unit and measured reliably. Other complex aptitudes that can be measured in tests are:

- Musical aptitude
- Manual aptitude

Where one or more of these ability/aptitude categories is required in a job, it is useful to test for them, provided the test results are seen for what they are – a glimpse of possible performance.

Abilities and management

One of the most difficult tasks in organizations is selecting managers. One explanation for this is that the findings relating abilities to managerial performance have been exceedingly disappointing. It is true that correlations have been found between intelligence and managerial performance, but only for average and just above average intelligence. Well above, or well below, average intelligence does *not* correlate with good performance. So managers who perform well are average to slightly above average in intelligence, but not too intelligent or too unintelligent. Studies relating other ability groups to managerial performance have been quite inconclusive.

Somewhat embarrassed that the behavioural scientists had not found useful information for those selecting managers, we investigated other ability/aptitude combinations. The belief has long been popular among academics and senior executives that managers can 'conceptualize', see 'the big picture', 'integrate the parts'. A capacity related to this skill has been called *field independence* or, by some management writers, the 'helicopter aptitude'. This is a complex cognitive spatial-visual ability which involves different ways of looking at situations. In 1974, we conducted a study which established a link between field independence and managerial performance in a drug company. Similar studies have been reported elsewhere.

Field independence is characterized by conceptual skills, isolation of essential issues in a problem, and independence from the problem. At the other end of the continuum, field dependence is characterized by poor conceptual skills, inability to isolate issues, and dependence on the situation.

Other researchers have found that field independence reaches a peak at about fifteen years of age, remains on a plateau until the mid thirties, and thereafter declines, as both men and women become more field dependent. This may mean that the best managers are aged between fifteen and thirty-five years! More realistically, it may mean we need some young managers among the older ones to get the best of experience and independence.

In our research, measuring this aptitude has presented a problem. So far, the tests used have not been able to separate average from really effective managers. Nevertheless, perhaps the old managerial expressions like 'seat of the pants management', 'play it by ear', 'rule of thumb', and 'common sense', were successful *if* the manager perceived problems from an independent position. Conversely, disasters could have been partly the result of these techniques used by field dependent people.

This research suggests that there *are* management abilities or aptitudes, but that so far we have been testing the wrong ones. As management is primarily an interpersonal activity, we should concentrate on perceptual aptitudes, rather than other abilities.

Motives, which do affect interpersonal skills, have provided much more useful data in identifying managerial talent. However, we have become so obsessed with abilities that selectors are reluctant to leave them or their commonsense theories – whether those selectors are in work organizations, universities, or colleges. Further, we became so obsessed with academic performance, intelligence, and reasoning ability, that we ignored the search for manual, mechanical, and musical aptitude. We are now paying the price for our obsession.

In summary, abilities/aptitudes *do* affect performance. Where possible, data on abilities and aptitudes should be available for predicting performance. However, that data should be viewed as an indication of *potential*. Whether or not potential is realized is primarily the result of the individual's motives and goals. Not surprisingly, research on motives and motivation has superseded research on abilities in our more recent attempts to predict behaviour.

Motives

There is a multitude of psychological theories about what motivates man. Is the force inside man, outside man, conditioned or not conditioned, goal directed or not goal directed? These are all very controversial issues in academic research into what gets people to want to work. Most people in organizations are not concerned with academic controversies and rely on their commonsense view of behaviour.

The simplest motivation theory suggests that man is motivated by a series of needs or motives. This theory argues that some of the motives are inherited and some learnt: that some are primarily physiological, while others are primarily psychological. Other theories deny the existence of needs or motives. Therefore, at one extreme the behaviourists argue that behaviour is a series of learned responses to stimuli, and at the other extreme systems theorists talk about all systems – individuals, groups, and organizations – having needs.

Motivation can be either a conscious or an unconscious process: the allocation of time and energy to work in return for rewards. Both internal and external stimuli lead to action. Internalized values, hopes, expectations, and goals affect the decision process of the individual, and thereby affect the resultant behaviour. Motivation is not an 'engine' built inside an individual – as so many training managers believe. It is the individual responding to a whole range of experiences, and responding as a totality, not as 'a need'. If we are threatened by physical force, the stimulus for activity is external. If the hormone secretions in our bodies operate effectively then we will wish to behave in physically satisfying ways. In both examples, some of the force is inside the individual, while some of the stimulus is external. How the individual will respond, how much energy he will expend, and how important are the consequences (rewards) are all factors which moderate his motivation.

There have been many attempts to classify personal moderators in the decision process. The most popular construct is the *need*, and categories of needs (e.g., body needs, safety needs, social needs, achievement needs) dominate the literature. *Goal* categories, remarkably like need categories, are also popular (e.g., money, status, power, friendship). *Satisfaction* theories are a variation of goal theories, but have produced even more controversial classifications (e.g., implicit and explicit rewards).

There is no space here to go into what is primarily an academic debate on theories of behaviour. I will contend that people are motivated to realize the outcome of ends or goals. Where I use the term 'need', I do so in the sense of ends or goals desired by the individual. I have difficulty in accepting a 'need' as a personality construct. However, desiring or wanting an outcome does reveal something about a person, and 'need' can be used to refer to that wanting. To many psychologists this view will be heresy, but I doubt if managers care what the energy force is called (need, want, goal, etc.).

Organizational psychologists adopt hierarchies of goals or needs, along the lines suggested by Maslow, McClelland, Ghiselli, and Likert. Maslow's need classifications are the most extensively used, mainly because they seem to fit organizations rather than because they have been empirically verified. We have little data to support the concept of a hierarchy of needs in which lower order needs are satisfied before higher (hierarchically) order needs. However, while need hierarchies may be difficult to accept, there is a great deal of data on the relevance of these needs or ends or goals for individuals working in organizations, and it is these data which are of value to managers.

The managers' dilemma is that, while they must accept the individual differences that exist among their staff, organizational (and particularly personnel) practices assume that such differences do not exist. The field of organization theory has been – and still is – plagued by the conflict between the individual and the organization. As the orientation of this book is towards organizations, it is important to deal with sameness or similarities between people, while acknowledging differences within groups.

Need categories

The five categories of ends or needs suggested below were developed from the views of several motivation theorists. They are the needs for:

- Physiological balance

- Safety, security, structure
- Relationships, love, identification
- Confidence, recognition, power, esteem
- Self-fulfilment, autonomy, creativity

Some of these goals or ends will be suppressed while others are pursued. If I am hungry, one of my physiological needs (food) is important, and I may become preoccupied with satisfying it. When a need (or goal or choice) becomes important, in response to external or internal stimuli, it produces in the individual strong internal pressures to achieve ends. It is the activity which results from this stimulus which makes people comment: 'He is a highly motivated person'. What people are saying is that the decision process of motivation has released a great deal of effort.

If the need remains important (is not satisfied) then we might see increasing concern in the individual, as he or she attempts to find alternative ways to satisfy that need. In the longer term, frustration of the need may lead to psychological and/or physiological disorders.

Let us examine each of the need categories in turn.

Physiological balance
The most basic and primitive of man's goals, this category includes the needs (or drives) for food, liquid, shelter, sex, sleep, oxygen, etc. There are hundreds of possible ends in this group, and it is not very helpful to keep adding to the list, because it is difficult to separate and test some of the physiological needs.

These physiological needs are inherited, but we learn how to satisfy them. There are hundreds of body needs, yet our bodies are incredibly well tuned systems. Whenever they get out-of-tune we try to restore the equilibrium. If I am thirsty, then I know easily how to remedy the disequilibrium by drinking water. But in many cases we are not able to identify what the cause is, and we go from one possible satisfaction to another, using trial-and-error methods to achieve balance. Hence, we may see an individual in a kitchen eating sugar, then something savoury, then something cold, because his system is lacking a particular salt or vitamin. However, the individual is unable to identify specific salts or vitamins, so he continues to search for food. Eventually one of his choices will return his system to a state of equilibrium.

16

Equilibrium is short-lived. As one need or goal is satisfied, another in the same or a different category will become important to the individual. The motivation decision process continues, and we see an endless succession of activities (including rest or inactivity) during the individual's waking hours.

Work organizations have shown little concern for employees' physiological needs. The International Labour Organisation and government legislation have been the major initiators of concern. Canteens, changing rooms, toilet blocks, and air conditioning are all devices to make the satisfaction of physiological needs easier. But it is only recently that work organizations viewed their responsibility as being any more than supplying basic conditions for physiological safety. More recently, pollution control, job redesign to reduce fatigue, and medical checks have indicated a greater concern for the physiologies of employees. Unfortunately, many employees have not responded with a similar concern for their own physiologies.

Strong physiological needs are typically found in manual and process workers and in some physical fitness occupations. Men and women appear to have similar body needs; what differences there are seem to be determined culturally rather than genetically.

In interviewing people for jobs, it is difficult (without tests) to assess body needs. Clues can come from sporting interests, manual interests, etc. People who have strong career goals (high achievers in an organizational sense), are not likely to play team sports, preferring golf, running, swimming, or squash. People for whom career is less important (lower achievers) are more likely to watch others play sport, even though their concern *for* their bodies is high; and their sexual experiences occur younger and, subsequently, more frequently. High achievers report less physical illness and spend less time discussing their illnesses. Conversely, the incidence of nearly every illness (including heart conditions) is higher at the bottom of the organizational hierarchy.

Safety, security and structure needs
Safety and physiological needs are so interwoven that it is difficult to separate them – and indeed, some researchers will not try. Here, 'safety' means the search for security, predictability, order, and, in organizations, for structure.

As safety needs are often so close to physiological needs, it is difficult to determine what is inherited and what is learnt. My research has revealed strong correlations between people with high needs for safety and structure and the following experiences:

- Unpredictable home life as a child
- Being the first child in the family
- An over-anxious mother/father
- Physical punishment in the home
- Rejection as a method of disciplining the child (e.g. 'If you don't like it here you can go and live somewhere else', or: 'Pack your case – we will not have you living here any more.')
- Complications at the birth of the child, or during the pregnancy
- Direct or indirect experience of the 'thirties depression
- Direct or indirect experience of the Second World War

Organizational controls have traditionally used 'safety' to control the behaviour of employees. If employees deviated from the required behaviour patterns, they were threatened with the sack (insecurity), isolation (insecurity), or promotional restrictions (failure and insecurity). This system has persisted for centuries. Even the Church threatened its members with the ultimate insecurity: damnation or purgatory.

My research has led me to believe that, although the strength of needs varies during our lifetime, if the child-rearing practices of a society are such that people develop very high preferences for security, then highly structured organizations with authoritarian management are the result. Conversely, when a generation evolves which has not been brought up on fear, or when fear is no longer an effective control, then highly authoritarian structures are less successful. Security appears to be one of the most stable of goals and is clearly related to childhood experiences.

A generation with less interest in safety, possibly the first in man's history, emerged after the Second World War. They were not thrashed at home (Spock helped here), they were the generation which saw the end of child-bashing in schools, the generation who were economically secure and well fed. Consequently, the age group under 30 years of age has significantly lower security needs than the age group 35 to 55 years of age; their elders are more concerned with preserving the current structure than with changing it. It is probably too simplistic to attach only child-rearing practices to this change. In addition, it is true that as people reach middle age, they become more concerned about security. I am less concerned about why the younger generation has emerged as it has than I am with the impact this group is having on organizations.

Lower safety needs have already meant less fear in giving direct feedback to bosses, a greater demand for measures of effectiveness, and, in universities, a revision of the examining and governing systems. It has also meant challenging traditional 'sacred cows' and, if necessary, using violence to expose hypocrisy and pretension.

The impact this group will have on structure in organizations is difficult to predict, but the signs are there already (looser structures, freer behaviour controls on dress, hours of work, relationships with bosses, etc.). What is difficult to establish is how much of the pressure comes from this group and how much from other variables which have similar effects (e.g., turbulent markets, managerial decisions, government actions).

Safety needs are also important in selecting people for programmed tasks, for large organizations, and for process work. People with safety as a goal have greater acceptance of order, definition, controls, job descriptions, etc. The more structured the task, the more it requires someone who enjoys definition and clarity. Conversely, loosely structured organizations (advertising agencies and entrepreneural ventures) attract people with lower concerns for safety.

If you are interviewing people for jobs you should include questions to give you clues about the strength of security needs. Clues are:

- Childhood experiences
- Birth order
- Discipline at home
- The school background (including day or boarding, state or private)
- Geographic location

More recent, and therefore more reliable, clues are:

- Low job mobility rate
- Nature of previous jobs
- Nature of organization (large/small, structured/unstructured, etc.)

People seeking security as a prime goal will be concerned about:

- Salary
- Superannuation
- Safety controls
- Programmability of task
- Security of tenure and location

Interviews may also give facial and gestural clues about the security and confidence of the applicant.

Organizations which traditionally attract people searching for security are banks, insurance companies (administration), universities, churches, gaols, and public or civil service. Ironically, many people who are attracted to large, safe organizations spend much of their time playing the 'knocking game', criticizing the very structure that attracted them and satisfied their security goals. Risk organizations are usually much smaller, less protective, and attract people who place security low among their priorities.

Relationships, love, identification needs
Some American research suggests that the search for relationships is developed in the first few months of a child's life and is determined by the way the mother figure (it may, in fact, be Dad) holds and caresses the baby. Other reseachers argue that the desire for love and affection is inherited and that subsequent experiences merely reinforce (or do not reinforce) that need.

As all parents, even if only initially when feeding the child, give a degree of love and affection, the question of what is hereditary and what is environmental in determining these needs is impossible to separate. More important, the strength of the goal in different people is great and this alone has a considerable impact on organizations.

People with above-average needs for social interaction are attracted to certain sorts of jobs: a group situation, working for other people, nurturing, or helping others. What is interesting in our research findings is that many people in personnel management or the behavioural science professions (clinical psychology, psychiatry, etc.) do not rate love and affection as being high among their personal work goals. This is especially true of our studies of senior personnel managers. We have found *security* and *power* are more important to them at work than relationships.

Identifying the strength of relationship needs in interviewing people for jobs is relatively easy. People with high needs will spend most of their time in groups. Males are more likely to associate with mates at the pub, football or the club. The extreme case will spend each leisure hour in the company of his friends, will dislike being on his own, and will tell you that his mates are one of his greatest sources of satisfaction. In contrast, the very high achiever will spend time on his/her own, in an office, or at a hobby on his/her own, will prefer loner sports like golf, swimming, or jogging to team sports like football.

Girls with high needs for relationships are likely to leave school with the prime objective of establishing a permanent love relationship in marriage. They are more likely to have fewer but very close friends than their male counterpart and to persist with family relationships longer.

We have found the following childhood experiences correlate with, but do not explain, the strength of the love needs:

- Absence of love and affection as a child
- A belief that boys should not be kissed or hugged while girls should be (this belief appears to have been particularly strong in Anglo-Saxon cultures in the 'twenties and 'thirties)
- Sequence in the family – later children have stronger needs for affection than earlier children
- Family size

Some studies of organizations have shown that many people are more concerned with relationships than they are with their achievement, or power, or self-fulfilment (career goals). They represent some 60 per cent of the work force and, not unexpectedly, they tend to remain at the base of the hierarchy – with their friends. Contrary to many erroneous assumptions, many of these people do not seek the sorts of strong 'ego and self-actualization' experiences that the executive class seeks. They are not motivated by the same goals, and we should stop making assumptions about their ambitions, hopes, and even their needs.

21

Man has a long history of projecting his own goal profile onto every other man. But what is success? Who gets the best deal – the highly successful executive, locked into his office on his own, or the chap on the factory floor, working, playing, and drinking with his mates? Perhaps the experiences of the factory employee provide rewards which surveys of his satisfactions (based on the expectations of high-achieving, career oriented, industrial psychologists) do not mention. Certainly, surveys report more dissatisfaction at the factory floor level, but we should ask ourselves what this means among people who appear to be more concerned about physiological, safety, and relationships needs anyway.

As some 60 per cent of the work force is occupied in processing work, identifying the right sort of profile for that work is important. The most important characteristic of the process worker profile is the strength of his or her need for relationships. Yet in job interviews, most of the questions are about schooling, parents, etc., which may or may not give clues to the strength of these needs. In an age where we talk about involving employees through worker participation in decisions, or semi-autonomous work groups, or project teams, etc., the most important needs to identify are the relationships and esteem needs. With practice, it is easy to develop questions which give a fairly accurate indication of the strength of these needs.

For many years the armed services, and more recently some banks, have directed some of their advertising at the lower achiever with strong relationships goals and lower career needs (esteem, self-fulfilment). Advertising offers 'mateship', 'relationships', or suggests 'Come join the 14 000 under 25'. In much of this recruiting, there is no mention of satisfying esteem needs through promotion or hierarchy climbing – just the opportunity to establish strong interpersonal relationships with a peer group; and, providing the match of profile and job is a good one, the result may well be a satisfied employee. Conversely, much of the technology we employ totally shatters opportunities to relate with others. Drivers in trucks, assembly line operators, service mechanics, would find little excitement in their work if they were looking for relationships – they spend most of their work day on their own, either because of the task or the technology or both.

Confidence, power, recognition, esteem

There are two groups of ends within this category:

- Self-respect goals
  power, confidence, competence, independence
- Recognition goals
  prestige, recognition by others, status, reputation

The need for self-respect is related to the emergence of the *self* concept in child development. As so much of personal development is the result of what others say or imply about one, the need to believe in and to have others say that one is 'OK' is not an unexpected outcome of years and years of living with the recognition (or lack of it) of others.

The use of recognition as a reward occurs early in a child's development. 'If you eat your dinner then you may watch TV.' From the time the child can understand the reward system, desired behaviour patterns are reinforced with rewards or recognition.

When today's child begins school, he or she is confronted by a new and highly complex reward system which has almost replaced the punishment system of 20 years ago. This reward system reinforces desired behaviour but avoids the negative effects of physically punishing 'bad' behaviour. Instead, today's child is confronted by a myriad of gold, silver, blue, green, and red stars, all denoting instant rewards for performance. Possibly no previous generation has had such a positive reinforcement in the classroom.

For some children, the onset of school is particularly crushing. For the first time, the child is asked to recognize that he/she is not as clever as some friends. In the traditional education system, that child may have been classified as a slow learner, and rather than positive rewards, may have faced negative feedback and endless punishment. It is not difficult to understand why he/she may have not developed strong esteem needs and even rebelled against the unchangeable 'system'. Factors which I have found correlate with strong needs for self esteem, confidence, and power are:

- Socio-economic backgrounds of parents – middle and upper classes
- Use of rewards as opposed to punishments in the family

- High standards or expectations of the parents for their children's performance
- High status and power needs of parents
- Deprivation – lack of recognition at all

Most of the research has found power needs to be the best predictors of managerial success. That is, managers who need to have influence over other people are more successful than those who do not have this goal. However, in this fourth need category, power is only one of the goals. People with strong egos may have strong desires for power, recognition, esteem, and status. People with strong egos do move to the top of organizations, but only the need for power correlates with managerial success; needs for recognition and status do not.

Unfortunately, most managers of organizations have not been able to discriminate power from other esteem needs. Consequently, people with strong needs for esteem, recognition, or power move to the top of hierarchies. But while they may be found effective at lower level jobs (or they may be seen to be visible, and therefore effective) they may not be very effective when they get to the top. Those who are successful at the top rate power as their major goal; whether others recognize or like them is secondary.

Jobs attracting people with strong ego needs (for power, recognition, status, etc.) are the professions (medicine, law, theology, engineering), and the jobs of academics and teachers, politicians, actors, entertainers, sportsmen, policemen (and other uniformed people), shop stewards, union officials, etc. Some are attracted for the 'dressing up' and recognition that ensues. Others are more attracted for the 'influence' the job gives them over other people's lives. Whatever the reason, we need to accept that in any social group there will be positions of power, and rather than denouncing power as a goal, we should learn to understand it and give it to those best suited to using it. The mind trembles at the thought of the number of individuals whose decisions affect our very lives who did not want power or know how to use it, being primarily motivated by the ego-enhancing spoils and tributes of office.

One of the difficulties in this analysis has been to separate the esteem goals from each other. Organizations and societies make the separation more difficult simply by mixing power and recog-

needs to not make very good bosses. They [...]
much of their subordinates, do not explain er[...]
expect, are loners, avoid fraternizing, and a[...]

Our research has found people with high [...]
ment in creative work (film directors, writer[...]
research academics), or as top 'loner' sport[...]
lysts, financial analysts, consultants, entre[...]
directors or politicians. The most obvious clue is prefe[...]
working alone or in small groups, as distinct from preference
(found in those seeking power) for working with others and
influencing their behaviour.

Organizations only absorb a small number of people with very
strong goals for self-actualization, because of their search for
novelty and change, their intolerance of mistakes, their 'flighty'
shifts from one job to another, and their aversion to formal
controls. Yet they are the innovators, the creators. They are
easily bored once the goal is nearly reached – finishing off
projects, or correcting errors in written work, or working up
systems or programmes do not come within their idea of creative
experiences. Similarly, repetitive clerical work is often excru-
ciatingly boring for them.

The easiest way I have found to get some idea of the strength
of the fulfilment needs in an applicant is the *acid test of goal
clarity*: a single page of paper, and five minutes to write down
what the person wants to achieve in the next five years. The
very high achiever will have no problem in answering the question, and may fill both sides of the paper. The process worker
does not think in this goal-directed way. He has difficulty in
declaring what his goals are for the next six months, let alone
five years. In extreme cases, I have found process workers who
do not think further than ten minutes ahead. They do not segment time into past, present, future – time is now. These people
are often called 'lazy' by managers. They are not lazy; they just
do not think, in the North American manner, of goals and time
schedules. There are more important short-term events in their
lives, like mates, fun, and love. The result is that the supervisor
of the group has to reinforce the production goals every ten
minutes. In contrast, the very high achiever is never without a
goal, is usually chasing multiple goals, finds work and leisure
inseparable, may neglect his family and friends, and seems complete in his self-sufficiency. He needs no bosses to push him into

27

, is often insulted if he is given a goal, and becomes
additional structural controls over his work. He is the
poet, entrepreneur, research scientist, long-distance run-
. He is alone, and that may be the price of self-fulfilment,
.d the danger in our mania with goal-directed behaviour. We
may be producing a society of high achieving loners, for whom
interpersonal relationships are temporary and blatantly secondary in importance.

Summary

This chapter examines the influence of two characteristics of
individuals – abilities and motives.

Abilities have been used widely to predict behaviour in organizations. The reliability of these predictions has been variable; yet our obsession with testing abilities continues. For some
jobs, specific abilities do correlate with performance. For management and supervisory jobs, there have been conflicting studies about abilities and performance.

Much more reliable predictors of performance come from
studies of motivation. Motives, needs, and goals are terms used
loosely in this chapter to refer to desired ends of an individual.
Five groups of goals or needs were discussed – physiological;
security – safety – structure; relationships – love; power – recognition – esteem; and self-fulfilment.

Chapter 2 applies this motivation framework to different sorts
of jobs and different sorts of people and then goes on to discuss
the changes that occur over time in people's motives.

For additional reading

For all reading lists the place of publication (unless specified) is
the United Kingdom.

On abilities
Campbell J. P., M. D. Dunnette, E. E. Lawler, and K. E.
  Weick, *Managerial Behaviour Performance and Effectiveness*,
  McGraw-Hill, New York, 1970.
Super D. E., and J. O. Crites, *Appraising Vocational Fitness*,
  Harper & Row, New York, 1965.

On motivation

Gellerman S., *Motivation and Productivity*, AMA, New York, 1963.

Gobles F., *The Third Force*, Pocket, New York, 1971.

Handy C., *Understanding Organisations*, Penguin, 1976.

Herzberg F., *Work and the Nature of Man*, Staples Press, New York, 1968.

Hunt J. W., *The Restless Organisation*, Wiley, Sydney, 1972.

Ibbetson J. F., and D. Whitmore, *The Management of Motivation and Remuneration*, Business Books, 1977.

Jarvis W., *Wake Up and Live*, Nelson, Sydney, 1975.

McClelland D. C., and R. S. Steele, *Human Motivation – a Book of Readings*, General Learning Press, New Jersey, 1973.

Maslow A., *The Farther Reaches of Human Nature*, Penguin, 1971.

OECD, *Emerging Attitudes and Motivations of Workers*, Paris, 1972.

Vroom V., and E. Deci, *Motivation and Management*, Penguin, 1970.

2 Individuals and organizations (II)

The previous chapter developed a framework for analysing an individual's goals or needs or motives. This chapter looks at different patterns of needs as found in the occupants of different jobs. These patterns may or may not be constructs of personalities. Whether they occur because of the organization, the role one is given, and the expectations of others, *or* because of an individual's background and experience is difficult to tell. My research suggests that people with certain patterns of motives are attracted to certain jobs. Subsequently, the job and the expectations of others about that job reinforce the pattern.

Different motivation profiles

The goals (or ends or needs) of individuals vary throughout their lives, depending on experience, the strength of the needs, and the opportunities for satisfying them. Changes in profiles of needs are inevitable, if only because the physiologically based needs alter as the body gets older.

In addition to variations based on age, there are substantial differences between people of the same age. For example, an 18-year-old university student has a different pattern of needs from an 18-year-old apprentice. What would be of great value to school counsellors would be some data on the motivation profiles of students, rather than the mass of data available on abilities and school performance. Similarly, in selecting university students, it would be preferable to know how motivated they were to succeed rather than merely knowing their results in a university entrance examination. Ideally we need motivation profiles as well as ability and performance indications if we are to provide useful career counselling for school leavers.

Using a questionnaire which asks for comparative strengths of the five need categories, we have been able to develop different sorts of profiles for different professions and for different jobs. The test asks respondents to rank the importance of the five needs to them in terms of their work; it does not ask for their importance outside work. In structure, the questionnaire asks for points to be allocated across the five categories of needs discussed in chapter 1. Rankings vary, depending on age, the importance of the goal, and the degree to which that goal or end is being satisfied at the particular stage of the individual's life. There is no space here to show all profiles, but three will illustrate the differences between people in markedly different jobs. We cannot explain why these profiles emerge; we can only identify them in samples of different job categories.

Relative importance of need categories. Example 1
Figure 2.1 shows the profile (an average) of shop floor employees. Notice that the most important goals for this group of individuals are the physiological, safety, and love categories. The career needs (ego, achievement, self-fulfilment) are not as strong. This person will be found in predictable, safe jobs where there are few opportunities for variation or creativity, where the basic need satisfactions are guaranteed, and where there are strong informal friendship relationships. This is not the high achiever in a Western sense but, as I suggested earlier, this group of people have interpersonal rewards, such as friendship, social support, and love. By placing these individuals in repetitive jobs, we reinforce rather than expand their profiles.

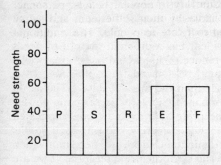

Figure 2.1 Ranking showing relative importance to respondents of the five categories. Raw scores have been converted to percentiles. Key: P = Physiological; S = Security, safety, structure; R = Relationships, love; E = Power, recognition, esteem (ego); F = Fulfilment, creativity, innovation, autonomy

Example 2

In contrast to the first profile, the profile shown in Fig. 2.2 is that of a very high achiever. He or she may be in creative work and will certainly work best on his or her own. Note the low priority given to love and safety needs. The strong goals here are for self-esteem and self-fulfilment. This profile represents less than five per cent of the adult population.

When bureaucracies become the patrons of creative people, they may so hedge individuals with red tape that creativity does not occur. Handling people with profiles like this one is an area needing much more research, because conformity in organizations and self-fulfilment are contradictory.

For example, if a government makes a grant to an artist who spends the lot on alcohol, should the grant be withdrawn? If an organization employs a creative high achiever who decides to work when she feels like it, who fails to follow even the most basic behaviour rules of that organization, but who produces excellent new product ideas, then does the lack of conformity matter? People high on self-fulfilment like to be assessed by their output, not by their willingness to conform. This is a basic contradiction for many of today's large organizations, as they are essentially conformist, compromising systems.

Example 3

The averaged profile of a large number of personnel managers is shown in Figure 2.3. Contrary to popular beliefs, personnel managers are motivated more by their self-esteem and safety needs than by their need to relate to people. The traditional

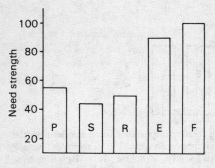

Figure 2.2

personnel function has been an inside, safe, protected function (hence the high needs for safety), but a function with considerable power (hence the self-esteem needs). A not unsimilar profile can be seen in accountants – they also are in safe, highly structured job situations, and measure *other* people's achievements. The average accountant's profile has slightly lower social needs.

What we need to develop is a range of motivation profiles for different sorts of jobs. From this we may begin to match people and jobs, not only on the ability-experience dimension of performance but, more importantly, on the motivation dimension. Further, as an individual's profile changes we can change the job to provide a better match.

Changes in profiles with age

From a very large survey of male respondents, aged from 18 to 75 years, we have developed average profiles for different age groups. The average for each age group provided the data for the following explanations of changing profiles.

For the purpose of illustration, we have exaggerated the differences. In fact, the movement of individuals' need structures may be much less. Where possible, we include some of the possible reasons for the changes. Because of the size of this exercise, only the *executive or potential executive profiles* have been included. We have not been able, at this stage, to produce a female career profile pattern, because the difficulty of obtaining an adequate sample of women in top positions.

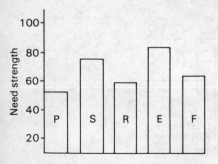

Figure 2.3

Stage 1   The 18-year-old male profile
Figure 2.4 shows the profile of matriculant students entering universities. There is evidence of the strong career goals (esteem and fulfilment), but note that the physiological and social needs are particularly strong. Safety needs are satisfied, reflecting the lower security needs of the age group currently under 25 years.

This male has recently been through puberty, is concerned with his body, and is experiencing greater freedom with his body. The high social needs reflect the importance of the peer group and the search for love relationships. From his first nursery story he, like most other children, has been promised a magnificent, romantic, love relationship. Television programmes reinforce the search for love; even the commercials promise the beautiful people a beautiful relationship. It is little wonder that the teenage male spends time preening himself for the magnificent culmination of 18 years of conditioning.

In contrast, the institutions of our society expect him to make career decisions when he is more likely to be concerned about his body, experimentation with his body, and interpersonal relationships. Perhaps career choices and entry to tertiary education should be delayed until physiological needs and love relationships are satisfied. Unfortunately, this may mean until anything from 18 to 40 years of age, depending on the individual's maturation and on his opportunities.

Stage 2   Mid twenties to early thirties
A quite dramatic change in need profile occurs at the time of marriage (or establishing a permanent relationship and living

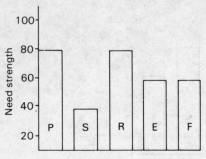

Figure 2.4   Stage 1 need profile

34

with someone else) as Figure 2.5 shows. The period it takes for the change in profile seems to vary greatly. Some profiles are still showing non-satisfaction of physiological needs two years after marriage; others stabilize before the marriage.

There appears to be a close relationship between identification of one's self with an organization and its labels *and* marriage. The process of deciding upon a career and feeling comfortable with an organizational role usually precedes a permanent relationship. Indeed, there may well be sense in delaying permanent or marital relationships until the individual has discovered what he wants to be.

The important fact is that the young, career-oriented profile has now emerged. It is fostered and strengthened by his bosses – by promises of even more self-esteem gratification, and more opportunities for self-fulfilment if certain goals are achieved. The ladder-climbing of the higher achiever becomes important.

The stabilization of the career profile gives the personnel manager the first real glimpse of the potential of the individual. This may be clear in an 18-year-old, or a 22-year-old, but it is most frequently clear only after a permanent relationship is established, in the early to mid twenties. The consequence of this finding is that measuring motives of school leavers may or may not be very useful in predicting future potential. In other words, the distorted ranking of the needs by teenagers does not provide very helpful data. It is not until 5 to 10 years later that the employer can be sure whether he or she has executive material or not. This places a very heavy reliance on the (much maligned) staff appraisal system of identifying talent in the 18

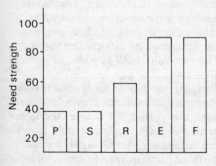

Figure 2.5   Stage 2 need profile

to 25 age group. Long cross-cultural studies, such as the Standard Oil study of executive potential, have found that socio-economic background and biographical data may be more predictive than motivational patterns in school leavers and graduates. Our research would support this finding – the prominence of physiological and relationship goals in teenagers makes career goals fuzzy at best. In this case, the socio-economic background of parents is a more reliable clue. It is still true, even in very upwardly mobile societies, that the executive/professional class reproduces itself. Similarly, the lower income classes reproduce themselves. However, when the individual reaches his mid twenties the executive profile does emerge, regardless of background, and predictability becomes slightly more scientific. In selecting future executives, it is this profile one should look for.

Stage 3 Child producing
The birth of the couple's first child will throw the profile into a new arrangement of priorities. High achievement needs become less important, and the physiological, safety, and relationship needs assume increased importance to the father.

We can only speculate on the reasons for this change in priorities. The birth of the first child is one of the most exciting and rewarding experiences of life. There is more talk about physiology, security, and love. Even before the child is born, one can detect changes in the individual's ranking of his profile. But the change is more marked when the child comes home. Now, there is a 24-hour concern for physiology – feeding, changing nappies, weighing, washing, cuddling, etc. – plus the concern of the couple to resume their sexual relationship. Traditionally, a greater concern for security gave insurance companies an opportunity to increase the sales of policies. The heightened awareness of his need for relationships reflects the inevitable concern in the individual for the child, both as a love object and as competition for his wife's love.

I have identified this change in the profile for several reasons. Often the father's boss becomes disenchanted with his subordinate's performance during this period. Of course, the father is likely to be more concerned about his wife and child than he is with his career. Another reason for identifying this as a separate stage is that the birth of subsequent children does not

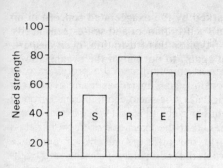

Figure 2.6 Stage 3 need profile

appear to have such a marked effect on the ranking of his priorities.

Variations between males at this stage are very great. The exceedingly high achiever's profile seems relatively unmoved by the birth of his first child. The lower achiever seems much more preoccupied with the child, as one would expect from someone with much higher concern for social relationships.

If there are no complications for mother or child, the ranking of priorities quickly returns to the achieving profile we saw in Stage 2. Six months appears to be the average for readjustment, but again there are wide variations. By the early thirties, the achievement profile reaches its strongest rankings.

Stage 4   Mid-career: 35–45 years
For most males there are questions in their mid to late thirties about what they are doing with their lives. For some, the period is one of reflection. The house, the car, the children, and the love relationship with his wife are all goals which have been achieved. There is often a sense of emptiness, and a greater concern for the second half of his life.

Most males appear to cope with the readjustment fairly well. But there appears to be an increasing number of male executives (estimated at 16 per cent) who do not. For this group we can call this stage *mid-career crisis*.

There seem to be two distinct stages in adjusting need priorities here. The first (see Figure 2.7) shows an increasing sense of frustration, of not achieving, of feeling locked into a career with no escape. It is marked by the exaggerated concern in his profile for the individual's self-fulfilment and self-esteem needs. The profile in Figure 2.7 typifies this frustration, even desperation to change, to begin again, to opt out of the organizational role he has acquired.

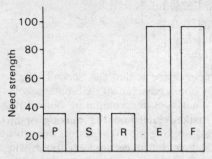

Figure 2.7 Stage 4a need profile

The second reaction is far more disturbing: from frustration to withdrawal. The profile collapses, the fire goes out and we see the high achiever begin to vegetate and psychologically to die. This profile (shown in Figure 2.8) is that of the male in mid-career crisis.

What happened to that striving 25-year-old? He recognizes that he will not make the top. It hurts. Since primary school he has been promised that if he worked hard, excelled, he would make it. What no one bothers to tell him is that opportunities are very few at the top. The very nature of hierarchies makes

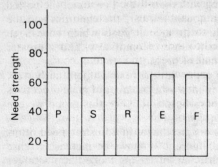

Figure 2.8 Stage 4b need profile

the period between 25 and 35 years one of rapid development, but thereafter opportunities become more and more scarce. In short, 'marvellous opportunities for advancement' was a lie – but he believed it.

This is not a new problem. There have been references to it for centuries. Dante (1265–1321) refers to it:

Midway on the Path of Life
I found myself in the dark woods
  (The Divine Comedy)

What is making the problem worse is that the Second World War and the post-war baby boom have meant that more people 'make it' earlier in life. What does the computing bureau do with its top eight people, who are all under 35 years of age? They have 30 more years of working life. What effect does this have on those underneath them in the hierarchy – those who were also promised? Waiting for kings to die may well be the lot of the post-war babies.

The problem is not restricted to the business executive. What does the doctor, or the veterinary surgeon, or the engineer find stimulating after 10 to 15 years in practice?

For the vast majority, success at the top of the hierarchy is not possible. Fortunately, the majority do not want it. But the high achieving society has so successfully produced high achievers that we may have more than we need. Organizations have little option other than to admit that they do not really know what to do with them. The mid-career motivation profile collapse appears to be the result.

Some organizations appear to avoid the problem by offering lateral movement, training, sabbaticals, special projects, etc., but even these attempts to provide opportunities for further achievement are restricted to those already at or near the top. For the bulk of middle management, the training course every 5 to 10 years is their only opportunity for resuscitation, and even this has the potential to stimulate, excite, and rekindle needs which subsequently become frustrated again.

The incidence of collapsed profiles is worst in those organizations where mobility upwards is promised to everyone – government departments, banks, insurance companies, service companies, universities, etc. It seems less evident in manufacturing companies where there is a rigid class structure (from unskilled labour to semi-skilled, to skilled, to managerial, and so on) and these class divisions are well known – not everyone is promised a path to the top.

Figure 2.8 shows the man in the mid-career crisis. Physiological needs become more important, as he talks more and more about his body. He becomes concerned about his weight, begins to jog and get his body into shape for new experiences, often diversionary sexual experiences. His increased concern for security reflects the fact that he is locked in, and has difficulty in seeing a way out. Relationships become important to him, as he may find his wife and children, who were neglected in the years of his high achievement, have developed life styles which do not include him. The family can sympathize with his problem but cannot solve it. It is a loneliness he cannot escape. Inevitably, his career needs begin to fall and the striving, achieving executive profile disappears.

Reactions to this crisis are many – preoccupation with the body and sensual pleasures, often to the extent of alienating his family, excessive drinking, drug taking, withdrawal, psychosomatic illness, psychological disorders.

From my current research, it would seem that between 16 and 20 per cent of middle and top executives do not completely recover from mid-career crisis. Most of these are plagued with psychosomatic disorders, heart problems, psychological problems, etc. Many will die before they are due to retire. Those who get to retirement may last only 18 months afterwards. It is the sense of loneliness and despair which is most distressing in talking to people who are unable to cope with mid-career stress. Labelling the problem will not help, but giving people the opportunity to discuss it is good therapy. The most important point for people to remember is that every man gets caught – even the managing director. Secondly, if goals are not achievable, then they can be revamped. Third, everyone suffers from disappointments, failures and rejections – we tend to imagine that it is only us.

The answer is to find other avenues for self-fulfilment: take up hobbies that were abandoned during the career obsession phase; enrol at the local college and revive the learning processes. Essentially, no one should depend on his or her organization to provide an endlessly stimulating and exciting path to self-esteem and self-fulfilment. Organizations were not created to do this; they are productive, repetitious systems, and opportunities for innovativeness are limited. We would be fantasizing if we imagined that, even by redesigning organizations, we could offer self-fulfilment on a continuous basis to every employee.

Stage 5   Mid forties to mid fifties

For the male who fought back from a mid-career slump, the profile will continue to show strong career needs but the social and love needs are likely to become more important. At this stage of his life, the male has adjusted to his organizational role, has developed other interests, and has made some plans for his retirement. This is the most difficult stage to generalize about. No particular patterns have emerged in my or other people's studies. Some recover, some do not. What makes those who recover do so is difficult to assess.

Stage 6   Mid fifties to mid sixties

This is the age of retirement. In the mid to late fifties, the physiological needs are ranked higher (see Figure 2.10). There may be several explanations for this. The male is in the age group where some friends die; his wife has been through the menopause, and he can no longer deny that his virility is diminishing; he may have had problems with his body already (hernia, heart, haemorrhoids, arthritis, heart murmur, etc.). At the same time, there is a need for more satisfaction of safety needs. Concern for superannuation, for the rate of inflation, for job security have all been cited in interviews with men in this age group.

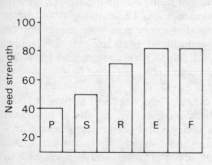

Figure 2.9   Stage 5 need profile

Social or love needs are also more important to him. The inevitable departure from the employing organization can be traumatic. With little ceremony, he is to be excluded from a range of long-term, daily relationships. In contrast, his wife has often developed her own circle of friends and activities which do not include him. Children have left or are leaving home; some are married. The potential loneliness of the aged becomes clearer.

In contrast, his career needs are less important to him.

Stage 7 Mid sixties to mid seventies
The trend seen in the sixties continues. There is increasing concern for body comforts, for health and welfare. The male and female become increasingly dependent. Fear of death or the unknown increases the concern for safety, and the isolation from children produces its own dependence. The achievement needs appear to hold the key to the life expectancy, yet so many retired people will do nothing to reinforce and develop their self-fulfilment goals at a time when they could do so many of the things they really wanted to do when they were younger. It is those who establish retirement plans, who keep moving and achieving, who live a fulfilling old age. Those who retire at 60 or 65 should not retire from living.

Old people's villages appear to be one way to prevent old age becoming a rapid and pathetic decline. Villages with group activities, outings, card games, community work, dances, competitions, are excellent therapy for reviving goal setting for day-to-day activities. At this stage, the time span becomes

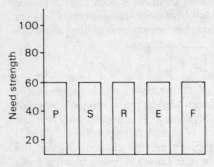

Figure 2.10   Stage 6 need profile

shorter, but the activity and goal orientation is reinforced by group members.

And so the end.

Need profile conflicts

So far, we have assumed that the individual can isolate his goals or needs and treat them separately. This is impossible. We all operate as wholes, not as five need structures; so if the body needs are being satisfied, the total person is involved.

However, there are conflicting goals – one will be satisfied at the expense of another. For example, the first-line supervisor who is promoted from his group of friends to be boss has the possible conflict of losing his friendships to satisfy his power and self-fulfilment goals. For many first-line supervisors the price is too great, and so they return to their friends, and their needs for relationships win the conflict.

The most frequently cited conflicts in my own research are outlined below.

Relationships or love needs versus self-fulfilment goals

This is a well documented conflict. Love needs involve relating to other people. Self-fulfilment is a loner activity and is difficult to satisfy with other people. Many wives blame their husband's work organization for this conflict, particularly if the work organization seems to win more frequently than the family.

This could be a fair accusation. Alternatively, the organization may have nothing to do with the conflict – it occurs in the person and he is not prepared to tell his family that his family ties are less important to him than his search for fulfilment of his potential.

Safety versus power-esteem

This is that familiar fear of taking risks, which produces the comment: 'Darling, what I could have done if it hadn't been for my need for security.' Unfortunately, it is usually only the first part of this sentence which is articulated accurately: 'What I could have done had they given me the chance.' Again, the organization (which *may* be the cause) is being blamed for a conflict within the person. He or she is not prepared to take the risks involved in greater opportunities for power or recognition or self-fulfilment.

Summary

Chapters 1 and 2 began by suggesting that motivation is a decision process in which individuals decide how much energy to use to satisfy needs or goals in return for rewards (satisfactions). This view can be expressed by a motivation function:

M = (Strength of needs or goals,

+

Energy expended

+

Importance of rewards or satisfactions)

We can take this into an organizational setting, and say that performance within an organization involves:

- Biographic background (age, sex, experience, education)
- Abilities
- Motivation
- Organizational setting (task, groups, structure, technology)

Biographic data is usually specified with the job. Abilities are important in jobs where specific abilities have been shown to be required (e.g., mathematical ability for a statistician). However, abilities have not been very useful in predicting managerial performance. At the best, collecting ability test results on an employee gives a glimpse of potential.

Far more useful in assessing one's own career and in predicting performance in organization are the needs, goals, and aspirations of employees. These first two chapters have looked at physiological, security, relationships, power – recognition and self-fulfilment needs and goals, demonstrated ways of identifying the importance of these needs to individuals, and related different importances to different jobs. What is important to an 18-year-old was shown to be radically different from what is important to a 25-year-old, and a 40-year-old. In looking at design of jobs in organizations, we assume nothing changes in the individual at all. We need to begin to design jobs on motivational data, not merely on productive capacity or neatness.

44

Chapter 3 takes the individual, puts him alongside another, and discusses the interaction between the two. In this way, we will begin to build an organization by analysing the interactions between individuals, remembering that interactions will be affected by *all* the variables discussed in this chapter, and especially by the individual's goals.

For additional reading

Goble F. G., *The Third Force*, Pocket, New York, 1971.

Jarvis W., *Wake up and Live*, Nelson, Sydney, 1975.

Schein E., *Career Dynamics: Matching Individual and Organisation*, Addison-Wesley, Reading, Massachusetts, 1978.

Sheehy G., *Passages: Predictable Crises of Adult Life*, Dutton, New York, 1976.

Soffer C., *Men in Mid-Career: A study of British Managers and Technical Specialists*, Cambridge University Press, 1970.

3 Individuals and other individuals

This chapter looks at the way in which people's perceptions and communications are affected by a whole range of signals which they send one another. It then goes on to trace the process of an individual's joining an organization and acquiring a role within it.

Attitudes and perceptions

Previous chapters looked at the way an individual's abilities and motives affect behaviour. Abilities tell us of potential performance. Motives provide driving forces to channel behaviour. *Attitudes* are the premises or positions the individual adopts about obejcts, people and beliefs.

When two people interact, the process of interaction includes their abilities, motives, attitudes, and experiences. Even before you and I meet, we have anticipatory expectations about what will happen; and in those anticipations our own motives, attitudes, and experiences are important.

An attitude is a statement of a position that an individual takes about an object, a theory, another person, or a belief. Hence, I have attitudes about the importance of your studying organizational behaviour if you wish to be a manager. I also have attitudes about managers, both generally and as people I know. Similarly, like you, I have attitudes about foreigners, about stockbrokers, about drop-outs, and so on.

Attitudes and motives affect the way I see or perceive people, groups, organizations, and objects. Indeed, it is difficult to isolate what exactly is affecting my perception or your perception at any one time. When we do meet, both you and I will have made anticipatory assumptions about each other. Subsequently we will make more assumptions.

By making assumptions, I am hoping that I can understand your behaviour. The more predictable the behaviour of others, the more secure I feel. The less information I have about you, the more difficult it is to make those assumptions, and the less comfortable our meeting may be, until both of us have collected enough data from each other to feel more competent in predicting subsequent behaviour.

For example, when you go to someone's house for dinner, you may have no data on the other guests. Not unexpectedly, the first half hour after the guests arrive is stilted, while the host assists in the data collection by introducing guests and dropping data about them, and by pouring drinks.

When we meet, we perceive each other as causing our own behaviour. Then we organize our perceptions to make motive – attitude – behaviour – effect links. That is, I add together clues I see and hear, and assume that you are motivated by X, and that this will explain your subsequent behaviour and the outcome of that behaviour. When pieces of data do not fit, we tend to discard them and preserve our neat logic, inevitably making mistakes and jumping to a multitude of false conclusions.

Once we have structured our experiences of each other into attitude – motive – behaviour – effect links we use adjectives (or 'traits') to describe them – for example, 'ambitious', 'charming', 'easy-going', 'lazy'. Finally, we structure the relationship further by collecting traits or adjectives together into 'personalities' or wholes and talk about 'types'. Then we feel much better because we have 'nailed' the other person by imposing *our* structure upon him.

What is even more disturbing is that, having linked some assumptions about me, my motives, behaviour, and perceptions into a label, the other person sticks to those labels and stabilizes his perceptions of me; and at the same time I am doing this to him. So what we all concentrate on in establishing interpersonal relationships is not the constantly changing behaviour of the other person, but a series of stabilized pictures which are filed away in a mental album of impressions or snapshots.

By this structuring process, we try to comprehend the attitudes, motives, and likely behaviour of the other person. From that, we hope to increase our capacity to predict behaviour; and the lower our tolerance of uncertainty, the more readily we produce snapshots of the other person.

Most of the time, we collect very little data about each other. We take the first few minutes of interaction very seriously and, on the basis of first impressions, begin to link motives, attitudes, and behaviour together. Even in interviews for jobs, the first impressions have been found to be vital in deciding on the applicant's suitability. As the data collection in the first few minutes is likely to concentrate on appearance, education, and experience, it is not surprising to find that recruiting officers have a stabilized 'snapshot' of the desirable employee. Nor is it surprising to find that the stabilized snapshot concentrates on appearance, education, and experience. Values, motives, and beliefs (from which one might predict subsequent employee behaviour) usually receive scant attention.

The rest of this chapter will look at how we collect data about each other: what signals we use, which are more important, and what happens when someone joins an organization of individuals interacting with each other.

How do we get data about each other?

When you and I interact, we transmit a variety of verbal and non-verbal signals to each other. Some of these signals are intentional; but some are not.

In communicating with you, I am the transmitter, and you are the receiver. The message is what I send to you; but it may not be what you receive.

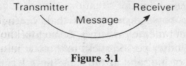

Figure 3.1

You and I are both restricted to four communication channels in collecting information about each other:

- Visual – using the eyes as receptors
- Auditory – using the ears as receptors
- Olfactory – using the nose as receptor
- Tactile – using the skin surfaces as receptors

If we meet each other in an organization then, like most other people in that organization, we are restricted to the visual and auditory channels. It is not acceptable behaviour in our society to start smelling each other, or feeling each other all over. This does not mean that we will not use the olfactory or tactile channels; it just means that there are more restrictions on our using them. So we talk to each other and pick up data about each other through our eyes and ears.

The olfactory channel *is* used and has been found to be important in making judgements about a person being 'good' or 'bad'! The person who comes to an interview smelling unfavourably may be seen to be a 'bad' applicant. Tactile clues will also be important, but will be restricted to shaking hands.

When we know each other better, we will use more tactile communications – such as pushing, slapping, stroking, and supportive gestures. In marriage, olfactory and tactile channels will be used extensively in our intimate relationships. One touch will convey a wealth of information.

In our organization roles we are usually restricted to visual (non-verbal) and auditory (verbal) clues about each other. Let us look at the non-verbal signals which affect perceptions.

Non-verbal signals
Proximity. Where you stand or sit will affect my perception of you. If the relationship is to be intimate, then we will be close. If you are applying for a job, then your sitting too close may irritate me, because I will expect to use visual and auditory rather than tactile or olfactory channels.

Proximity varies with the situation. If we are having a party, then physical proximity, confined space, background music, and dim illumination will help in the 'getting-to-know-each-other' phase. We are unlikely to see a similar scene in union-management negotiations for new awards. Distance will have replaced proximity, and barriers to tactile communication (for example, tables and chairs) will inhibit opportunities for touching.

Posture. The way a person stands also gives us clues: the position of the arms and the leg stance. Height and good posture are assumed to be 'good' signs for people motivated to succeed in work organizations. As both height and posture are largely genetically determined, it is difficult to see what they have to do with a learned motive to achieve, apart from cases where tall children are told they will succeed.

Physical appearance. Physical attractiveness differs from culture to culture. When I meet you I have commercialized pictures of attractiveness which have been 'sold' to me from birth. These pictures relate to height, physique, face, hair, hands, and so on.

Clothes are only relevant within a particular culture and, within that culture, in particular organizations or professions. For example, if you arrive in my business dressed as a surgeon, or priest, or barrister, then we may initially have problems of communication.

Physical appearance has become a mass-produced obsession; a search for beautiful people. In some jobs, what you are is secondary to how you look.

Facial and gestural movements. Emotions, attitudes, and beliefs may be transmitted through facial expressions. Some of these clues have universal significance: weeping, blushing, turning white, and pupil dilation all indicate various emotional states. Gestures are much more diverse because of the number of different possibilities. Some merely reinforce verbal signals, while others convey much more information than verbal signals. Next to the face, the hands and arms give the most important non-verbal clues, and their functions are different from facial expressions. Hands and arms are used for illustration, for replacing speech, for indicating emotional states, and for grooming oneself. Facial expressions may do all these, and in addition may indicate understanding, concentration, and attention.

Direction of gaze. Eye movements tell the transmitter something about the receiver. Interaction usually begins with a period of eye contact which appears to signal from me to you (and vice versa) that we are ready to relate. Thereafter, direct eye contact is intermittent (25 to 75 per cent of interaction time) and is longer for the listener than for the transmitter.

In summary, proximity, posture, physical appearance, facial and gestural movements, and direction of gaze are all non-verbal clues picked up through the visual receptors (eyes). From this data I (the receiver) will make assumptions about your behaviour.

Fortunately, by using verbal signals we have the chance to test our series of pictures of each other.

Verbal signals

We can classify most speech under five functions:

- Egocentric utterances: 'I have just been called to head office.'
- Questions: 'On what flight are we booked?'
- Influencing others: 'Don't confirm the tickets till I tell you.'
- Conveying information: 'Flight 234 at 11.15, Monday morning.'
- Establishing and sustaining relationships: 'We must have you over for dinner before we leave.'

We 'dress' the function of our conversation with a multitude of verbal signals about ourselves. The words we use, our accents, tone, volume, and speech errors give more clues about us. The structure of sentences, the use of repetition, the linking of thoughs or ideas, the variety of words used, and the grammatical structure of sentences yield yet more clues. The use of these verbal clues varies according to the person with whom we are conversing. The training officer conducting a programme for foremen will use very different words and sentence structure from those he uses when he is working with top management. Indeed, one of the most damaging behaviours affecting inter-personal relationships can occur if he misjudges the nature of the group and uses inappropriate words or sentences.

Linking non-verbal and verbal signals

Usually our verbal signals are reinforced or supported by non-verbal ones. The non-verbal signals expand or clarify the verbal. Yet in our day-to-day lives, we are witnesses to communication breakdowns, misinterpretations, blockages, where the transmitter's attitudes, motives, experiences, language, postures, etc., do not link together in a consistent message; or the message itself has inaccuracies; or the receiver's attitudes, motives, and perceptions make him so filter the message that the intended information does not get through.

Communication breakdowns are the most prevalent symptom of organizational problems but, frequently, they are symptomatic of something else: most employees do not leave for work each day with the intention of causing a communication bottleneck. Yet, while other factors cause most of the breakdowns, it is undeniable that, in an organization, your perceptions of what I am saying and my perceptions of what you are saying are often *the* cause of a whole chain of communication problems. Some people are just much more sensitive and perceptive in receiving data than others.

We can improve interpersonal communication in the following ways:

- By signalling continuously attentiveness and responsiveness to the signals of the other

It is infuriating to talk to someone if he spends all his time staring out of the window.

- By continuously sharing speaking and listening

If you are trying to tell someone something, it is very distracting if he keeps interrupting you in the middle of a sentence.

- By signalling attitudes and intentions towards one another

It is off-putting to try to communicate honestly with someone who remains totally bland, giving no verbal or non-verbal clues as to agreement or disagreement.

- By using gestures which are consistent with speech

It is highly inconsistent if your boss tells you to stay calm, while he himself rushes about, nervously playing with his clothes, his pen, or his desk drawers.

- By using gestures only to illustrate speech

It is annoying to have to discuss marketing strategy, for example, with someone who continuously grooms himself.

- By providing continuous feedback on how the message is being received.

If there is no response, no feedback, a dialogue becomes a monologue.

If these behaviours in other people annoy you, remember that you are guilty as well. Indeed, organizational life encourages us to give incorrect feedback, to be less than honest, to pander to our superiors while neglecting our subordinates, to play a multitude of political games. In a hierarchical structure, where success is seen in terms of promotion but where opportunities are limited (and become even more limited the higher you rise), then playing the power game is inevitable. However, games lead to communication breakdowns: I tell you, my boss, what I think you should hear, and leave out much of the rest; and you, in turn, are telling your boss what you think he should hear, and leaving out the rest. While bosses control the careers of subordinates, this filtering of communication will continue.

What we do with the verbal and non-verbal signals

You and I receive signals from each other and interpret them. If you have influence over me, I may try to predict what signals you would like to see or hear, and consciously send them to you. If I send an inconsistent signal, your verbal and/or non-verbal signals will tell me to explain or correct that signal; and while you are collecting and structuring data about me, I am doing the same about you.

We both draw inferences about each other as we order our perceptions into tidy links. Labels are slapped on to people with little regard for accuracy. Unfortunately, we need language to communicate; and language creates labels. Without language and labels, verbal communication is impossible. However, what is more worrying is that, once labelled, we are likely to live up to that label. For example, children who are told they are stupid live up to that expectation. Children who are told they are 'sickly' are sickly. Fathers who tell their boys that they will be engineers should be delighted with their success rate, at least initially (many subsequently flood into business schools to get out of engineering). Managers who see union leaders as aggressive, pig-headed, and irrational relate to union leaders in such a way that they elicit aggressive, pig-headed, irrational behaviour. Labels become self-fulfilling prophecies.

We have also devised 'grand' labels on a national scale – like 'Tony is Italian' – and that in itself leads to stereotyping. Similarly, Jewish, South African, Australian, American, Russian, or European trigger national snapshots of traits.

This passion for stereotyping illustrates yet again our need to structure our perceptions and to reduce the infinite variety of incoming information to manageable levels. Interaction is easier if the essential labels, such as socio-economic status, are established; and, when meeting people, we have a series of acceptable ways of establishing minimal data levels, such as socio-economic status: 'Do you live near here?' 'Do you work in the city?' It might be easier if we all presented a resumé of ourselves rather than waited for the questions.

The most blatant stereotyping occurs because of sex differences: 'Men are more intelligent', 'Women are more emotional', 'Men are physically stronger', 'Women are more creative', etc. It is remarkable that this sexist labelling continued up to the 'sixties, even though most of the research on differences attributable to sex did not support these labels. Thereafter, women, understandably, began to get very angry, and attempted to 'liberate' themselves from a whole bag of stereotyped labels.

How accurate are the labels?
Some characteristics make for great inaccuracy in our perceptions of one another:

- If our motives are involved, our perceptions of verbal and non-verbal signals become more distorted
- If you and I are emotionally involved, distortions are greater
- If I am dependent on you (boss–subordinate), then your perceptions of me are more distorted
- If our relationship is very aggressive, our perceptions of each other will be more distorted
- If you or I have psychological disorders, distortion of our perceptions of each other is increased

Our perceptions of each other may become more accurate if:

- I know you well over a long period of time
- You and I are peers (rather than boss and subordinate)
- Our interaction is two-way (I talk to you and you talk to me)

Interpersonal relationships at work

Organizations are characterized more by two or three people working together than by larger groups working together. Yet, while models of group behaviour are well developed, we still do not have a model of interpersonal relationships. What we do know is that relationships are strengthened by three behaviours:

- Imitation
- Reciprocity
- Reinforcement

Imitation occurs if I send you verbal or non-verbal signals and you respond with similar signals. For example, we meet and I tell a joke; you respond with a joke; or we may wink at each other.

Reciprocity occurs when I help you in some way and you reciprocate by helping me.

Reinforcement occurs when you reward me (respond positively to my signals). I tell my joke and you laugh genuinely and enthusiastically.

In addition to these behaviours, organizations have other ways of forcing and reinforcing relationships. Verbal signals can be controlled, broadcast, and edited. Formal devices are designed to reinforce expected behaviours and, where deviations do occur, members employ these devices to correct those deviations.

Joining an organization

I decide to join an organization. I believe that I have something to contribute in the way of ability, aptitude, skills, experience, and potential, but I also have goals, motives, and hopes which I perceive this organization will satisfy. The employer buys a contributor to goals or tasks, but also buys a person, even though those tasks only require a part of me – the part of me that can do the job. The employer's expectations and my expectations will be different and inevitably compromise will characterize our relationship from the day I join until the day I depart.

Even before I decide to take the job, I develop naïve expectations about what it will be like. If I know very little about the firm or the people in it, then, to reduce my uncertainty, I will invent my own snapshots of what to expect. The disorientation of actually entering the organization shatters some of these naïve expectations. I am confronted by an explosion of non-verbal, verbal, written, and tactile clues. I can only reduce the uncertainty and hell of those first few days by learning relevant data quickly; but some of the data takes months to emerge, let alone learn, and the pain of joining is the pain of gathering enough written, verbal, and non-verbal data to know the ropes. I know, and the employer knows, that I have a role to play, and I want to learn it as quickly as possible – to reduce my uncertainty to certainty, and to merge myself into the rest of the 'cast' of actors.

The process of role acquisition can be studied at four stages.

Stage 1 is an anticipatory stage. It occurs before we actually arrive. We take written and verbal data provided by personnel departments or by interviewers, as well as highly generalized data about the company or department. The more naïve our expectations, the greater the chance of our leaving. Employers have a vested interest in telling the truth, or at least not telling untruths, in job interviews.

Stage 2 is the formal phase. From the moment you or I enter the organization, verbal and non-verbal signals are being transmitted about required behaviour. Formal signals are often grouped together in an induction programme, and so anxious are we to reduce the total uncertainty to something we can understand that we will swallow the formal induction without even a whimper. The more important security, structure, and definition are to us, the more readily we will absorb the formal signals about expected behaviour.

Within hours, the new recruit may have agreed to objectives, tasks to perform, hours of work, codes of behaviour, boss–subordinate relationships, work territory, and so on, all in exchange for specified rewards, usually monetary, and unspecified promises, such as promotion. A legal and psychological contract has been established.

Stage 3 is learning the expectations of one's work associates. Informal values, norms, and expectations are just as important as the formal ones. Through the verbal and non-verbal signals of informal relationships, we acquire the social props to our identity. We are so lonely in the process of entry that we accept the informal group dictates with little evaluation. Group norms about work, work rates, dress, conformity, and so on, are soon added to our concepts of the role we are to play.

56

Stage 4 occurs much later in the entry process. It may be months later, when naïve expectations have become realistic beliefs. By then we feel comfortable; the stress of joining the organization is over; verbal and non-verbal signals are synchronized and ordered; we know the formal and informal expectations; and we are making our contribution to the output of the organization. In return, as agreed on joining, we receive regular payments of money and intrinsic satisfaction from our work. In this pleasant and mostly satisfying environment, the personal stage of role acquisition occurs. We begin to change the role to include our own expectations of what it should be. We may even use our own verbal and non-verbal signals to persuade others to change the formal requirements to bring them closer to our own expectations.

By now, we have two contracts – a legal contract, and a psychological contract. The psychological contract is a contract of expectations between 'them' and 'me' – it links what I expect from 'them' and what they expect from 'me' in the role I am to play.

Roles

A *role* combines the cumulative formal, technical, informal, and personal expectations about a job. *Role* is the link between individual and organization. *Role conception* is how I see the role I am expected to play. *Role performance* is how I actually behave. A *role system* is the cumulative expectations and behaviours of the actors or players in the organization. The role system is the arena where the actors play out their motives, hopes, and dreams. It is the arena of verbal, non-verbal, olfactory, and tactile signals, of emotions, of decisions. It is the arena where expectations change, some gradually – for example, formal expectations – others quite rapidly – personal or informal expectations. It is the arena where some actors impose their will on others in an endless power game in which others are imposed upon and allow that imposition to continue for personal reasons (rewards, money, promotion, or love).

It is impossible to describe the role system other than momentarily, because it is always changing; but when we speak of the role system we freeze that dynamic interaction for a single moment, take a picture, and know that a moment later the role system will be different.

Role stress

Acquiring a role raises problems for the individual.

Living up to other people's signalled expectations is often a pleasure – pain experience: pleasure in the recognition we receive for satisfying other's expectations, pain in the sense that we lose some of our independence and freedom. For this reason, roles may never be totally satisfying.

The result of this conflict between them and me is stress. *Role conflict* occurs where more than one role is required in the same situation. *Role ambiguity* occurs where others' expectations are badly signalled or received and remain unclear. *Role overload* occurs where expectations of others are too high. *Role underload* occurs where expectations of others are too low.

Role sets

When I join an organization, I do not have relationships with everyone. Indeed, I am most likely to have relationships only with a relatively small number of people on a day-to-day basis. These are people such as my boss, his boss, my peers and, if I have any, my subordinates. At the most, this may amount to 20 people; and of these there will be fewer than 10 with whom I have most relationships. This small group (within the larger group – the organization) is called my *role set*, and it is their transmitted expectations which affect my role performance most of the time.

Those members of my set who have most influence on my role performance have more power to influence me. Hence, my boss is more likely to produce a change in my role performance than one of my peers. My boss has my career in the palm of his hand – it is amazing how powerful he can be! Conversely, my peers are more tolerant, more willing to accept me for what I am, rather than for what I might produce or become in the hierarchy. However, if they decide that I have violated our psychological contract then they, too, have great power to influence my behaviour. Power and influence are what role systems live on. If power is important to me then I will try to acquire it. The next chapter discusses power and its acquisition and use in organizations.

58

Summary

When people interact, they emit a range of verbal, visual, olfactory, and tactile signals, using the eyes, ears, nose, and skin surfaces as receptors. All this data is channelled through the process of perception. You and I filter these signals through our own motives, expectations, attitudes, and experiences. We structure the data into simplified snapshots, attributes, 'traits', and types, and attempt to predict behaviour from the structuring process.

Proximity, physical appearance, direction of gaze, and facial and gestural movements all affect our perceptions of one another. Speech patterns, use of words, accent, volume, and so on, are verbal clues which we add to our structuring behaviour.

If we take these characteristics of perception into an organizational setting, then the verbal and non-verbal signals still provide data for interpersonal relationships. However, formal induction procedures and the allocation of a job to perform can stereotype the signals a great deal more efficiently.

New employees join a *role system* of interacting players, whose perceptions and expectations establish norms of required behaviour. Role systems live on influence and power.

For additional reading

Argyle M., *Social Interaction*, Tavistock, 1969.
Argyle M., *Bodily Communication*, Methuen, 1975.
Hinde R. (ed.), *Non-Verbal Communication*, Royal Society and Cambridge University Press, Cambridge, 1972.
James M. and D. Jongeward, *Born to Win: Transactional Analysis with Gestalt Experiments*, Addison-Wesley, Reading, Massachusetts, 1971.
Molesworth V., *Factors in Effective Communication*, West Publishing, Sydney, 1964.
Van Maanen J., 'Breaking in: A consideration of organisational socialisation' in R. Dubin (ed.), *Handbook of Work Organisation and Society*, Rand McNally, Chicago, 1975.

4 Individuals, roles, and power

This chapter sets out to analyse the lifeblood of all role systems – power. It talks about where it comes from and how to acquire it, and also suggests ways in which we can all reduce the negative or destructive use of power in organizations.

What is power?

Power is the capacity to affect another's behaviour. *Influence* is the effect. Power is a resource; influence is the result of using that resource. Power is the ability to choose outcomes in the light of our own interests; influence is the actual achievement of those outcomes.

Power is acquired by individuals through expertise, physical appearance, information, or authority related to a position. When a policeman stops me for speeding, he has influenced my behaviour. I stop because the policeman has power. He acquires that power from the authority of his position, from his verbal and non-verbal signals about influence, and from the legal but unpleasant fines he can slap on me.

Authority differs from power, but contributes to it. Authority refers to a formal or legitimate right to control resources – people, money, materials, equipment, information, for example. Authority relates to a position in an organization and is structurally bound. Some writers refer to authority as *positional power*.

What is appealing about power is both its scarcity and its potential in influencing other people's behaviour. To possess power is to have the ultimate 'ego-trip'; people recognize power and strive to acquire power at the expense of someone else. Authority is given; but I can work to increase my power even if the organization does not reinforce it by giving me more authority.

Three variables determine the amount of power an individual acquires:

- The resource

This is something that is possessed or acquired by a person. It may arise from knowledge, appearance, strength, money, hypnotic charm, authority, skill, previous experience, leadership skills, past record of performance in the organization, etc.

- Dependence

Having the resource is only part of the relationship. Other people must need that resource or be dependent on it, even if that dependence arises from fear of reprisal. That is, power must be recognized or conceded by other people, if influence is to result.

- Scarcity

If the knowledge, or hypnotic appeal, or money, or skill is readily available from others, then the capacity to influence is reduced. The international sportsman, the famous opera singer, the international banker, acquire power through a skill which is in scarce supply.

The word *power* has connotations of immorality and deviousness. This interpretation dominated the American literature from the 'thirties through to the 'fifties. Power was a dirty word. One explanation was that both Hitler and Mussolini adopted power theories as the basis of their totalitarian societies. From the 'fifties on, there has been an increasing recognition that groups, organizations, and societies rest on power and that we need to understand this behavioural phenomenon.

If you or I are going to affect the outcomes of an organization, then we must use ourselves. These assertions of the self lead to power and to influencing other people's behaviour. Unless we can devise productive organizations of passive individuals, then we need to spend time letting managers understand the acquisition and use of power. Power can transform individuals' interests into coordinated activities that accomplish worth-while ends. It can also lead to destructive conflict on an international scale.

Bases of power

There have been numerous classifications of the bases or sources of power.

- Coercive power

Identified by most researchers, this is power based on fear. It depends on the application, or threat, of physical sanctions, such as pain, deformity, or death. Our education system was until recently based on coercive power, with all the reinforcements of pain (cane, strap). This power relies on a subordinate's concern for his/her security.

- Remunerative power

Also recognized by most writers, this power derives from control of rewards and resources. In organizations, this power comes from a manager's control over salaries, promotions, status symbols, etc. Although there is no threat of pain in a physical sense, this control system can be psychologically painful. The withholding of salary increases, of promotions, of status symbols, can be nearly as upsetting as physical punishments.

Conversely, recognizing good performance in a job with rewards reinforces the performance, provided the reward is important to the individual and he sees a relationship between the reward and his performance. For example, most parents use rewards as a base for their power to influence their children.

- Legitimate power

This is authority as vested in a position and used by the occupant of that position. Authority is a legal or institutionalized right to control resources (people, money, materials, information, equipment). Hence, the managing director has authority (or positional power); he has control over nearly all the resources of the organization. He reinforces this power with remunerative power.

Related to authority or legitimate power are additional trade-offs which stretch the power far beyond the authority written into a job description. For example, information can be withheld (often in the name of security); delays in processing applications reinforce authority; restructuring jobs, procedures, regulations, stretch the original allocation of authority. After long periods of occupancy of a position, the personal role acquisition phase can lead to an extension (legitimately and/or illegitimately) of authority, sometimes through almost imperceptible tactics. And the more important the resources controlled by the occupant of that position, the greater potential he or she has to stretch his or her power. For example, the clerk at the reception desk of a fully occupied hotel has infinite *power*, yet the formal description of that job would indicate very little *authority*.

These 'hidden assets' of legitimate power, regarded by some writers as principal power sources, have been ignored in most of the writing on power. One difficulty in dealing with them is proving their existence. For example, a boss's secretary may have the task of allocating his time for appointments. From that innocuous statement of task arises amazing power: she may tell me that he is not in and make it impossible for me to get through at all, and she can pursue her own likes and dislikes of his subordinates. Yet if I confront her with descriptions of her tactics, she denies the accusation, claiming that everyone has equal opportunity to have an appointment.

Each of these three power bases (coercion, remuneration, legitimacy) derives most of its influence from organizations. Once the occupant of a position withdraws from that position he loses these power bases. However, there are sources of power which derive from individuals rather than from organizations, and these bases are transferable to other situations.

● Expert power

The possession of important technical information is the basis of all specialists' power. The dependence of others on one's expertise or skill is basic to power derived from what one knows or can do. For example: the TV repairman has great power when the television set breaks down; the plumber has great power if the water supply bursts in the middle of the night; a doctor has considerable power if called to deliver a baby at 2 a.m. in the morning.

Knowledge is power, and in our society we have extended this to mean education. In our mobile society, there are two means of acquiring upward social mobility and, thereby, increased power: knowledge (education), and wealth.

Expert power depends on scarcity, and will be reduced if others acquire the skills which support it. Hence, experts have a vested interest in surrounding their skills with jargon, 'black magic', and mythology to preserve their scarcity. They can further reinforce their power by game-playing – manipulating the uncertainty surrounding their expertise; and by enshrining their expertise in secret societies or associations.

Expert power can be reduced in organizations by hiring other experts (reducing dependency), or by bringing in consultant experts. It may also be reduced by increasing the knowledge of other members through training.

The fights between staff personnel and line managers are aggravated by the higher level of expertise attributed to staff personnel and the reliance of line managers on 'experience', which has lower ranking in terms of expertise. I am not sure why we give such a low rank to experience, especially when ten years' experience on a job must be as educative, if not more so, than three years doing a degree.

- Referent power

If you admire someone to the point of imitating him or her, then that person has referent power to influence your behaviour. In all organizations there are heroes and stars whom others try to emulate.

Over time, the expectations of subordinates become major determinants of the managerial styles of their heroes. If others depend on you, then you must live up to their expectations, lest you lose your power. For example, a drunk chief executive at the staff Christmas party threatens the dependency of his subordinates and thereby risks losing his power.

The irony of referent power is that the role performance I find myself playing, in living up to others' expectations of that performance, may be quite removed from the role I would like to play. For example, foremen have been labelled and stereotyped as tough, resilient, task-oriented bosses. Most of those I have tested have high social needs and, underneath their rough exterior, are gentle people. Yet the role they play to live up to the expectations of their men and their role preference are quite contradictory. It may not be possible for some of them to 'play it straight' any more.

Traditional figures for referent power were built into our religions. They were (are) magnificent human beings whom we should all emulate. Today's heroes are more frequently pop stars or football stars than religious figures.

- Personal attractiveness

This power is related to expert power and referent power. Some people have charisma or such an attractive presence as to command attention. We often see examples of this power in social situations where a person with no position or expertise attracts attention by appearance, presence, charm, poise, conversation, warmth, or sexuality.

This power is elusive, undefinable, and temporary, and most people who find they have it reinforce their ephemeral charisma with position or expertise. After all, attractiveness does fade.

- Political power

Andrew Pettigrew has identified another power resource, which he calls *political access and sensitivity*. My view is that this is a subset or hybrid, emerging from expertise and legitimate power. However, I would like to discuss it separately because of its importance in organizations. Further, while it is normally related to a position, it does not entirely depend on expertise or position. For example, a process worker may, through audacity or charm, get access to all levels of the hierarchy.

Having access to power centres of an organization, or to the powerful elite of a society, creates power for oneself. Hence, for those seeking power, there is an endless struggle to reduce the distance between themselves and the more powerful. The greater the distance (the less the accessibility), the less political power. In all organizations, and in society as a whole, becoming politically involved with the power elite is important to those seeking power. It is fashionable to ridicule this search for membership of the establishment, as if there were something indecently opportunist about it. But all organizations (whether corporation, union, church, club, juvenile gang, or commune) have an elite, and the overthrow of one establishment will herald the beginning of another, as the power struggle begins again. One fatal mistake a would-be member of an establishment might make is to join an establishment just before its overthrow.

There are a multitude of games people play in organizations to acquire power. Some of them are listed below. All could be classified into one of the categories cited.

Acquiring power

Those who have power have used legitimate as well as illegitimate and often devious means of acquiring it. Here are some of the most common methods.

- By acquiring the expertise the organization requires – preferably in advance

W. H. Auden has argued that opera singers and prostitutes survive revolutions because of the scarcity of their skills and the market for those skills.

- By joining the leading department, and not one which is in decline

In every organization there is a department or division which is 'on the make', one which is seen to be better than others in reputation and results. Often, reputation depends on technology (take, for example, the rapid emergence of data-processing departments and their glamorous image in the sixties) or skill (the current re-emergence of industrial relations).

- By acquiring the values, attitudes, and behaviour codes of those with power

Establishments, like any other group, have acceptable standards of dress, behaviour, and manners. To reduce the distance between oneself and the more powerful, one must learn these codes.

- By performing

Very high performance in the current job is important in securing internal visibility and a more powerful position.

- By increasing people's dependency

You may do this by controlling resources or services, or listening to the problems of the more powerful.

- By establishing relationships with external but powerful people

This may involve claiming friendship with power figures in our society, the implication being that one has powerful friends.

- By using the names or positions of the powerful: 'I need the information now – for the Minister.'
- By inferring the needs of the powerful

This leads to statements like 'The managing director may need the information' or 'I think he will need that information', or 'The boss is likely to need the information.'

- By entertaining

Wining and dining the powerful is a familiar ploy. Even implying that one entertains the powerful is sufficient: 'We had dinner with Sir Leslie last week.'

- By increasing external visibility

This is especially important among competitive organizations, by publishing, appearing, and being vocal at conferences and reunion dinners.

- By oozing self-confidence in speech, dress, and manner

Verbal communication can be especially effective in increasing visibility.

- By dropping data about expertise and experience: 'When I was marketing director in New York . . .' 'When I was at Harvard . . .'
- By generating myths and legends based on the past

All power figures are talked about by the less powerful. Myths and legends abound about the boss, the Prime Minister, the famous musician. Usually, admirers generate the myths, but the smart politician or managing director or the person on the make generates his or her own myths and feeds them into the grapevine.

- By acquiring assets and wealth, or even implying that one has acquired assets or wealth: 'We have a house in the South of France'
- By working for higher degrees and thereby increasing expertise, internal and external visibility, and scarcity value
- By developing such social skills that even the most boring company director believes people are fascinated by his repetition of his own myths and legends

- By using one's family (wife and children) to multiply one's impact on an organization
- By recognizing the importance of patronage

Careers need patrons, and choosing the wrong patron can have negative results. The paternal tendency for patronage, to support the up-and-coming younger person, is still strong in organizations, despite all the 'justice' of appraisal schemes.

- By broadcasting one's achievements in non-work activities: 'I won the race on Saturday – on to the finals now'
- By learning the niceties of political, organizational games
- By developing skills not used in the work organization but socially approved

For example, the champion swimmer's reputation in his work organization depends on swimming, not on what he is employed to do.

- By attaching oneself to worthwhile and socially responsible non-work organizations (children's research fund, the blind, the church)
- By choosing the right parents

Socio-economic background has been less significant in some countries than in Europe, but in certain industries, class and school are still important.

- Finally, by recognizing that most studies of career show that they do not develop in carefully planned, logical sequence

Most careers are the product of chance – being in the right place at the right time. So the final tactic for those seeking power has been to watch the fickleness of chance, and when chance made an offer, to take it.

Those who wish to learn more of the power game should read Berne's book: *Games People Play* (see Additional reading).

All the tactics listed above can be seen in organizations, and those who use them most are either at the top or on the way to the top. Listed as they are, they may appear nauseating and exaggerated, but we really cannot blame individuals for using them in a system which promises power and influence to all, and then restricts both to a few. If an individual hopes to realize the rewards of the achieving society, then he or she will be seen to use these political tactics: the illegitimate ways to improve one's chances of success and power.

Further, we should remember that the games generate conflicts which energize the role system, and make it very productive. Without conflict, organizations may well die, just as families and marriages without conflict die. However, if conflict becomes destructive, it destroys, and much destructive conflict arises from the power game (for example, unresolved strikes, and boss-subordinate sulks).

The effect of power game playing on organizational effectiveness can be quite damaging. In a system where the boss has the power to determine the future careers of subordinates, the filtering of communication upwards through the hierarchy is inevitable. This leads to a vicious circle in which important communication is filtered out by power seekers so that the structure (which causes most of the problems) is reinforced to flush out the filtered information, thereby making the filtering worse. It is only in flatter, smaller organizational units that we see a sharp decrease in both the game playing and the filtering.

Filtering to preserve power

Apart from data required for control, most upward communication in organizations can be categorized into four groups.

1 We send up data about ourselves and our problems.
2 We send up data about others and their problems.
3 We comment on, or suggest refinements to, the procedures, policies, and regulations (the structure).
4 We suggest strategies for current problems and what needs to be done.

As organizations increase in size, the necessity to predict and control the behaviour of the whole organization inevitably leads to more structure, more controls, more requests for information. Further, the larger the system, the greater the struggle for power and influence. Not unexpectedly, we all learn to filter out data which puts us in a bad light, and we learn to tell the boss what he wants to hear. Studies of a vertical filtering of information have found four reactions from members.

1 *Put it in writing*. We send written details up the hierarchy in case we have to prove that we have completed our tasks. A multitude of memos circulate in the role system, simply to justify our behaviour in the event of a breakdown. If a breakdown does occur, we rush to our files and extract the relevant memo which shows that we *did* tell the boss what was happening – i.e., we covered ourselves.

2 Because power is the promotion of the self, we send up the hierarchy *positive data on ourselves*, and forget to send the negative data. In other words, we tell our superiors how good we are.

3 We send in *negative data on our peers* – those who are competing against us for more powerful positions.

   The 'But-syndrome' is a common indicator of negative filtering. It occurs all over the hierarchy, but is seen in its most blatant form at the second level. This form of game playing begins with praise for a peer, but ends with negative feedback on that peer. Usually the negative feedback begins with 'but'. For example: 'We were very lucky to get Harry from the opposition because he is the top marketing man in the country – but he knows nothing about our products and still has a lot to learn.'

   Or, even more shattering: 'He means well' – the innuendo being: 'He fails.'

4 We try to *reduce the distance between* ourselves and our boss by using first person plural pronouns, and talk of what 'we' (that is, he and I) will do in the future. '*We* could always write to head office, boss, and ask them to let *us* have more data. *We* could really make this place swing if only they gave *us* the data to work on. Couldn't *we*?

   By implication, the use of 'we' attaches the less powerful person to the more powerful, and power is equalized.

These four methods of filtering, promotion, and covering oneself occur in all large organizations. But the early symptoms occur in organizations with 100 people. The reverse also holds: the smaller the organization, the less prevalent the problems, and the more constructive the conflict.

Imbalance of power

Organizations depend on a balance of power such that no one individual had dictatorial power. In an age when ownership and management of large corporations are less incestuously linked, if not separate, the balancing of power is possible. However, very costly imbalance does occur between individuals, between groups, and between management and unions. Work organizations still represent the best example of centralized, concentrated, and largely unopposed power, despite all the 'participative' movements. An imbalance of power between individuals can be reduced by

- Withdrawing

The person with less power leaves, retires, sulks, or resigns.

- Coalitions

Those with less power form a unit to counter the power of the more powerful. These are fragile solutions, that are always threatened by instability. Kings form coalitions with favoured groups – most usually their second level. However, if the king rejects coalition (or team work), then he is in danger of being isolated from the power game and from the data he needs for managing. Two factors are reducing the isolation of kings. One is the uncertain market, and the second is increased union power. As a result, the incidence of top management coalition has increased, with many senior groups managing as a permanent taskforce.

- Collusions

These are a subset of coalitions, but predominantly defensive, harbouring unconscious motives. They tend to be very temporary and unreliable, but are effective for very short attempts to reduce imbalance.

- Continuous interaction

The less powerful interacts continuously with the more powerful. By ingratiating himself with the more powerful, the less powerful equalizes the power. For example, the personal assistant to the managing director, by isolating his boss from his functional heads, can make the MD totally dependent.

71

In more primitive societies and in totalitarian systems, physical isolation and death are ways of restoring the balance of power. In work organizations, we do not have physical punishment or death as strategies (although one wonders how many heart attacks are triggered by losses in the power game). We use more subtle methods to 'kill' people, if only psychologically. We can ignore them, not speak to them, not send them any correspondence, put them into the organizational gaol called 'special projects', golden handshake them, humiliate them, bypass them in the hierarchy or in promotion. We can deny them access to the powerful, not appraise them, move them laterally, refuse to increase their salary, or just extend the time scale for their next big 'chance'. We can send them to purgatory (often a colonial outpost) or leave them in purgatory longer. We can give them the most boring job but tell them how well they can do it. We can start rumours about their competence, sanity, paranoia, or sicknesses, or merely broadcast that 'he means well'; or, if the direct approach is unwarranted, we can attribute sickness, insanity, infidelity, and so on, to members of his family. In short, we can eliminate by psychological means, thereby restoring the balance of power; and, for a decreasing number of organizations, if all this fails, we can fire them – physically eliminate them. Ironically, the use of dismissal is being restricted more and more to middle and top managers – the very people who used this technique so liberally in the past with lower echelons.

The drama of power

Zaleznik and Kets De Vries recently argued that the power struggle in organizations leads to three life dramas. There are other dramas in the power struggle, but these are among the most frequent:

- Parricide
- Paranoid thinking
- Ritualism

Parricide is the drama of stripping the king of his power. Subordinates fantasize about what they would do if they were in control. Several enjoy the same fantasy. Add a major organizational setback, and fantasies become possibilities and the power struggle ensues. The struggle results in the 'death' of the king. Age is often a reason for parricide – the aging father figure will not relinquish the reins, so a palace revolt takes them from him. Subsequently, there is likely to be a further power struggle; the potential death of the old king units the second level together into a temporary coalition, but once dead, this common enemy is gone and internal struggles occur for the throne.

Paranoid thinking is a distortion of thought and perception of which all humans are capable. But this drama follows a collusion which breaks down. It is characterized by jealousy, suspicion, attributing malevolent motives to ex-members of the collusion. Behind the suspicions there are often truths, but they become distorted as the paranoid thinker becomes convinced of his own integrity and the dishonesty of others. Paranoia is second to depression as the major psychological disorder of executives.

Ritualism is the drama of creating and elaborating structures to delay decisions, subvert power, defend oneself. Sometimes it is no more than an obsession with literacy – putting everything in writing. It may, however, develop into ceremonies – such as imported problem-solving techniques – which delay facing the issues. Ritualism is a further attempt to present rationality in a highly emotional, conflict-motivated, power-based role system.

Many of the organizational problems of the power game were expressed some years back by Argyris, in his theory of inter-personal competence. He argued that the pretence to be rational and to follow the rituals of the system produced dishonesty, lack of trust, and incompetence in interpersonal relationships. At the time, he argued that we needed to increase the degree of trust by using T-groups, to transform destructive conflict into con-structive, energizing conflict. Nearly 15 years later, we find a whole host of behaviourally-based devices on the market, de-signed either to reduce the impact of structure on individuals in the power struggle and/or to lead to power equalization. Not surprisingly, the results in reducing negative games have not been startling. Power struggles continue, and will always con-tinue, because organizations are political systems which attract people seeking power. Moreover, those political systems can be incredibly productive. However, because so much conflict is destructive, we are learning to assess the state of conflict and the power struggle, and if necessary to use instruments to min-imize the negative effects. For example, 15 years ago, few top management groups regularly participated in off-site, soul-baring exchanges. Today, many top groups have regularly booked sites where they 'let-it-all-out'. Fifteen years ago, there were very few off-site union–management exchanges. The number of these has increased exponentially. Fifteen years ago, who talked of worker participation or involvement, or redistribution of power? Yet every major industry and government department now has some vague thoughts about power redistribution, if not equalization. Smaller organizational units, decentralized authority, plus a new generation which is increasingly suspicious of the destructive, executive-masked power seekers and even rejects the power struggles of its parents, are all significant changes. And if the analysis of organizational power lets us understand the sources and abuses of power and the levels of constructive conflict, this is a very worth-while field of study.

Limits to power

So far this discussion has treated power as if it could be acquired by anyone, without restrictions. There are in our society, however, increasing limits on the concentration of power. Certainly, concentrated wealth is in the hands of the few, and the separation of ownership and management has been excessively overstated; upper classes own and manage, if not together, then within a class. One area where a change has occurred in the power game has been in the awakening of concentrated industrial or union power, which rested like a sleeping giant for nearly a century. Now that the giant has flexed its muscles, management is concerned about the balance of power and the dangers of concentration. However, this does produce the necessary accumulation of capital to permit us to finance more of our ventures.

What limits the concentration of power?

● Organizational boundaries

Power is rarely transferable across these. The managing director or union officer is powerful within his own organization, but far less powerful in a court of law.

● We have had a long history of humiliating those in power

We search diligently for some fault in them – their Achilles heel

– and, having found it, we broadcast our discovery, usually with negligible supporting data. This produces a strange contradiction: lack of respect for those with power, yet a history of submissively responding to their commands.

● Legal restrictions

Restrictive trade practices legislation is only one of the multitude of restrictions on concentrated power.

● Limits of time and energy

Few people realize the time and effort involved in being a Minister of State, a permanent head of a government department, a governor of a prison, a cardinal in the church, or a managing director of a business. For most of the people in these positions, work is a seven-days-a-week activity. Of course, most of them thrive on it, but younger people are beginning to wonder if the rewards for having power, and the influence one can have on others, are worth the costs, especially in terms of family relationships. Are wealth and power more important than love?

● The individual's search for harmony

Where power imbalances occur, the individual uses one or more of many checks to correct that imbalance; and with an increasing awareness among subordinates or union members of their potential power, abuses of power may be prevented.

● Power exists only if other people recognize it

We have had some interesting political examples over recent years when power was unceremoniously withdrawn from politicians. Similarly, in work organizations, willingness to endure a dictatorial boss or union organizer is diminishing.

Managers and the use of power

Power is vital to organizations: it makes role systems productive. Yet it can be so destructive that managers need to understand rather than decry it. Here are some guidelines for managing power and influence:

● Try to be honest with others

There is among animals a *norm of reciprocity*, by which if A

75

does a good turn for B, B will return that good turn. I have found that if A is honest with B, in most cases B is honest in return. We need to ask people what they want from organizations, highlight areas of conflict, and negotiate compromise solutions. Many individuals are still frightened of honesty, lest it should indicate weakness. Managers can do a great deal to encourage and reward honesty and clarification of personal goals.

- Avoid unnecessary power struggles by clearly defining goals and authority rather than functions

Structure is essential for organizations, but invariably designers of structure become involved with controls rather than concentrating on ends.

- Do not be afraid to experiment with structure

People who want power do make better managers. Often the wrong people are given management tasks simply because that is the way to move up the hierarchy. Conversely, power struggles run rampant if the structure (particularly the hierarchy) is tampered with continually.

- Explain to people that organizations are compromises of many needs, expectations, and attitudes, and that negotiation is essential

For example, taking on a union with the intention of humiliating its officers (more recently referred to as 'union bashing') does little to help the eventual compromise.

- Understand that not only senior executives (with powerful ego needs) want power

Power to influence the behaviour of others is something we all enjoy, yet it is denied to the majority. Two sensible policies are:

1 To involve the people in decisions that affect them. Share power with them.
2 To give those who seek power the chance to influence other people's behaviour. The tendency of senior managers to 'hog' power (often on exceedingly trivial issues) does not improve working life for the majority. For example, union delegates are also motivated by the need for power, and

management's delusion that one day the union movement will cease to want power is a contradiction of management's own motives. We need to rotate positions of power so that more people who seek it may have experience of possessing it.

- Recognize that there are, as Anthony Jay has noted, yogis and commissars, or philosophers and kings, or experts and managers

In the power struggle, power gained through expertise is different from power gained through authority over resources. Some who seek power through expertise (such as some philosophers, yogis, architects, surgeons, or academics) may not make very good kings, commissars, or managers. Conversely, kings, commissars, or managers may make poor philosophers, yogis, or experts. Yet in organizations, we promote through a single hierarchy in which philosophers compete with commissars for greater power, recognition and reward. This unnecessary struggle could be avoided by allowing the organizational rewards to relate to performance rather than position in the hierarchy, so that effective philosophers or yogis can be 'promoted' (rewarded) without moving into the hierarchy of commissars and kings.

Recognition of the search for different power bases among individuals would save unnecessary struggles. The advertising industry and parts of the media approach sanity in separating experts and managers into two hierarchies, thereby avoiding situations where they compete against each other. Even universities, which exist to develop and transmit expertise, require experts (academics) to become managers to be promoted beyond professorial rank. Not surprisingly, when those experts become managers, their lack of managerial experience is often blatantly obvious.

- Recognise that organizations include different groups with different expectations

Harmony between those groups is temporary – power struggles and conflicts are inevitable. Organizations are pluralistic, not unitary as so many people want to believe.

Summary

Role systems exist for interpersonal relationships, which depend on influence, which depends on power. Power is a resource, while its effect is influence. The effects of influence are cooperation, conflict, love, hate, fear, jealousy, and all those other emotions encountered in role systems.

People in the role system acquire power through a variety of organizational and individual characteristics. Position in the hierarchy creates authority to control resources – and in a system of scarce resources that creates positional power. Other non-formal sources of power within role systems are coercion, charisma, access to the more powerful, and expertise. Whatever the source of power, the struggle between individuals for more is inevitable in a system which promises power and influence to all, but restricts both to a few. Illegitimate methods of increasing one's power are the result.

Games are played to impress, to win friends, to increase visibility, to influence those above oneself, to create dependence, to present oneself in the best light, or to present others in a less favourable light. One consequence of the struggle for power is conflict. Most of the conflict is constructive, stimulating members of the role system to greater productivity, creativity, and cooperation. However, much conflict becomes destructive, reducing productivity, alienating members from the role system, isolating the powerful from their subordinates, and separating member from member.

Power and conflict energize role systems. Without both the resource of power and the consequences of power – influence, conflict, cooperation – organizations may die. So the dilemma for the manager is how much power, how much influence, how much cooperation, how much conflict to allow. Too much conflict may become destructive and destroy the system, but too little may be unconstructive and lead to organizational malaise. Managers need to understand the sources of power, the needs some people have for power, and the fragility of balance in role systems. From this information the manager is in a position to negotiate, confront, ignore or stimulate the productive – and individually rewarding – processes of role systems.

For additional reading

Abell P. (ed.), *Organisations as Bargaining and Influence Systems*, Heinemann, 1975.

Argyris C., *Interpersonal Competence and Organisational Effectiveness*, Richard D. Irwin, Homewood, Illinois, 1962.

Backrack R., and M. A. Baratz, *Power and Poverty*, Oxford University Press, New York, 1970.

Berne E., *Games People Play*, Grove Press, New York, 1964

Cartwright D., *Studies in Power*, Institute of Social Research, Ann Arbor, Michigan, 1966.

Clegg S., and D. Dunkerley, *Critical Issues in Organisations*, Routledge & Kegan Paul, 1977.

Fox A., *A Sociology of Work in Industry*, Collier Macmillan, 1971.

Fox A., *Beyond Contract: Work Power and Trust Relations*, Faber and Faber, 1974.

Jay A., *Management and Machiavelli*, Hodder & Stoughton, 1967.

Maccoby N., *The Gamesman*, Simon and Schuster, New York, 1976.

McClelland D., *Power: The Inner Experience*, Irvington, New York, 1971.

Mumford E., and A. Pettigrew, *Implementing Strategic Decisions*, Longman, 1975.

Swingle P. G., *The Management of Power*, Lawrence Erlbaum, Hillsdale, New York, 1976.

Zaleznik A., and M. F. R. Kets de Vries, *Power and the Corporate Mind*, Houghton Mifflin, Boston, Massachusetts, 1975.

5   Individuals and groups

Previous chapters looked at the individual's goals and motives in joining a role system in an organization. I explained that, on arrival, he or she is confronted by written, verbal, and non-verbal signals about the role he or she is expected to play. The relevance of those signals will depend on the power of their source – hence, at this stage of role acquisition, one's boss has considerable power to influence.

Another source of power which will affect the entry and subsequent role performance will be the groups that person works with, drinks with, strikes with, laughs with, connives with, fights with, etc. Power acquired by individuals in groups is a major influence within role systems.

Many students of organizational behaviour study organizations as a multitude of groups, some official and recognized, others unofficial and unrecognized. I prefer to study organizations as a collective of individuals performing roles within a role system. From my observations, very few people do in fact spend *all* their work day in a group. However, from time to time groups form and then disband, and in that process influence the behaviour of individuals. And with the current shifts towards smaller organizations, semi-autonomous work groups, power equalization, and team building, a knowledge of group behaviour within organizations has become a major part of a manager's education.

This chapter will draw on research from all over the field, from group dynamics, laboratory groups and organization development groups. Only data which is useful in understanding organizational groups will be cited – a criterion which eliminates much of the available laboratory research which has limited value in studying role systems. Inevitably, some of the findings are more supported by research than others. Some of my comments are my own 'gut' feelings, because there are areas (e.g., groups and industrial relations) which sadly lack research findings.

What is a group?

A group is any number of people who are able to interact with one another, are psychologically aware of one another, and who perceive and are perceived as being members of a unit.

Usually the number of people is fewer than ten, and most frequently fewer than six. To a great extent, tasks determine group size in work organizations. A group is more enduring and supportive than two people interacting socially but is looser or less structured than an organization.

It is useful to examine groups in terms of such characteristics as group norms, structure, and roles. An analysis of these characteristics suggests highly generalizable observations which will provide a framework by which managers can analyse groups in their own role system.

Norms

The most consistent finding on groups is the emergence of norms about shared patterns of behaviour. Norms begin as our own expectations, which merge or converge with others' expectations to produce a group norm. Norms relate to behaviour, but there is also convergence of expectations, attitudes, beliefs, and feelings among members of the group.

The process of norm development in work groups is exceedingly complex but we do know something about the process:

- Norms develop about the task – i.e., the work the people were hired to do
- Norms develop about non-formal goals of the group – e.g., sport, or informal relaxation
- Norms develop about internal regulation within the group, about interactions, power, language, and discipline
- Norms develop about opinions, attitudes, and beliefs – about unions, management, non-members of the group, politics, religion, and territory
- Norms develop about physical appearance – work and non-work dress, use of safety clothing, lockers, lunches, and even carrying bags

The process of 'establishing' the group norm inevitably means modifying the expectations of some members. However, members will subsequently deny they changed their own expectations as much as they did. Explaining or rationalizing our own behaviour to make it appear rational is a characteristic of all behaviour, but especially of group behaviour – we can kid ourselves about anything if (as group members) we need to.

When you or I enter the group from outside, group norms are already shared by members, and our contribution to those norms is initially negligible. Unlike laboratory studies of groups, the work group is not created and permanently disbanded, but recurs over long periods of time. Consequently, norm development occurs over very long periods, and often very old behaviour patterns are preserved long after they have ceased to be relevant. You or I may notice these norms when we arrive, and question their relevance, but if group membership is vital to our role acquisition, we will accept the irrelevant norm merely to establish our intention to conform and thereby hasten our acceptance by the group. This sharing of expectations about acceptable behaviour ensures conformity.

The degree to which you or I will conform to group norms will depend on

- Our desire for agreement on our membership
- Our wish to avoid displeasure and possible isolation or punishment
- Our belief that the norm reflects our own view (congruence)
- Our doubting our capacity to stand alone
- Our belief in the group's goals

The degree of conformity to group norms in most organizations is considerable. Role performances are closely controlled, dress is controlled, speech is controlled. The disadvantage of this control may be the loss of individual initiative and creativity, but we have to weigh that cost against the cost of non-conformity.

Not all norms affecting our performance in organizations emerge within the role system. Societies also have norms which exist for a whole range of acceptable behaviour patterns. These norms arise from the culture of our society and are carried into organizations as well – they relate to universally accepted behaviour patterns – salutations, manners, dress, etc.

In contrast, group norms of members in a role system of an

organization are more subtle and relate to behaviour within that specific role system. However, the purpose of these norms is the same as societal norms: to reduce variability in behaviour, and to produce conformity, dependability, and predictability. Writers on groups who decry conformity but refer to 'positive conformity' as 'cooperation' are indulging in verbal games. Whether the organization is a university, a car manufacturing plant, a hospital, or an army, its existence relies on conformity, predictability, and dependability. Shared expectations or norms about what behaviour ought to be within a group are important in providing that conformity.

Research on conformity has shown that individuals with higher levels of ability conform less to group norms than those with lower levels of ability; individuals with high social needs for identification with a group conform more readily than those individuals for whom groups are not a rewarding interaction; highly authoritarian individuals conform more than less authoritarian.

Norms provide the base for the structure of any group. They are the first structured perceptions or snapshots of interpersonal relationships as members feel they should be. Subsequently, these 'structured' perceptions are elaborated into 'structured' roles which members play within the group. My behaviour in and out of a group is different. If I want group members' approval, I will accept the dictates of the group about my behaviour, even though I would not accept that influence in a one-to-one relationship. I will agree to decisions which are quite contrary to my own standards. I will modify my behaviour to conform to the expectations of the group and I will do so in a much shorter time than has been the experience of clinical psychologists working in a one-to-one relationship. What has happened to me in the group is that my own structured perceptions of myself and others have been modified into a series of simplified snapshots called *group norms* and expectations which are only marginally mine.

Too frequently in analysing role performances in organizations, managers forget the significance of a group as a source of power and influence on individuals. A boss tries to understand, say, how Harry, who proudly wears a company's 35 years' service badge, can walk out with his work group in an industrial dispute. The error the manager makes is to try to correlate

Harry's performance on his own with his performance in a group
. . . they are two entirely different performances.

Group members' perceptions of expected behaviour are concerned with bits of behaviour, rather than with behaviour as a
continuing phenomenon. On these bits of behaviour a structure
is developed, with norms as the structural foundations. On top
of norms, the group members develop expectations, implicitly
or explicitly, about the role that each of them is to play. In an
evolutionary way, the group members establish their own
psychological contracts with one another.

Group roles

Many roles will be performed by members within the group –
however, studies of groups have repeatedly found two roles
which recur:

- The task leader role
- The socio-emotional or maintenance role

The task leader role is a structuring, organizing, goal-setting,
and often dominating role. It is generally occupied by one person, but sometimes split between two people – a task leader
(manager) and a task leader (expert), where the manager does
not have the expertise but acquires power through his capacity
to get the task done.

The emergence of the task leader role in the group leads to
a second role: the socio-emotional or maintenance role. This is
concerned with supportive responses, seeking consensus, resolving conflicts, and avoiding group disintegration. Like the task
leader role, this may be split between several people. However,
the degree to which the role is absorbed by several people
appears to depend on the strength of the task leader role. That
is, if the group is dominated by one person, then to restore
balance to the group, most other members, for reasons which
are difficult to understand, may adopt a compromising, team-
building posture. The less dominant the task leader role, the
less spread, or even clear, the maintenance role. However, I
have seen cases where the reverse holds – the less clear the task
oriented role, the clearer the socio-emotional role.

In most work groups, both roles emerge clearly. They may be
played by two people; they may be played by more than two

people; they may also be played by one person who performs both task and maintenance roles. In their own way, and depending on the stresses within the group, the members will almost intuitively sort out a set of relationships which will provide both the leader roles and thereby establish a *balance of power*.

If the member playing the task leader's role leaves (the player is transferred to another location) then the group members will restructure and the roles will be reallocated. The time this balancing of roles and influence takes will depend on the people, their perceptions and expectations, the task, and the internal stresses. In a work group, a new structure will emerge within one or two weeks.

Structure and the balance of power

Unless there is a high staff turnover, the structure of work groups in organizations is invariably clearer than in studies of groups in laboratories. The early processes of structuring and allocating power which appear in laboratory studies have been resolved long ago. Roles are more finely delineated and other social roles have been allocated: the comedian, the best drinker, the union link, the arbitrator, the encourager, and the pacifier. Disturbing the group structure has, consequently, more repercussions than most managers realize. The entire fabric and balance of power within the group may be shattered if someone is pulled out. Certainly, in time, group equilibrium or balance will return, but there are many occasions when the cost of the group's disequilibrium is greater than the cost of not transferring that member.

The structuring process in *formal* work groups is affected by the hierarchy of authority and the managerial style of the boss. Because a person has a title such as 'leading hand' does not mean that there will not be a task leader role among his or her subordinates. What it does mean is that, if the leading hand adopts a very warm socio-emotional managerial style, then an 'informal' or 'unofficial' task leader role may emerge in the work group. Moreover, the balance of the roles is central to the output of the whole section. If the section works effectively, we may see the leading hand promoted and the unofficial task leader formally recognized and promoted to the position of leading hand. This strategy assumes a reciprocal rebalancing of power in the work group through the emergence of a maintenance role. In fact, a very different set of relationships may emerge, and not without some intra-group conflict.

The methods for gaining power in a group have been receiving more and more attention. Why, for example, does Betty win the role of task leader? In work groups or informal groups similar sources of power to those mentioned in chapter 4 are found – expertise, visibility, position, strength, etc.

Work groups have long time periods in which to assess the claims for power from task leaders. They can review the data on a person's past power, they can check the would-be leaders 'drops' or information leaked to establish expertise or experience ('When I worked in America I found . . .') For this reason, they may make fewer mistakes in choosing the roles members are to play in the group. Laboratory groups or social groups rarely have this opportunity, and it is somewhat alarming to me that members of laboratory or social groups accept 'drops' or claims for expert power without any attempt to check the data.

If power and influence explain the emergence of the task oriented role, they also explain the emergence of the socio-emotional role, but this process appears to be more complex. For example, Spillane has found that this role need not emerge at all in experimental groups. I have found that both roles usually emerge in work groups, but the roles, not individual performers, are the important variables. That is, the socio-emotional role may be spread across several people rather than confined to one person, just as the task role may be divided between people.

The more dominant the performance of the task leader role, the more the remainder of the work group are forced (or agree) to perform socio-emotional, supportive roles. This condition is also found in formal hierarchies; if the king is dominantly task oriented, he or she is supported by a group of warm, friendly people, who are often called 'weak'. In this example, these 'weak' people make it possible for the king to be effective by balancing his power. The major disadvantage of this balance of power occurs with the death of the king, which is usually followed by a long and painful period of restructuring and thereby rebalancing roles within the group. This sometimes means eliminating what are left of the original actors. Power balance is the key to understanding role relationships in groups.

Group power and influence

Informal, friendship groups occur most often across the hierarchy – peers, rather than bosses and subordinates, are friends. It is true that in very loose, open hierarchies, different hierarchical levels do form friendship groups, but this is still the exception rather than the rule.

The influence of the friendship group is greatest at the base of the hierarchy, where relationships between members are strongest. Conversely, members at the top of the hierarchy do have informal relationships, but there is little friendship involved; senior managers' informal relationships are based on convenience rather than love.

The power of groups to affect the behaviour of members should not be underestimated. You and I are affected by groups throughout our daily lives – in work groups, committees, families, or friendship groups. The ultimate control of the group is total rejection, a form of isolation few of us can endure for long.

This process of influencing behaviour in groups can be traced. When a deviation from the expected behaviour occurs phases of control will be seen.

Phase 1. The initial tolerance. The deviation is noted by members of the group. They may seek an explanation ('Why are you doing that, Harry?') or members may make excuses ('She hasn't learnt the ropes yet.'). Whatever the technique (and it may be total silence), other members of the group have registered the deviation and the implied message is, 'OK, we note the deviation. Now let's be sensible and not deviate.'

Phase 2. Attempts to correct. The members have noted the continued deviation from group norms and deliberately attempt to correct the behaviour. 'Don't keep doing that,' 'Put your clothes back on again,' 'You don't have to go home yet,' 'Have another beer,' etc. At this stage, members of the group are still tolerant, but are signalling verbally or non-verbally that the deviation must cease.

Phase 3. Verbal aggression. Other group members are becoming more annoyed by the deviation. Verbal messages become more hostile, more aggressive, and the threat of rejection may be offered: 'If you can't do it this way, don't do it at all' (fail and go elsewhere). Verbal aggression is more likely to occur than physical aggression with groups whose members come from middle or upper income families. Lower income groups use more physical aggression.

Phase 4. Physical aggression. As a control, this is limited by other group norms (e.g., no physical aggression). It is more likely to be used on the factory floor than in the boardroom (where the process is often more subtle but no less damaging).

Phase 5. Rejection. 'Get out.' As soon as the individual is rejected (physically or psychologically), the group members will rebalance power and roles, eliminate the deviant's contribution, and, if necessary, readjust its norms. Probably the most frequently used rejection is total silence.

In many cases, members of a group ignore all the niceties and reject immediately. Or the group may take step 2 and then go to 5. In other words, the phases are sequential but not necessarily consecutive.

The power of the peer group has been known to managers and union officials for many years, and both managers and union officials use that power to influence the behaviour of employees. What is particularly different about work groups, as opposed to others, is that the norms and standards are central to the rewards the members receive. If a deviant decides to produce more than the group norm, then all members of the group are threatened. Similarly, if the employees feel industrial action is warranted, they will not tolerate nonconformists because nonconformists weaken the group's position. Work groups are very much a case of 'one in, all in'.

This power and influence in work groups intrigues managers, mainly because they would like to manipulate groups and use group power. Power comes from within the group and depends on many variables. Probably the most important clue to power in a group is the degree of *cohesion*. Cohesion is affected by:

• How often the group meets

As work groups meet every day, they represent the second most cohesive group in most people's lives – second only to the family.

- The attractiveness of the group to members, in terms of objectives, satisfactions, and productivity

Members of informal groups in work organizations usually have vague objectives, and are less cohesive and often erratic. Members of formal groups are very goal oriented and groups are deliberately structured to achieve goals.

The 'attractiveness' of a group refers to the interpersonal attractiveness of members of the group for one another. Members may be attractive because they offer the opportunity for affiliation, recognition, security, or because the goals are significant to the member, or the expectations are strong that the group will satisfy that member's goals and motives. Group members reinforce their attractiveness by incentives – offers of more love, security, fun or affiliation. Research on job satisfaction has consistently shown that the degree of group cohesion is important in predicting the performance of a group. The 'mateship' syndrome is a particularly strong factor in most work systems, and productivity can be increased, satisfactions increase, and absenteeism decreased simply by reinforcing group attractiveness and cohesion.

The layout of the office or plant, the boss, the opportunities for interaction, and noise levels also affect the cohesiveness of the group. Most laboratory studies of group dynamics analyse the number of verbal signals to indicate cohesion and structure. This method is not very useful for informal groups in organizations, as there may be a great bond between a group of people despite verbal signals at work being very few. Often an informal group will rest alongside a machine, literally sitting on the factory floor, even though a canteen is available. In an entire lunch-hour, those same members produce only half-a-dozen verbal transactions between them, yet a multitude of non-verbal signals binds them together in a group. After work, at the pub, verbal interactions increase rapidly. It is this bond which the 'achievers' at the top of the hierarchy have great difficulty in understanding. In contrast, mainly because of their obsession with constant verbal signals, highly career-motivated people fill silences with socially acceptable noises.

Top managers' goals also affect cohesiveness and hence group power. Managers seek productivity, but claiming productivity as the only goal of a group may be a mistake. Each current process within a group is the cause of subsequent outcomes, including productivity. Holding only the final outcome to be significant denies the continuous shift in members' motives, attitudes, satisfactions, and interactions. Interactions are continuous and on-going, and it is the interactions now that are important for the cohesiveness of the group. It is the social reward of cohesiveness *in the group now* which affects productivity, *not* the pursuit of productivity itself. Productivity is the outcome of having a rewarding time in the group. The means to productivity is group cohesiveness and group satisfaction. Conversely, if productivity goals are achieved, this reinforces commitment and the feeling of group cohesiveness.

Conflict in groups

As groups depend on the allocation of roles (and power), they depend also on the consequences of power – conflict, cooperation, trust, mistrust, etc. Conflict is inevitable. It is also highly desirable and constructive in any social system, whether it be an organization, a group, a family, or a friendship. Constructive conflict energizes relationships in role systems; they might disintegrate if we were ever able to eliminate conflict.

Conversely, destructive conflict is injurious to social systems, and we should aim to eliminate the destructive, negative forms of conflict which pervade many work organizations.

Intrapersonal conflict occurs in an individual where there are equally attractive options but only one may be chosen. Interpersonal conflict occurs between two or more persons when attitudes, motives, values, expectations, or activities are incompatible and *if those people perceive themselves to be in disagreement*.

Constructive conflict can be very beneficial to a group. For example, conflict may:

- Introduce different solutions to the problem
- Clearly define the power relationships within the group
- Encourage creativity and brainstorming activity

- Focus on individual contributions rather than group decisions
- Bring emotive, non-rational arguments into the open
- Provide for catharsis, release of interdepartmental or interpersonal conflicts of long standing

Conversely, if conflict is destructive, it may:

- Dislocate the entire group and produce polarizations
- Subvert the objectives in favour of sub-goals
- Lead people to use defensive and blocking behaviour in their group
- Result in the disintegration of the entire group
- Stimulate win–lose conflicts, where reason is secondary to emotion

It is difficult, in analysing organizations, to know when intra-group or inter-group conflict is destructive. Sometimes, what seem to be very heated and destructive conflicts have very positive outcomes. For example, while a strike would normally be seen by managers and union members as destructive conflict, it can provide a focus for attention and an opportunity for catharsis.

The release of tension in organizations is probably one of the most neglected areas of research. In all societies the crowd, religion, and ritual have provided important social mechanisms for the release of tension. Organizations are only now beginning to appreciate the need for tension release, and some apparently very negative and destructive conflicts when released have positive effects.

Just as destructive and constructive conflicts are often very similar, competition and conflict are also difficult to separate. Competition is a form of conflict, a pre-condition for conflict, but conflict need not be competitive.

Most conflict occurs in groups because of differences among members in motives, attitudes, and feelings. The greater the involvement with those motives, attitudes and feelings, the more difficult it is to change people's perceptions and to resolve the conflict. Motives and attitudes about power are usually at the root of conflict but they do not necessarily cause conflict. Other factors – such as the seating plan, the location of the meeting, the task, status differences, and the leadership roles – are all influential in releasing differences.

Loss of equilibrium within a group may occur because of a variety of behaviours which lead to communication blockages. Some of these behaviours are usually destructive rather than constructive:

- Restricting information: a member of the group implies he knows the answer to a group problem but is not telling
- Lying: deliberate distortion of the facts to preserve a position in the group
- Paring: breaking into sub-groups rather than solving the conflict as a group
- Put-downs; put-downs of others or of self. The put-down of others, through verbal or physical aggression, may maintain the structure of the group. Self put-downs may get sympathy and de-fuse opposition – the 'poor-me' game
- Fight: win–lose conflicts which are difficult to resolve
- Flight: run away, sometimes literally to leave the group. More frequently, 'sulk' behaviour, withdrawal: leave the room, pretend to sleep, move physically away from the group, say 'I'm not really interested in the question'
- Making noise: speaking to be heard rather than to contribute. Often very fuzzy, undisciplined. Common in training groups
- Expertise: stopping contrary views by 'dropping' expertise. 'When I was in Paris, I talked with the Minister.' Using legal or scientific jargon to dazzle
- Suppressing emotions: Rather than letting the emotional blockages out, the person demands logic, rationality. 'Let's not get emotional,' 'Please let's act like adults.' This is unfortunate, as much of the blockage is emotional and should be expressed
- Changing to topic: changing the focus from topic to topic, or from person to person

There are many other variations on these tactics. People learn to use tactics which work for them. Hence, the person who uses the sulk response ('poor me') will continue to use it because it has been successful in the past.

All of us who work regularly in groups should try to identify our defensive and constructive behaviour. I have found that most people have no idea how they behave in a group, and are often most upset when they watch their behaviour in groups on television video replays. And the closer to the top of the hierarchy, the more surprised they are – high achievers learn to achieve on their own and rarely work in groups.

However, we should not get conflict and defensive behaviour out of perspective. If we need to watch for too much conflict in a group, we need also to watch for the reverse. Too much cooperation and agreement can produce a 'love-in', where completing the task becomes secondary to enjoying interpersonal processes. And, while interpersonal relationships are the most important relationships in our lives, members of organizations do need to produce something or complete a task. The difficult questions for a manager are: How much conflict, and how much cooperation? How much love, how much discord? How much process, and how much content?

Inter-group conflict
One of the most frequent forms of conflict in organizations is inter-group conflict: sales versus production, personnel versus finance. Much of the inter-group conflict occurs simply because we separate people into functions, such as sales, production, or personnel. Another cause is the fact that very different people, with different attitudes and perceptions, are attracted to each functional group.

The worst form of inter-group conflict is what is called a 'win–lose' conflict, in which the competing groups seek to win and in which there can only be one winner. Where this occurs, destructive conflict is usually the outcome.

What happens in this situation has been well documented:

- Each group becomes more cohesive, as members close ranks
- Each group becomes more task oriented
- Each group alters the leadership roles to strengthen the task oriented role at the expense of the maintenance role
- Each group becomes more structured, and demands more loyalty and assurances of solidarity
- Emotion, rather than reason, dictates group decisions

In looking at its competitor, each group

- Distorts perceptions of the 'enemy'
- Distorts perceptions of its own members, minimizing weaknesses within itself and concentrating on strengths
- Increases its hostility towards and decreases interaction with the enemy

If one group does win the competition, that group remains cohesive, releases tension through playful activities, and remains highly cooperative, but may become complacent.

The losing group tends to splinter; conflicts come to the surface; blame is allocated. Of winner and loser, the loser group is likely to learn more from the experience, and to evaluate its performance for future activity.

Resolution of conflict

As much conflict is constructive, the goal of a manager should not be to eliminate it. When conflict is dealt with openly, members are stimulated to seek solutions, to resolve differences, to be more searching and creative. However, much conflict in organizations is not confronted openly, but ignored. We can divide responses in handling conflict into one of the following categories:

- Denial/withdrawal

A manager attempts to get rid of the conflict by denying its existence: 'I don't think we have any problems.' If the issue is not critical, then this may be the best way of dealing with the conflict. However, as the causes of the conflict are not identified, denial may result in the conflict growing to a level where it becomes unmanageable.

- Suppression

The manager smoothes over the conflict. 'We don't really have any major differences, do we?' It is inevitable that organizations have conflict. To preserve relationships between members, suppression may often be the only feasible strategy to adopt – some people just dislike one another.

- Dominance

Power and influence may be used to settle the conflict. In a hierarchical structure, the use of dominance or power to resolve differences is inevitable. There will always be a 'last word', if only for the resolution of conflict. The advantage of dominance is that the answer can be found quickly. The disadvantage is that the method divides the members into winners and losers, with all the disadvantages of win–lose conflicts.

● Compromise

Negotiation may take place between the groups. Organizations depend on compromise. The very act of joining an organization is an act of compromise between what the individual wants and what 'the system' requires. Yet compromise often gets clouded in emotive adjectives, as though it is always a 'good' strategy. Whether we call it bargaining, negotiating, or compromising, this style of conflict resolution has disadvantages. For example, individuals tend to inflate their requests to allow for the compromise. Second, compromise is seen by members as a weakening and, hence, commitment to the decisions is less. Nevertheless, in a pluralistic organization compromises are inevitable.

● Integration or collaboration

Emphasis is put on the task rather than on defending positions. Everyone expects to modify his or her views. Group effort is seen as superior to individual effort. Differences are acknowledged and respected.

Group decision making

Some groups are very decisive, very productive, very creative, and very satisfying for their members. Others are the reverse. The remainder of this chapter looks at the process of decision making in a group. As we design more and more committees, task forces, teams, and production groups in organizations, we should remember that there are advantages and disadvantages in using groups as decision-making devices.

In our enthusiasm to 'group' people in organizations, we should ask, 'Is the group the best form?' 'Will the group give the best answer?' Groups have been found to make 'better' decisions in *some* situations. This may be because the group 'averages' its answers, which eliminates the extreme positions some individuals may adopt on their own. Other advantages of groups as decision-making devices are:

95

- The heterogeneity of experiences and skills in a group compared with one person
- Groups can generate far more and better quality ideas in brainstorming than can individuals working on their own
- A division of work or effort is possible
- Groups can generate more information on a problem
- Members can detect each others' errors
- The motivational arousal of being in the group decision

On the other side of the argument, groups have been found to make disastrous decisions. Some of the reasons are:

- Members were too alike (homogeneous)
- Failure in group discussion to detect the skills and experiences of different members
- Too many members (especially over seven) leads to restraints on participation
- The effect Janis refers to as 'group think' – 'a determination of mental efficiency, reality testing and moral judgment that results from in-group pressures'
- Search processes focused for short time spans on the problem
- Tangential discussions are time consuming
- The problem was technical and complex and known only to a few
- Time was lost because of the social issues in the group. Individuals working on their own concentrate on the task, not the task plus social interactions
- One member used coercion or expertise or position to dominate the others and conformity pressures were strong enough to eliminate constructive criticism
- Conjecture led the group into irrelevancies and time was wasted
- Members were so heterogeneous that they could not communicate

Janis's concept of 'group think' points even more at the dangers of group decision making at board level. His research leads him to conclude that 'group think' is characterized by:

- The group's belief in its invulnerability: 'If we all work together we can't go wrong.'

- The group's belief in its own morality: 'We are doing this for the benefit of everyone.'
- The group's belief in its own rationalizations: 'We had to lay off the 2000 at our other plant so we could save the jobs at other sites.'
- The group's belief in its own generalizations. 'We know the unions will agree.'
- The group's belief in its own uncritical thinking: 'Let's not go over it all again. We have thoroughly examined the alternatives.'
- The group's belief in its own unanimity in decisions. 'We have agreed, haven't we, to go ahead.'

To these I might add my own observations in working with groups in change programmes.

- The group's belief that all persons have expressed views and that the decision is a consensus of divergent views
- The group's concern for an answer at any cost rather than no answer
- The group's failure to identify expertise among its members

To guard against bad decisions in groups, we should all watch for these characteristics. Drawing them to the attention of the group is likely to lead to instant denial. A much more effective technique is to suggest to members that you have a break from the task. This breaks the cohesion and may give individuals time to reconsider. We can also save a lot of problems by carefully choosing tasks to be given to a group. Here are some of my own guidelines.

Guide for opportunities for group decision

- Give the group a concrete, not an abstract, task
- The task should have a definite beginning and end and reports on the effectiveness of the decision should be fed back to the group
- Give the group sufficient autonomy to carry out the task
- Reward the group as a whole (rewarding individuals negates the advantages of the group)
- The structure of the task for the group should at least include:
  a precise statement of the objective(s)

a precise statement on the method of presenting the group decision(s)

time and cost limits

- The task should require a variety of skills and experiences, not those of an expert. (Often an expert would be much more competent than a group).
- The more able the members, the better the decision
- The more aware the members are of group processes, the better the decision
- Cooperative groups are better problem solvers than competitive ones
- Creative groups, where members choose one another, make better decisions
- Where the leader roles lead to coordination to overcome the slowness, tangential discussion, loss of focus and other inefficiencies of groups, better decisions result
- Restrict the size of the group to five or six (although the empirical data is conflicting on group size)
- Select problems where the administrative cost and time *or* the social benefits support a group solution – that is justify the choice of a group

Too often, groups are selected for tasks with no forethought about benefit to the members or to the organization.

A group's problem-solving capacity is directly related to the interaction within the group. The interactive process moves through phases, and it is important to extract decisions at phases of maximum interaction.

Stages of group problem solving are:

- Orientation

The relationships of one member with another have to be worked out. Members are disoriented, not able to solve problems realistically. Questions of roles and power have not been resolved – balance has not been achieved.

- Deliberation

The interactive process of the group is brought to bear on the problem. This is the research, data analysis phase. Roles emerge, task and maintenance role performances are clearer.

Claims for power (expertise, experience, etc.) are signalled by members.

● Conflict

Individuals formulate their positions. Unfavourable comments are frequent. Polarization of attitudes occurs, and a reaction to the emergent roles and power distribution. Further counter claims for power are made.

● Emergence

There is a reduction in the amount of conflict, and fewer unfavourable comments. Ambiguous comments permit a shift in ground. Roles for task orientation and maintenance orientations are implicitly allocated to individuals – i.e., power is distributed and balanced.

● Trust

This stage is marked by the sharing of honest communications. It is the best phase for problem solving, where personal animosities (or organizational games) are minimal. Balance has occurred within the group. Role allocations are accepted by role performers.

● Reinforcement

Argument is minimal, as members become aware of the inevitability of the decision they are to make. Balance has been superseded by problem solving as the focus of attention. Decisions are made.

These phases of group problem solving should not be seen as a model to follow. The pattern may vary widely in specific groups. For example, trust may not occur between the emergence and the reinforcement phases at all. If it does, that is when it is *most likely* to do so. Similarly, conflict may not occur overtly, and after the deliberation phase the trust phase may lead straight to a solution (reinforcement).

As all of us spend time in groups, we can monitor group processes. Two important questions can be asked:

● What contribution do I and other members make to the task (i.e. content)?

- What contribution do I and other members make to group interaction (i.e., process)?

By conducting self-critiques within groups, teams, and boards of directors, we can eliminate a lot of the disruptive behaviour in ourselves and others. Unfortunately, too few groups will attempt that sort of critique without the aid of a behavioural scientist. Team-building techniques are now commercially available to conduct group critiques, and all groups of individuals who work intermittently together should, from time to time, conduct a group analysis. More frequently there is total preoccupation with task completion, and the senior executive often dominates his group so that his subordinates make only minimal contributions. Alternatively, the training officer's preoccupation with the processes within his training groups may be just as one-sided when they degenerate into mini-psychotherapy clinics, where solving interpersonal problems outside work becomes more important than the organization task. Somewhere between these extremes is where groups operate best. Just as most parents evaluate their influence on their children, just as most married couples spend time analysing their relationship, so, too, do we need to regularly assess what is happening in work groups in organizations. Only in this way can we get the best from work groups in task completion, problem solving, and decision making, and avoid the worst: failure to complete tasks, terrifyingly bad problem solving, and horrendous decisions.

Summary

This chapter began by identifying a group as any number of people who interact with each other, are psychologically aware of each other, and who perceive themselves and are perceived by others as being members of a group. Norms are the basic structural controls that group members devise for themselves. Norms are standardized expectations that members have about one another's contribution to the group. These expectations arise from the convergence of perceptions of one another's roles. Two roles which reappear in most groups are a task oriented leadership role and a socio-emotional maintenance or human relations role. These roles result from agreement on the allocation of power and influence within the group.

When both roles have been absorbed by members, the interpersonal relations in the group reach a level of equilibrium or balance, and concern for getting the task done becomes central to members.

Control within groups is related to both the leadership roles and to the norms of expected behaviour. Deviation from the group norms will lead other members to insist on conformity; if a deviant continues, then the ultimate painful threat to that deviation is rejection. As groups involve individuals influencing one another's behaviour, conflict (especially about power) is inevitable. Much of this conflict is constructive, energizing members' contributions. However, much of the conflict is destructive. Destructive conflict occurs where interpersonal relationships break down entirely, or where the openness and trust for members for one another decreases.

The next chapter looks at all the variables affecting an individual's behaviour in an organization. It concentrates on the role system and extracts the norms, rules, pressures, machines, etc., that affect performers within the role system. Most of these influences have already been cited – from chapters 1 and 2 (on individuals), through chapters 3 and 4 (on individuals interacting with other individuals), to chapter 5 (on individuals interacting with other individuals in groups).

Chapter 6 is about individuals interacting with other individuals in organizations.

For additional reading

Argyle M., *Social Interaction*, Tavistock, 1969.

Bales R. F., 'The equilibrium problem in small groups', in T. Parsons, R. F. Bales, and E. A. Shils, *Working Papers in the Theory of Action*, Free Press of Glencoe, New York, 1953.

Bullmer K., *The Art of Empathy in Interpersonal Relations*, Human Science Assoc., New York, 1975.

Cartwright D., and A. Zander, *Group Dynamics*, Evanston Row, Peterson, New York, 1953.

Cooper C. (ed.), *Theories of Group Learning*, Wiley, 1975.

Dunphy D., *The Primary Group*, Appleton Century Crofts, 1972.

Fisher B. A., *Small Group Decision Making: Communication and the Group Process*, McGraw-Hill, New York, 1974.

Hare P., *Handbook of Small Group Research*, Free Press of Glencoe, New York, 1962.

Janis I. L., *Victims of Group Think*, Houghton Mifflin, New York, 1973.

Kolb D. A., I. M. Rubin, and J. McIntyre, *Organisational Psychology: An Experimental Approach*, second edn, Prentice Hall, Englewood Cliffs, New Jersey, 1974.

Schein E. H., *Organisational Psychology*, Prentice Hall, Englewood Cliffs, New Jersey, 1965.

Shepherd C. F., *Small Groups*, Chandler, San Francisco, 1964.

Spillane R. M., *Authority in Small Groups*, unpublished Ph.D. thesis, Macquarie University, Sydney, 1976.

On team development

Fordyce J., and R. Weil, *Managing with People*, Addison-Wesley, Reading, Massachusetts, 1971.

Harvey D. F., and D. R. Brown, *An Experimental Approach to Organisational Development*, Prentice Hall, Englewood Cliffs, New Jersey, 1976.

Shepherd Clovie C., *Small Groups*, Chandler, San Francisco, 1964.

Zander A., *Groups at Work*, Jossey-Bass, San Francisco, 1977.

6 Organizations

Chapter 3 discussed relationships between two people, and the verbal and non-verbal signals that one person transmits to another. These signals we perceive as falling into a pattern, and we use these patterns or impressions to predict and explain other people's behaviour.

When a person joins an organization, he anticipates what will be expected of him. On entry to the organization he is confronted by an explosion of verbal and non-verbal signals. Some signals relate to required behaviour, others are merely suggestions of possible behaviour. There is no easy way to acquire roles; the humiliation of entry, of being desperate for data, of being without social supports, may be vital to the process of role acquisition. In time one adopts the expectations (formal and informal) of those in one's role set and one performs a role which, for most of the time, conforms to the expectations of oneself and of others.

This chapter sets out to develop a framework for analysing the influences on individuals in an organization. Of necessity, the framework or model is over-simplified, simply because all the influences are so interrelated through the individual's perception of them as to be impossible to separate. However, in the face of this complexity of motives, expectations, attitudes, influences, etc., of role systems, a framework is essential if managers are to understand some of the important interrelationships. I will discuss these influences on individuals as being: external, formal, informal, technical, and personal. Most of these influences on role performers have already been discussed in previous chapters, so my purpose here is to link much of the earlier discussion into a framework. As we have discussed personal influences such as motives, expectations, values, etc., in several other chapters, I will only briefly refer to these influences here. The focus for assessing influences will be the role system.

The role system

Organizations are coordinated role performers, producing a service or product. Role systems are interlocked role performers who have shared expectations about their own and others' behaviour. Most of these shared expectations can be extracted from the members and analysed as variables affecting behaviour. Hence, there are formal expectations about what I, as a role performer, should do. Similarly, there are informal expectations which represent my friendship and interest relationships with other role performers. There are physical limitations on my role performance, and these I have grouped as one variable, the technical system, simply because the major components of this influence is likely to be plant and equipment. Finally, people external to the role system have communications with me and therefore there are external expectations. These variables (formal, informal, technical, external) exist mostly in the heads of organizational analysts – that is, they group like expectations together (rather as we group like tasks together in designing work) and analyse those groupings. For example, the formal structure represents expectations (some of them written) about status, authority, rules, regulations, rewards, careers, promotions, appraisals, schedules, etc. And while, as a role performer, I know there is a 'system' or 'they', I am unlikely to have the relevant expectations grouped as neatly as analysts of organizations. Similarly, while I, as a role performer, may recognize that group norms are influencing my behaviour, I am unlikely to have these categorized as informal or formal norms. I am much more able to see the influence of external or non-member expectations and, although I may not think about it very often, I will be aware that the machinery I work with does have an impact on my behaviour.

The variables of organization analysts are collections of *like* norms, attitudes, beliefs, expectations, extracted from the role system from the behaviour of role performers. I will discuss them as being separate, and I will also argue that as variables we can manipulate them, rearrange them, change them – but what I am really saying is that the norms, perceptions, attitudes, beliefs, machines, external communications, can be changed, reinforced, etc., depending on the power one has to change those attitudes, beliefs, machines, etc., within the role system.

A further development of role systems is to believe that the interacting individuals constitute a system themselves. That is, the system or organization is itself a living, dynamic whole, in which the individuals are merely players. Or, from another perspective, the system is more than the sum of the parts. This view, known as *systems theory*, is a highly controversial one among academics and other theoreticians. I will use 'system' to imply the whole and will draw illustrations from systems theory, but my reason is the practical advantage of looking at an organization as a social system rather than because of any commitment to systems theory.

My own view is that organizations are linked or coupled mosaics of role performers, mostly working on their own, but from time to time working in groups. Very rarely does the entire membership of an organization occupy centre stage and sing or act together. Mostly we operate within role sets which are loosely linked to each other. Balances of power occur within and between a plurality of role sets which, in a power allocation sense, become dynamic.

It is difficult to conceive of an organization as a single system; it is easier to view it as a series of linked sub-units. Whatever dynamism occurs for the whole occurs because of the sub-units. And to suggest that the sub-units are analogous to the different parts of the body and to pursue this analogy to conceptualize a 'body corporate' gives extremely false impressions of the degree of linking between the role sets. Linkages are contrived through formal, informal, and technical devices. Basically, organizations are about individuals interacting intermittently.

Role systems have important characteristics. First, their members engage other people. Second, members' activities have a degree of coordination. Third, most action of the role performers is purposive or goal directed. Fourth, role systems (through individuals) take inputs from an environment, transform those inputs into products and/or services, and export them to customers. We can represent this as in Fig. 6.1.

There are six resources that role performers import from the external environment:

- Other people
- Finance
- Materials and equipment

Figure 6.1

- Ideas
- Information
- Energy

More resources are imported than are strictly needed for the transformation, to allow for breakdowns in production, reserves, and changes in orders.

Some transformations made in organizations by role performers to the resources are considerable – like steel transformed into cars, for example. Other processes are minor – like those in a clothing importing firm, where role performers do no more than add a new label to the item imported. Other minor changes include changing the packaging, wrapping the input, changing money, and charging for a service.

Once transformed, the product or service is exported from the role system by role performers specifically employed for marketing and distributing the product. Usually we classify organizations by their outputs: a steel company, an advertising agency, a butcher's shop, a building contractor, a bank, a university.

Once the transformed input (now the output or product) is placed in the market, role performers wait for feedback to see whether clients or customers like the transformed input. Feedback to role performers from external buyers creates an information network from input to output; to this extent, organizations are information systems, and the degree to which role performers collect, hear, and perceive feedback tells us something about the degree of *openness* of the system. Very closed systems block out external communicators; open systems receive verbal and non-verbal signals from non-members.

Openness

Early management theorists assumed that organizations were closed systems – i.e., that the role performers were not affected by non-members, external to that role system. In this way, traditional theorists were able to suggest ways to design organizations without any concern for changes in the market place.

More recent research has shown the need to study the members of organizations as exposed, subject to the pressures from other individuals in other organizations and groups. The boundary of the organization is not the front door of the building or the factory, nor is it the extent to which members move in and out of the physical limits of the organization. Organizations are coordinated collections of people or role performers, and the boundary refers to the relationships between the people and the lack of relations with non-members. Hence, the sales manager of an organization can extend the boundary of his organization all over a continent merely by flying from one place to another.

Organizational members develop mechanisms to reduce the number of feedback channels across the boundary from the market place. They do this through interaction in the role system. Structural devices such as restricted telephone lines, restricted channels for letters, or restricted entry through the reception areas for non-members are some of the more apparent ways to reduce the possible barrage of pressures (communications) from non-members.

External influences on the organization arrive as communications (verbal, visual, olfactory, and tactile) from individuals or machines outside. The selection of messages penetrating the role system is exceedingly difficult to control, simply because each member is receiving messages (verbal or non-verbal) from non-members. Each member brings these messages into the role system of interactions and transmits some of them to others.

The impact of the external environment on organizations has only recently been investigated. In the highly complex industrialized economy we live in, many role performances, much of the structure, and some of the technical system of an organization appear to be determined more by forces *external* to the organization than by those inside. Customers, suppliers, government agencies, competitors, and the inter-organizational dynamics of the market all have an impact on the organization we are examining. Even relatively closed organizations (such as the

107

monastery) are at the whim of the market, simply because the market place controls the source of survival, new members. Total self-sufficiency or independence is impossible for an organization – it *must* import resources and therefore is dependent on the external environment.

External pressures

The cumulative external influences on an organization will be called *external pressures*. They are one of the major variables for analysing organizational behaviour. It is important to identify and monitor them because they act either as a constraint or as an impetus for action and change in organizations.

Most members of organizations do not try to anticipate, react, or adapt to external pressures. Instead, they focus on their jobs and play out their roles, and only as changes affect their jobs or possibilities for promotion or for further rewards do they anticipate environmental pressures and prepare for them. Not unexpectedly, such isolated, individually-based reactions from members of a role system are unlikely to result in a clear overall strategy for adaptation. Organizational death among business firms is as prevalent today as 50 years ago.

Reactions within the role system to changes in external pressures appear to depend on the vertical and horizontal links between role performers. Where role performers are tightly

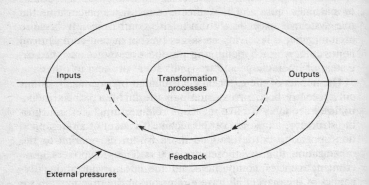

Figure 6.2 External pressures on the system

linked into a team, and where links between teams are strong, the capacity of role performers to adapt is better than where they are only loosely coupled together.

Where external pressures are recognized by members, there is a multitude of possible responses. First, we might just accept that we cannot predict the rate or direction of external change, and remain inactive. Second, we might accept some uncertainty, but react on whatever information we can get; what information we cannot get, we ignore. A third response is proactive: we take the information we can get from the environment and make plans and forecasts to deal with it. A fourth response is to interact with the environment: we try to clarify the uncertainty or lack of information about what is going on and, if necessary, to make changes to the environment.

If external pressures on role performers continue, there will be changes in the way the members perform. Roles will be modified. Initially the way to change the role will be by seeking structural answers, redesigning jobs, tightening controls, etc. Most of these devices occur initially as a result of informal huddles, and members attempt to resolve a question of power by rearranging authority. If the pressures continue, we are likely to see individuals modifying their own perceptions of what role they will play. They short-circuit formal devices, change standards, establish new priorities, and attempt to confront sources of power other than authority.

If pressures on role performers continue still, then personal changes to roles may mean loosening the structure, not because it is decided that some of the controls are unnecessary, but because members bypass them as they shift from a reactive to an interactive phase. Where this occurs, organizational survival is possible; where the learning process does not occur, the organization may die.

The degree of change that occurs in members depends on how stressful they find the external pressures. If the marketing department is seen to have 'external relationships' as their function, and if the market is kind, relatively certain, and predictable, then the level of stress within the marketing department and in other departments will be low. If external pressures were suddenly increased and became uncertain, hostile, and unpredictable, then reaction and proaction phases would probably precede the adaptive phase, simply because not enough role performers *felt* sufficient stress to adapt: 'It is a marketing problem. They have to solve it.'

Phase 1 of reaction would be recognition of the threatening environment by marketing people. Phase 2 would be a reactive redesign of the marketing structure. Phase 3 would be proactive, as attempts were made to involve others in planning strategies. Phase 4 may see a political struggle, as power shifts from marketing to another role performer (usually the king) who interacts with the environment. And so change winds its way through the role system. Not unexpectedly, for some organizations this is too slow, and disintegration occurs.

The degree of the reaction to external pressures is related to the motives of the role performers. If the organization attracts people seeking security, safety, and predictability, then environmental uncertainty is incompatible. They ignore the uncertainty, or seek structural devices to stop it. Structural devices may do little to increase the degree of integration of role performers into adaptive teams – indeed, it may hamper 'team work', with a consequent decrease in capacity to adapt. Conversely, risk organizations attract people with low security needs; there is less structure, more willingness to endure stress and uncertainty, and more capacity to adapt.

Further, role performers have varying degrees of insulation from external pressures, so that the pressures do not affect all members equally. On the boundaries of the organization, the salesmen are most exposed to external pressures. Well inside the boundaries, the people in production and accounts are more insulated and do not perceive external pressures to be as threatening. External pressures are not, as so many writers imply, a single uni-directional force; they are complex, of variable intensity and are perceived quite differently by different members of the same role system. As I said earlier, most members prefer not to receive them at all – it is more comfortable.

However, an organization is not just a piece of flotsam, bobbing on a turbulent sea of environmental uncertainty. Some organizations are in highly competitive markets (computers, consultants, estate agents). Others appear to be in highly competitive markets, but use power lobbies, cartel arrangements, contracts, dependencies, etc., to protect themselves from excessive external pressures. And the members of yet others have such power within the environment that they are relatively unaffected by external changes (monopolies, government departments, etc.). This last group of organizations may dictate pressures for *other* organizations. Not unexpectedly, they attract people with high needs for predictability, security, and structure, and are relatively predictable, safe, highly structured organizations. The vast majority of role performers do not deal with non-members, do not anticipate external changes, but remain preoccupied with their jobs. In this way, some government bureaucracies can survive electoral upsets, foreign and home government investigations, and even revolution, relatively unaffected by these experiences. Such power to survive, fortunately, is a feature of very few organizations.

Internal variables

The transformation of inputs into outputs becomes a highly complex part of the organization. Indeed, at various stages in the development of organization theory, parts of the process alone have been called *the* organization. For example, 'the organization' of the finishing process in a factory, or 'the organization' of the community fair. Unfortunately, this double use of the word *organization* had led to confusion. These administrative processes will be referred to as structures, and only the entity as a whole will be called the organization.

Input transformation is achieved either by individuals or by individuals working machines, and the personality of each and every one of those individuals is brought to the organization each day. The abilities, experiences, and motives of the individual, together with his perceptions and expectations, are the inputs to the transformation process – individuals on their own, individuals interacting in twos and threes, and individuals in groups are what constitute role systems.

But the moment we place two people into a working relationship, we create a whole range of *situational variables* which will affect their performances. It is these situational variables which transform temporary role systems into more or less permanent organizations. Let us look first at individuals as performers in role systems.

Individuals and structures

The process of transforming inputs into outputs creates a pattern of behaviour in members which we can study. The expectations and the behaviour of individuals as they do their work and interact with one another are called the *role system* of the organization. It is here that the observer can see much of what makes the organization interesting: the stresses, the successes and the failures, the love and the hate, the freedom and the fear, the powerful and the powerless, which characterize behaviour in organizations.

Chapter 3 explained that, when an individual joins an organization, he or she is asked to play a part in the role system. This part is called a *position*, which is a collection of tasks which have been planned (explicitly or implicitly) for one person. Contrary to many earlier theories, this planning of positions, in the early years of the organization's life, is not a highly logical activity. It is a very *ad hoc*, unplanned procedure of trying new and better combinations of skills, machines, motivations, and abilities.

An excellent example of the implicit, trial-and-error structuring occurs in a family. When Fred marries Myrtle, they form a group, or *dyad*. Assuming they have not lived together before, Fred will develop expectations about Myrtle's behaviour and Myrtle develop expectations about Fred's behaviour. Little by little, they are prescribing positions for one another. Without very much debate, they fall into a pattern of structured inter-relationships based on shared expectations. For example, Fred always showers first, and Myrtle makes some coffee. When Fred finishes showering, Myrtle showers while Fred dresses. Fred then gets the newspaper, the milk, and makes the toast, while Myrtle dresses. Anyone can observe these recurring behaviour patterns within his or her own family. After a period of time, any observer of Fred and Myrtle could produce a manual describing the jobs or positions Fred and Myrtle have in the dyad. What the manual is describing is the emergence of shared expectations, or *structure*, and the power relationships between these two people as they perform their roles within the physical constraints of their house and the relational constraints of other roles.

Already there are numerous situational variables affecting

both Fred's and Myrtle's role performances. First, their own motives, abilities, interests, perceptions, expectations, etc., can be considered as one variable for analysis. For the purpose of studying organizations, we can collect these personal characteristics together into a single variable – *the individual variable*. (Other writers may call it the *people variable* or the *personality variable*.) It consists of the influence of personal motives, perceptions, and expectations on role performances. See Fig. 6.3 for an illustration of this concept.

A second variable for analysis, *structure*, may also be extracted from Fred's and Myrtle's situation. They have begun to structure their relationship into predictable patterns of behaviour.

As we add more people to Fred and Myrtle's unit, the parts or positions they all play will be more clearly defined, and the constraints on behaviour will increase, simply because the group is more complex and the transformation process requires more structure. For example, the family of two will be less structured than the family of ten. The family of ten may have a whole series of codes simply for using the bathroom in the morning.

In this same trial-and-error manner, processes become structured in organizations. The structure is initially the same as Fred's and Myrtle's: the combined expectations of the members involved. Later, members create positions and fill them with people who spend their entire day structuring the processes and roles of other people. Organization and Methods specialists turn what has often been a trial-and-error procedure into a specialist function. Words like *authority* (or legitimized power) replace

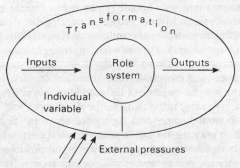

Figure 6.3 The individual variable

such less structured concepts as *relationships*. People in positions of power allocate authority to control resources (people, money, materials, etc.) to other people, and, partly by this allocation, power relationships are determined. The fluidity of the very small organization begins to disappear; structure replaces trial and error in determining behaviour. Indeed, from a free-forming relationship of two, where organizational manuals and other trappings of the structure are absent, we now begin to see that process by which a formal structure, using pre-determined authority delegations, may eventually programme the behaviour and determine the formal relationships of thousands of people. In the ultimate, the formal structure may produce totally programmed behaviour (e.g., the soldier on the parade ground).

A minimum structure is a division of roles in the role system into two major categories:

- Task oriented roles – goal and structure oriented
- Relationships oriented roles – socio-emotional oriented

When Fred and Myrtle began living together, it was likely that one of them acquired a structuring role to play, and the other spent more of his or her time playing a supporting, maintaining, human relations role. Personality factors do affect the allocation of the parts to be played but, at times, by mutual agreement roles will be swapped. In very crude terms, there will be a 'dad' part and a 'mum' part in any role system. The allocation of parts does not depend on sex, but, I believe, on roles played in parental family, birth order, and relationships with other members of the family.

As cited in chapter 7, some 43 per cent of male executives tested in our research have favoured playing the relationships oriented part in work organizations. It is possible (although rather over-simplified) that, in their marriages, many of these 43 per cent have wives who play the dominant or task oriented role – and despite the music hall jokes about such marriages, the relationship may well be a balanced and successful one.

The emergence of these two role performances was identified first in individuals (some showing a preference in their management style to play the task or output oriented part, while others preferred to play the supporting, warm, approachable role). Subsequently the phenomenon was seen in groups (task leaders and socio-emotional leaders), and more recently in our own studies in organizations we have found that two roles (not necessarily played by two people) emerge. In a subtle way, we allocate power or permit ourselves to be influenced by others along two dimensions – probably because we see this distribution of power in our parental family.

When a third person enters the relationship between Fred and Myrtle, the allocation of roles is thrown into some disequilibrium and a period of adjustment follows, when the three people sort out their expectations about influencing one another's behaviour. Once this is resolved, a new or modified structure emerges. Similarly, with the arrival of numbers 4, and 5, and 6, the structure is modified again, and the new relationships become established. By the time 15 have joined the system, the structure is much more complex, with more rules and sanctions. But as influence has previously been face-to-face, this is no longer possible for most of the time, so written signals are added to verbal signals about what is expected and who has positional power (authority).

It is inevitable that structure in role systems is always in arrears of emergent expectations; it is modified officially in organizations only after changes in behaviour have already occurred. In small groups, the structure is the cumulative expectations of members and it approximates their expectations *now*. In organizations, as they increase in size, the cumulative expectations about the official structure drift further and further away from what is 'now.' For this reason I have divided structure into two variables – *formal* and *informal* structures.

Formal and informal structures can only be adequately differentiated by time. Formal structures are those official or legitimated expectations which are known to and shared by most people. As an organization increases in size, it becomes more and more difficult to ensure that all performers share the same expectations – it takes longer to establish what they are. And for this reason, formal structures fall further and further behind what is 'now' in time. Elaborate and intricate devices are used to bring members up to date with official expectations. In contrast to this, informal expectations relate to relationships now, within one's role set and friendship group.

Increasing size and complexity

When the organization includes 10 to 15 members, relationships become segmented because of the communication difficulties when 10 or 15 people are all relating to each other at the same time. Interests, friendships, tasks, and technical systems all influence the emergence of these sub-groups. These groups are based on relationships 'now', on liking, attraction, and fun, and are usually referred to as *informal groups* – quite unofficial, unsanctioned, yet essential for organizational survival. This rich network of unofficial relationships develops for many reasons, one of which is to link formally separated units together.

With the emergence of informal groups within the total group, solutions to task problems are often found informally, and subsequently many of these solutions are formalized: 'From now on, so that this problem does not recur, let's always place our orders by Thursdays.'

The intricate relationship between the formal expectations and informal expectations is continual . . . informal relationships produce formal solutions, which in turn (because they are official or formal) produce more informal relationships. By the time the group has 15 members, clear formal structural devices have appeared. In a small business, the founder–boss has probably moved himself physically away from the other 14. He has begun the process of reinforcing status by withdrawing and reducing the number of communication channels that can reach him directly. He isolates himself from the others and may place a secretary in between his office and the location of the other 14 members.

By the time the organization has 30 people, members will have devised further structural devices. Separate tasks or functions of the transformation process will appear; more written controls will have evolved, sales may be separated from administration; accounting is likely to emerge as a separate function. This evolutionary process of specialization is known as *functional differentiation*, and it occurs continuously in role systems, as like tasks are grouped and new power centres emerge. Leading functions also evolve; one function in the process (e.g., sales) seems to have more power and influence than any other function.

Within each of these functionally structured sub-groups or couplings, (accounting, sales, production), the structural evolution continues. Norms develop, and task oriented and main-tenance of relationships roles emerge. Often these roles are spread over several people, but they emerge none the less.

In an organization of 60 people, the members will have a formally structured production function, an accounting function, and a sales function. The order of emergence depends largely on external pressures and on the skills of the founder–boss. Entrepreneural founders with sales skills may hold on to that function themselves, rather than allow others to perform that function. Further, entrepreneurs who have a high tolerance for risk are likely to hesitate in appointing an accountant, who may be seen as a non-risk-taker, over-concerned with security.

The last recurring business function to be differentiated is personnel. It is usually differentiated in organizations of between 100 and 200 people, but the tasks of this function are handled within the accounting function and remain with the accounting staff for a long time. Sometimes the function does not become separated from accounting until there are between 500 and 700 people, and usually then it is separated because of the series of 'people' crises rather than a planned introduction of the function.

By the time the organization employs 1000 people, the majority of formalized, structural devices have appeared. Hierarchy and authorities are defined and charted, job descriptions describe positions and authorities, there are appraisal schemes, complex reward systems, career plans, and a whole host of implicit and quite explicit behaviour codes. There is a multitude of accounting and production controls to ensure that the feed-back loop of the system will allow members to notice deviation from plans.

The technical system (equipment, plant, buildings, etc.) introduces a range of further formal controls on behaviour. We already have a highly complex and structured organization, and it is not uncommon to hear, in informal group discussions, 'It isn't like it was in the good old days when we all knew each other and had lunch together.'

And that is true – it is not like it was. Something has been lost by growth. The 'system,' or the accumulated norms of formally required behaviour, has acquired power through a process of structural design. The self-regulating small group that began this story has been superseded by a formal structure more powerful than most of the members working in it. And many informal groups have developed to satisfy members' needs for fuller, less structured relationships. The formal and informal structures have been extracted from the role system as identifiable influences on behaviour in Figure 6.4.

Informal structures

Once the members of an organization begin to structure the process for getting the job done, informal or friendship relationships develop. There is some debate as to whether informal relationships emerge first and the formal structure second, or the reverse. My observations suggest that it depends on how planned the system is when it starts. Some founders of organizations have explicitly designed a structure when they ask members to join (e.g., starting a new political party). Other, less planned, situations see informal relationships emerging first, followed by formal structural relationships.

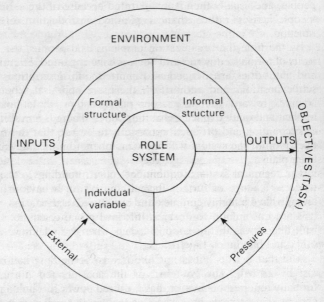

Figure 6.4 Formal and informal structures and the role system

Informal relationships appear to be essential for organizational survival. Based on our needs for close relationships, these affiliations lead to friendship, interest and work relationships which are unofficial, emotional rather than rational, and are very satisfying to all of us. Indeed, one of the personal objectives of most people at work is to form a truly cooperative team, where honesty and support prevail rather than dishonesty and lack of trust. Attempts to redesign jobs and organizations try to re-create this elusive climate.

Informal groups usually have fewer than five people. The most common number is two, but groups can range up to seven or eight. Within each group, a structure emerges in a manner similar to that described for relationships in formal structures. Expectations of one member about the behaviour of other members and the expectations of others about the first member lead to a degree of structure which is implicit rather than explicit, but nevertheless very binding.

The degree of structure in groups and the controls in those groups was discussed in chapter 5 on group behaviour.

The number of informal peer groups in organizations is greatest at the base of the hierarchy and least evident around the top. People with high needs for relationships and low esteem or fulfilment needs are more likely to be found in production rather than managerial tasks. It is these people who form the strongest and most enduring informal relationships.

This high need for interpersonal relationships, plus the fact that the structure is most rigid at the base of the hierarchy, leads unskilled workers to form extremely tight informal groups, which persist into non-work situations. Further up the hierarchy supervisors and managers may be less concerned with relationships. Careers and self-fulfilment are more important to them, so we see fewer informal relationships based on friendship. Relationships do exist informally, but these relationships are based on ladder climbing rather than love and friendship.

Informal relationships usually occur across the hierarchy – between peers, rarely between boss and subordinate. There are two reasons for this lateral, as opposed to vertical, structuring of informal relationships. First, as informal relationships are based on openness, they may be difficult between boss and subordinate in a formal structure where the boss determines the future career path of the subordinate. Conversely, the subordinate has been raised in a society where the boss was different, superior, often god-like. If the boss presumes to be the same as the subordinate, then he is no longer different, and the subordinate may feel cheated – where is the god figure? For this reason, subordinates will encourage the boss to participate in their social functions, but they and their boss will seek out their own peer groups for longer-term relationships.

Calling this variable of organizations the *informal structure* draws attention to the fact that the multitude of small groups where people chat and relate to one another and express themselves openly are linked into a very complex network. If the occasion arises where such a network is needed, linkages will be made between the groups. However, most of the time group members are not concerned about other groups, and groups are entities whose behaviour is erratic and difficult to predict.

Some people belong to a variety of groups (friendship, work, lunch, etc.) and are able to transmit messages to several groups. Through such linkages, the informal grapevine can link quite different and unrelated groups into a whole network *if* the information being transmitted affects everyone. If the information affects only one department, then it is likely to remain in that department. But if the king is very ill, then the linkages between diverse and often geographically widespread groups are made without too much planning or noise. Within hours, the entire membership of the organization has received the message. Hence, the informal structure can be analyzed as a whole, but is rarely seen as a whole.

The past 70 years has seen many abortive attempts by managers of organizations to squash informal relationships. The most frequent methods have been to disallow talking, or to keep changing group membership. These were extraordinarily stupid tactics. As the majority of the work force seeks strong relationships, is it common sense to prevent such relationships? Further, as informal discussions are often highly creative and innovative, attempts to prevent such relationships stifle a major source of creativity. Enlightened organizations actively encourage informal relationships through work group structures with considerably reduced formal constraints.

In summary, then, we can divide structure in organizations into formal and informal. One represents the rules, regulations,

120

controls, hierarchy, and the other the norms, controls, and roles of friendship and interest groups.

Why do we structure relationships?

Probably we do so because we structure our perceptions of people, things, and situations. The tendency to structure is related to security needs. We seek to reduce uncertainty and create order. Religious teachings suggest that it is because God created order and we try to emulate that order – the physiological cell is a highly structured and ordered system. Another possible reason is that we perceive our world in patterns. Another possibility is that from birth we are in structured situations, with the distribution of power to the task and the maintenance roles allocated between mother and father. The child is subordinate. Another reason for structure is to communicate – communication is impossible without some semblance of structure. Finally, we have learnt that getting tasks done is easier if a structure is defined – so structure helps get work done.

Whatever the process by which structure is developed, psychological comfort and conditioning seem the most plausible causes. In the family, a child soon discovers the hierarchy of mum, dad, child. In extended families, play groups, and kindergartens, he sees more examples of hierarchy. Once he reaches school, he enters his first major organization outside the family. Here there is a clearly defined formal structure, with a headmistress or master, a teacher, and the children. Even the children are formally structured into first grade, second grade and so on. And within each class there is a structure among the children, based on ability, muscle, behaviour, social class. If a child has not understood hierarchy and authority (or positional power), we reinforce it over and over again.

They move from kindergarten's top class to the bottom class in primary school, and the ladder climbing begins again; third form, fourth form, etc. Having mastered this hierarchy we go through the process again: the high school child, previously at the top of the hierarchy in primary school, is moved to the bottom of the hierarchy in high school and the process begins again – first form, second form, right up to sixth form. And for one final reminder, the university student is placed on the lowest rung of the hierarchy and given the dubious title of 'Fresher'.

121

With this sort of vertical thinking and conditioning, and the recurring evidence that structured processes appear to be more efficient and 'successful' than unstructured processes, it is not difficult to see why we continue to repeat the same basic ingredients of structure over and over again. As order relieves our fear of insecurity and uncertainty, we are able to satisfy a need by structuring our relationships. And we see people doing just this in any situation involving more than two people. At dinners, at parties, at schools, at football matches, the observer can watch the mania to structure. Over time, he can divide structures into the formal or the informal. The advantage of this characteristic of structuring in man is that he produces a relatively predictable and ordered society. One disadvantage is that trying to reduce or change the structure becomes difficult, since all the members of an organization are in various ways contributing to the growth of that structure.

The technical system

As members structure the process of transformation of inputs into outputs, it becomes clear that some mechanical devices would be more effective than additional human contributions. Into the process we place machines, and link the machines to one another through the contributions of individuals. Each machine we introduce in turn adds more formal structure because it produces behaviour controls, often documented in operating manuals on how to get the best from the machine. Buildings, office walls, machines, plant, computers, telephones, typewriters, calculators, etc., contribute to the efficiency of members' performances, but also add to the complexity of the formal structure. As these physical influences affect behaviour, I have separated them as a distinct variable called the *technical system*.

The technical system may be a major determinant of the shape and complexity of the formal structure. For example, a massive paper-making machine will determine the behaviour of all the people who work around it. It will also determine what jobs are to be done, how many people will be required, what skills they will need, and how they will interrelate. However, more recent research has suggested that the relationships between the technical system and the formal structure is *not* a direct one. Other contributing factors are the size of the technical equipment, the size of the organization (in terms of the number of people) and the external pressures. Figure 6.5 presents the five major influences or variables affecting role performances with the role system.

Summary

The components of a productive system are:

- Inputs
- Processes
- Outputs
- Feedback

The members themselves form a role system within the organization, and their interpersonal relationships lead to the emergence of *structure*. Structure occurs both formally and informally. Informal relationships compensate for the constraints imposed by the formal structure. The *technical system* makes it physically possible to transform the inputs into outputs, and the technical system aids the feedback loop.

Figure 6.5 shows the major variables of our model of an organization. Unfortunately, figures are two-dimensional and lack the dynamism of the real world. However, by considering all these situational variables we begin to understand the com-

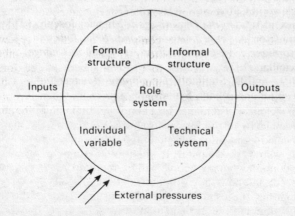

Figure 6.5 The technical system

plexity of predicting individual performance. Not unexpectedly, predicting organizational performance is even more complex.

The next chapter looks at the final major variable of organizations: leadership, or managerial style.

For additional reading

Bowey A., *The Sociology of Organisations*, Hodder & Stoughton, 1976.

Byrt W., *People and Organisations*, McGraw-Hill, Sydney, 1971.

Child J., *Organisation: A Guide to Problems and Practice*, Harper & Row, 1977.

Evan W. M. (ed.), *Interorganisational Relations: Selected Readings*, Penguin, 1976.

Farace R. U., P. R. Monge, and H. M. Russell, *Communicating and Organising*, Addison-Wesley, Reading, Massachusetts, 1977.

Handy C., *Understanding Organisations*, Penguin, 1977.

Hunt J. W., *The Restless Organisation*, Wiley, Sydney, 1972.

Kast F. E., and J. E. Rosenzweig, *Contingency Views of Organisation and Management*, SRA, Chicago, 1973.

Katz D., and R. Kahn, *The Social Psychology of Organisations*, Wiley, New York, 1966.

Korman A. K., *Organisational Behaviour*, Prentice Hall, Englewood Cliffs, New Jersey, 1977.

Townsend R., *Up the Organisation*, Michael Joseph, 1970.

Warmington A., et al., *Organisational Behaviour and Performance: An Open Systems Approach to Change*, Macmillan, 1977.

Yuill B., and D. Steinhoff, *Developing Managers in Organisations*, Wiley, Sydney, 1975.

7 Leadership

The discussion so far has moved from individuals, to groups, to organizations. At each level of analysis, the motives, expectations, and attitudes of individuals have been vital in understanding what may be happening. Of the *major* influences on role performers within role systems, one influence remains to be discussed: the role played by the *leader*. He or she is the vital link between a multitude of role expectations faced by individuals and their role performances – between what is expected in the organization and what actually occurs. In this sense, the role of the leader could be the most important variable of all.

For centuries, man has been attempting to find out why some people are better at performing the leader role than others. In this century, there has been an avalanche of research on leadership, but most of this research has been of little use to the practitioner. Indeed, there are few areas of the behavioural sciences which have been so persistently disappointing in producing useful results for practitioners. Some writers have suggested abandoning the concept of leadership altogether, because it has outlived its usefulness. Others feel too embarrassed to discuss it in public.

Leadership is a process which involves the leader, the led, and the situation. Studies of leadership have tended to concentrate on one of these three variables. First, the personality of the leader. Second, the personalities of the led. Third, the characteristic of the situation: tasks, structure, pressures, technology, etc. More recently, a deviation from this pattern has been to study the actual behaviour of the leader in the role system. This approach has been labelled *leadership style*. After a brief discussion of the personality or trait theory approach, this analysis will concentrate on style, as the approach most likely to be useful.

I see leadership as the embodiment of the commonweal; as an outcome of a man or woman's capacity to sense and prescribe what a situation requires and to encourage others to perceive and pursue that prescription. Management, on the other hand, does not require such situational sensitivity as it literally means 'keeping the show going'. Some managers are leaders; some are not. Conversely, some leaders are terrible managers.

At this stage, I am making a traditional distinction between leadership and managing. This chapter looks at leadership as a behavioural process within role systems. So is managing, but managing has been defined traditionally to include a planning and evaluating function as well. While leaders do plan and evaluate, most research concentrates on the interpersonal relationships of leader and led. Managing, on the other hand, has only recently been seen as primarily interpersonal. In this sense, the distinction I am making is fallacious; I make it only for convenience in discussion. Managers are leaders; leaders are managers. This overlap is seen most clearly in style theory, which comes under two synonymous labels; leadership style and managerial style.

Traditional theories of leadership

Trait theory
Some people seem better at leader roles than others. Traditional leadership studies attempted to produce a profile of personality characteristics from which we could identify those people. This led to 'Christ-like' qualities being offered as a basis for selecting school captains, officers in the armed forces, executives, executive cadets, and any other occupant of a leader role.

School systems throughout the world built much of their curricula on the assumption that we could develop certain desirable characteristics in people and, therefore, could mass-produce future leaders. Among the desirable characteristics were honesty, courage, decisiveness, intelligence, and maturity. Subsequent research on the relationship between these characteristics and success in leader roles has been very disappointing. There is very little empirical data to support the personality trait approach to leadership and selection. People who use personality tests in selecting executives have yet to justify their claims with empirical data.

My own research has shown that those who make it to the top and thereby to positions where leadership is vital are above

126

average in intelligence (but not too high above average), are healthy, are from middle to upper class backgrounds, have high power needs, and are more often first born or first son. But we have also found that these characteristics are not necessarily the predictors of 'good' leaders. Many who make it to the top are not good leaders, so, while we can identify a few personality dimensions which do correlate with moving up the hierarchy, the same characteristics do not necessarily correlate with being effective in leader roles. There is certainly some truth in the cliché, 'Con men make it to the top'; chapter 4 mentioned some of the political games they play.

In short, there is no set of personality traits from which we can predict successful leaders or, conversely, from which we can predict non-leaders.

Yet organizations depend on identifying potential and promoting that potential. In fact, they are so dependent on this process that assessment centres to identify talent have become multi-million-dollar businesses. Appraisal systems also rely on desirable personality traits. So to find that there is no one set of characteristics which could be used for these purposes is not very helpful for practising managers. What it does mean is that the use of traits in appraisal should be reduced, and other criteria (such as criteria of job performance, self assessment, interpersonal relationships, motivation to succeed, etc.) could replace these nineteenth-century elitist and militaristic personality traits, which still dominate so much of our culture. More and more we are learning that there are factors, other than individual characteristics, which may be more important in determining successful leadership.

Style theory
Over the past 20 years, research has shown that the personality of the manager is merely *one* variable in predicting leadership effectiveness. Other factors are:

- The situation he has to manage and his perception to it
- The people in that situation and their perceptions of it
- The organizational constraints on the situation (formal structure, technical system, environment, number of people involved)

Because of the number of variables involved, Fred may be a

very successful leader in one situation but quite ineffective in another. Children learn very early in life to seek out those situations where they excel and avoid those areas where they do not. Similarly, managers seek out situations where they will succeed and feel most uncomfortable in situations where they feel, or others feel, they cannot succeed.

Because of the shortage of people with the Greek-god profile suggested by trait theory, style theory has superseded trait theory. This approach looks at what the leader or manager *does*; how he/she behaves in response to the demands of the situation, including the expectations of subordinates, his/her own perceptions and expectations, and the possible use of his/her own abilities and experiences.

Early attempts to label leadership style produced a continuum between two extreme behaviour styles:

Democratic . . . . Autocratic

These two styles were seen to exist almost as though the situation had little or no bearing on managers' use of these styles. In the economically insecure world of the 'twenties, 'thirties, and 'forties, an organizational combination that was very effective was:

- A bureaucratic structure
- Repetitive technology
- Rewards satisfying security needs (pay, superannuation, sick pay, etc.)
- Closely restricted informal relationships
  and
- Autocratic managers

With the changed circumstances of the 'fifties and 'sixties – including high external pressures, the rising standards of living, and a consequent satisfaction of safety needs – increased pressure for alternative combinations of the variables of organizations emerged. These new pressures also meant different managerial styles. This in turn led to an increasing search to identify alternative but effective leadership styles (Fleishman, Fiedler, Reddin, Blake and Mouton, House, and Vroom and Yetton).

Among the important studies of leadership behaviour were those conducted at Ohio State University in the early 'fifties. This research found that the two dimensions (democratic and autocratic) were not supported in the way previous theories had argued. Fleishman claimed the two dimensions of leadership style were:

- Initiating structure
- Consideration for others

That is, there was consistent evidence in studies of leadership of an initiating structure – getting organized and pushing the work through – factor, *and* there was a people, or human relations, or consideration for others factor. Both factors can be evaluated in an individual by using a simple questionnaire. The factor can be described as below.

Initiating structure. This reflects the extent to which an individual is likely to define and structure his role and those of his subordinates towards goal attainment. A high score on this dimension characterizes individuals who play an active role in directing group activities through planning, communicating information, scheduling, trying out new ideas, etc.

Consideration. This reflects the extent to which the individual is likely to have job relationships characterized by mutual trust, respect for subordinates' ideas, and consideration of their feelings. A high score is indicative of a climate of good rapport and two-way communication.

A second clarification of this research was that the two behavioural dimensions are not opposites on a continuum, but are both found in differing degrees in the behaviour of all people. However, most people have more of one dimension than the other. Third, the Ohio studies found that the two factors were independent of each other – that is, what a person has on one factor has no influence on what he or she has on the other. I have represented this claim in Figure 7.1. Later research has supported the two factors. Bales found the same dimensions in group behaviour (task leader and socio-emotional leader) and Zelditch found similar two dimensions in marriage (task specalist and maintenance specialist). More recent research has questioned the independence of the two dimensions. Some studies conclude that the two dimensions are related, other studies show they are not. For our purposes here it does not matter: all bosses display behaviour which can be described by these factors and, therefore, these factors are useful for categorizing leader behaviour. Some managers have more task or initiating structure orientation while others have more consideration or human relationships orientation in their leadership behaviour. Yet a third group are equally oriented on both factors.

Blake and Mouton (1964) produced a style grid for classifying different combinations of these behaviour factors on the two axes. They added to the confusion by renaming the axes: Concern for people and Concern for production. But they clarified combinations of behaviour on the two factors by isolating, from empirical data, five idealized leadership styles. Reddin has extended this sort of classification further and developed a matrix of styles. He has also related those style categories to a large number of situational variables – task, structure, technology, etc. Another attempt to extend the classifications of relevant styles comes from Vroom and Yetton, who use different decision strategies, from autocratic decisions to delegating decisions to groups, and ask managers to relate these decision strategies to 18 contexts.

My own belief is that these extensive reclassifications suffer from the same problems as the type theories of personality – we merely divide human beings yet again into behavioural types. My second reservation is that the empirical tests of style theories have not been encouraging, especially when related to performance. Their major contribution has been the data they give managers about themselves and their leadership style – and even on this issue I have reservations, mainly about the style tests used.

In summary, the two original Ohio dimensions keep recurring, suggesting that they (of all the style dimensions) have practical

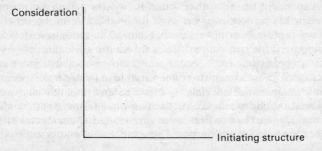

Figure 7.1 The two dimensions of leadership style

value. But how the dimensions are related is controversial. Refinements of these dimensions have related them to situational factors. For example:

- Under high pressure for production, initiating structure tends to be more effective
- If the group size is small, consideration is more important than initiating structure, if satisfaction is important
- If employees have strong needs for safety and structure, then they prefer bosses who initiate structure
- If employees have low needs for structure, they prefer consideration

However, the findings from research are often quite confusing on these propositions. The work done by Fred Fiedler at Michigan University has been more conclusive.

Fielder's variation on the theme
Fiedler's approach relates the style of behaviour of the manager with his perceptions of his least preferred co-worker and/or his most preferred co-worker. Self ratings on either the least or most preferred co-workers are taken from a questionnaire. The respondent is asked to think of the person with whom he can work least well, and to fill in the scale about *that* person. In this way, data about the actual respondent and about his leadership style are collected relative to a specific situation and to specific people.

There is considerable similarity between the consideration–initiating structure dimensions of Fleishman *and* Fiedler's least preferred co-worker scale. There is also considerable similarity with Likert's four systems of management, Bowers and Seashore's four dimensions of leadership, and Reddin's dimensions of style. All theorists have found similar behaviour dimensions; where their theories differ is in the number of other variables they include. Certainly, Fiedler has probably given the most comprehensive, multi-variable explanation of leadership style, although Peter Saul's Australian study provided a much wider examination of organizational variables and their relationship with style. He found that style factors and organizational variables (structure, technology, environment, etc.) varied from organization to organization in predicting organizational effectiveness. This research would suggest that attempts to develop five or ten style types are gross over-simplifications of leadership behaviour.

Probably the most pungent criticism of style theorists is that the instruments they use to collect data to support their propositions are unreliable. Fleishman and Harris's Leadership Opinion Questionnaire, Fiedler's LPC Scale, Reddin's Tri-Dimensional Grid, Blake and Mouton's Grid Questionnaire, Likert's Survey of Four Systems of Management can all be used with the same people and produce different results. The easy explanation for this result is that the scales are measuring different facets of leadership behaviour. An alternative explanation is that the instruments themselves are dubious measures of the behaviour dimensions of style. In assessing a manager's style, I would be reluctant to rely on any one of these instruments; as a minimum I would require from him/her a self-assessment, their superior's assessment, their peers' assessment, their subordinates' assessment, their motivation profile, and some data on the organization variables. With that data I would have some confidence in labelling his/her managerial style in *that* situation. Perhaps the source of controversy over leadership style studies is the instruments or questionnaires or tests rather than the theories.

The current situation with leadership research

The two dominant areas of research remain the trait approach and the style approach. But there have been many modifications in the last ten years. Indeed, the 'seventies saw a new wave of theoretical and conceptual attempts to understand leadership. The path-goal theory looks at the relationships between the leader's style, his subordinates' expectations, task complexity, and environmental factors.

Path-goal theory postulates that it is the motivational function of the leader to assure his subordinates personal rewards for accomplishing work goals. The boss can do this by clarifying the paths to the subordinates' desired rewards, and by removing blockages. It is also the function of the leader to improve opportunities for personal satisfaction by showing consideration and support.

This theory has its foundations in the goal–reward theory of motivation, which is particularly applicable in the American culture, where the relationship between reward and performance is highly praised and understood. In cultures where goals, rewards, and paths are more diffuse, the theory has less value.

Further refinements of this approach have increased the number of situational variables and related these to the dimensions of style. At this stage, the most developed situational variable is what is called *task structure*. For example, we can propose from path–goal theory that, for subordinates with lower levels of education, with weaker needs for achievement and autonomy, with superiors with greater technical and administrative knowledge, and where bosses have control over extrinsic rewards, then:

- If the task is not highly structured or repetitive, an initiating structure style of management helps subordinates clarify their goals and paths and achieve extrinsic satisfaction
- Under conditions of high structure, high repetition, then the initiating structure style lowers levels of satisfaction and leads to conflict

Another popular approach is developing among *contingency theorists*, who include not only task and individual variables but also organizational variables, such as structure, technical system, personality characteristics of subordinates, environmental variables, etc. This is the approach I prefer, and it is developed throughout this book. In some situations, certain combinations of the style dimensions and the situational variables seem important for effective leadership. In other situations, other variables seem important and a different combination is needed. Certainly, as Saul found, there is no *one* successful combination.

Possibly the important variable is the manager's perception of and sensitivity to the situation. His style is a response to the situation he perceives and his perception of that situation may be the key to leadership. Certainly, whether he adopts one leadership style or another is as dependent on the expectations of his subordinates as on any other variable. Therefore, research which relates style, situation, subordinates' expectations, effectiveness, and capacity to perceive and evaluate situations is necessary if we are to understand leadership. After all, the manager is only one variable. Why should he be so remarkably different from other people? What is significant may be his capacity to read a situation, pick up the verbal and non-verbal signals from his subordinates, and provide the impetus to produce a cohesive team.

In a pilot study of 80 managers, Eric Walton and I found that in highly complex managerial tasks, the most effective managers were initiating structure oriented in style, and could differentiate the situational variables clearly. This capacity to differentiate, to rise above the situation and perceive it in its environment has been popularly referred to as the 'helicopter' ability, and is now included in some corporate appraisal schemes. It is a cognitive or perceptual capacity which reaches maturity in the teen years and remains strong till the late 'thirties; thereafter it declines; the helicopters glide to the ground, becoming more dependent rather than independent of the situation.

Research on the perceptual skills of leadership is still very tentative, despite the lavish claims from some consultants. There is very little empirical data. However, this view of leadership offers a linkage between three approaches:

- Style theory
- Situational determinants (including subordinates, expectations, tasks, environments)
- Individual skills and motivations of the leader

For this reason it is worth pursuing. We already have volumes of studies supporting the style dimensions; more and more situational variables are appearing in the literature. Yet most approaches to leadership *do not* discuss the relationship between the style, the situation, and the leader. Most research discusses two of the three sets of variables.

For the practitioner, the best advice for selecting potential leaders is to collect data in these three areas. Style data is readily obtainable. Situational data (especially about superiors, subordinates, and peers) has been neglected, and even consultants and personnel managers spend too little time collecting data on the tasks, the structure, and the people in a situation for which they intend selecting a leader. And even the psychologist's forte, data on the leader-elect, has tended to be marred by an obsession with personality data rather than data on perceptual skills, motives, style preferences, etc.

Finally, the source of the most promising data is not in psychological tests, or expensive organizational analysis, but in the appraisal data which has been collected on the individual for many years. As one international study found, appraisal of a person in a variety of company situations is still the most reliable method of selecting future managers.

Style analysis of managers

My own studies – using the Organisation Attitude Questionnaire, motivation tests, self-assessment, peer group rankings, and the Leadership Behaviour Description Questionnaire – have shown managers to be almost equally divided on their style bias between initiating structure (concern for production) and consideration (concern for people). Forty-seven per cent in managerial positions in our studies are more concerned about getting the task done than they are concerned about people. Forty per cent of male managers show higher concern for people than for the task; that is, they are more consideration (or maintenance or human relations) oriented. We have found 13 per cent of male managers are equal on both factors.

The relevance of style is a relevance of balance. Groups or teams in organizations attempt to achieve a state of balance dependent upon the styles or behaviours of the role performers. This kind of balance may be *the* major factor in leadership effectiveness, so we will look at it in some detail here.

Balance in social systems

A group made up of people who are only prepared to play a task oriented role is likely to fail to achieve its ends. A group of people who only wish to play the maintenance of human relations oriented roles may also fail to produce a result, depending on the task. In organizations, people shift their styles to meet the needs of the situation and to create peaceful co-existence or a balance of power and influence most of the time. In this way, the balance of a team is restored. (Reddin has referred to this as *style flex*.)

Balance in this context refers to a situation in which the relations among the members fit together harmoniously; where there is no stress for change. Conversely, if imbalance occurs, then members will attempt to change their relationships to restore balance.

Balance should not necessarily be seen as desirable. Tensions

135

within groups are often constructive, creative, cathartic. Balanced relationships can become boring and from time to time managers may change their styles to produce imbalance, conflict, and creativity. However, most groups will quickly develop tactics to restore balance, to find consensus rather than conflict, and by that process prevent the disintegration of the family, work group, project team, etc.

Style is a personal response to group balance – the reward might be stable, mutually satisfying interaction in the role set. In a simple example, most families will have one adult who prefers to adopt the task specialist role most of the time, and another adult who prefers to adopt the maintenance or human relator role most of the time, depending on the situation. (See the Fred and Myrtle case study in chapter 6). If one of these adults withdraws, the members of the family will redress the imbalance in power, and the missing role will be adopted by another person or divided between two or more people. A common example: if the father usually adopts the consideration oriented role and withdraws, either the wife (who may usually play the initiating structure or task oriented role), or one of the children, will adopt the missing role. When the children are very young, the imbalance occurs often if the father is away frequently on business. When the husband returns, his wife may comment, 'Thank goodness you are home, I have had trouble with the children.' In other words, an imbalance of power and influence occurred in his absence. One of the apparently essential roles was missing. Most frequently, as the children get older, one of them will take over the human relations specialist role if and when father is away. Less frequently, the wife plays both roles. The only problem with children adopting roles is when the missing parent returns and presumes that the child will be willing to relinquish his or her adopted role. For example, conflict is often the result where a task oriented father withdraws and then returns and tries to re-establish his dominant role. How many fathers cause the lament: 'Why is it the children start fighting as soon as you come home?'

Sex category has much to do with the allocation of tasks within the family. But it has less to do with the acquisition of power. There is no reason at all why the female should not be the task leader, and in nearly half the families she is. The only irony of this situation is that our culture encourages the task

136

oriented female to play the maintenance or nurturing role of mother, while a consideration oriented husband goes to work. He may be a much better 'mother' than she would be.

One ironic complication of the taking of roles in families has been the tendency of the dominant, or task oriented, member to express a desire to withdraw from the role set entirely, as if he or she loses interest once securely dominant. Also, he or she is likely to claim less sexual satisfaction from the relationship. A second complication in marriage occurs where females are dominant, but social conditioning tells them to be sexually submissive. Fortunately, the conditioning is less effective in behaviours not related to power in a sexual sense. If our culture decrees that the socialization of children into boys and girls should make boys dominant and girls submissive, then we should change the values supporting that cultural norm, because it does not work; almost half the males prefer, as adults, to adopt a consideration, human relations role. So much for all that 'kick the football', 'bash him', 'boys have no emotions' stuff of the 'twenties to 'fifties. My own belief is that sex, birth order in a family, and the roles played by parents are the major determinants of adult role preferences, including styles. After all, the first role set we experience is the family. The number of male dolls on the market today would indicate that many parents are no longer terrified that their sons should adopt a nurturing, human relations role in their adult lives.

First-born children and first-born sons have a much higher propensity to seek and adopt task oriented roles in organizational life. Third- and fourth-born boys and girls have a higher propensity to play the human relations role in organizational life. However, before we divide the world too simply, there are many, many deviants from these findings, depending on distance between children in families, mother–father relations, etc.

So far, the assumption has been that family roles are fixed. But the requirements of the situation (especially the task) are just as important in determining role adoption in a family as in organizations. We may see a female who habitually adopts a warm, nurturing, supportive role in the family, but who adopts a task oriented, dominant role in a crisis. Conversely, even task oriented male managers learn to be sensitive to the atmosphere in their families, and learn to shift quickly and use a human relations oriented style when appropriate.

The arrival of in-laws in a family totally changes the distribution of power and forces compromises, role shifts, and accommodations if the unit is to remain relatively conflict free. In our cell-society of mum, dad, and two children, we may be in danger of losing the style flexibility of the extended family and be unable to merge, temporarily, with other people into a single unit. Having people to stay becomes too great a hassle!

When a male or female leaves home to enter an organization, he or she is likely to adopt a different leadership style. The situation will be different, the task different, the rewards different, and the expectations of subordinates different. Quite often, the shift in style is dramatic, suggesting that the situation, rather than the individual's motives, goals, etc., is the dominant variable in understanding the style shift. However, most frequently we tend to adopt a preferred style, which we modify only slightly as we move from one situation to another. Blake and Mouton suggested we have a preferred style and a back-up style. This research suggests style is basically a personality factor and shifts in style reflect sensitivity to the situation.

Even if the shift to a back-up style is only slight, there is a period of adjustment which is sometimes distressing. For example, many males who have adopted a leadership style at work appear to find it impossible to move back to their family role without the help of alcohol at the pub. Those who do not use the pub as a diversion may find it takes them 20 minutes or more (plus a beer or a scotch) to move back into their family and adopt their family role. It is extraordinary that if a child comes to stay with us, we all make allowances for the child to move in, adjust, adopt a new role. Yet how many families have conflicts simply because no provision is made for the re-entry and change in role of the male or female, or the newly employed eldest child. 'What's wrong with her/him/Dad/Mum tonight?' In a society which permits multi-roles in widely different role sets, it is to be expected that stress occurs because of role confusion. I am always a little put out by people who see me lecture and ask 'Do you go on like that at home?' Of course I don't.

In summary, I believe an individual's preferred mode of leading is largely a personal behaviour pattern developed over long periods and influenced by many childhood, familial, and organizational experiences. However, the appropriateness or relevance of the style adopted is a function of the degree of

138

perceptiveness or sensitivity of the individual to the demands, tasks, expectations, etc., of the situation.

If the situation needs a new balance of power the leader will modify his own style or the task or the styles of the other actors. By such sensitivity he continues to lead . . . to embody common purpose for the common welfare. 'Style' is the result of personal, situational and perceptual factors.

If we now look at organizations, we will find a similar search for equilibrium, power distribution, and role balance.

Equilibrium in organizations

Identifying styles (whether by observation or by testing) is vital in understanding the workings of an organizational unit or of the whole organization. Whatever the preferred style of the king, there will be accommodating styles among those supporting him. The dictator supported by acquiescing, supportive, human related subordinates has been well documented in history. Figure 7.2 illustrates an example of balance from a study of managerial styles among the top group of a chemical company. This group was in balance most of the time. And this sort of combination is often very effective. Similarly, if the king prefers to play a human relator role by choice, then we will find a task leader (sometimes known as 'Harry-the-Hatchet-Man') supporting the king at the second level.

Just as small groups and families establish levels of balance, so too do groups in organizations. Combinations which are effective vary considerably because of the number of roles each person may adopt in response to the situational demands. Strongly task oriented people can adopt conciliatory, human relator styles when confronted with conflict between two other task oriented members of the group. In this way, the group balance (rather than disintegration) prevails – shock waves are

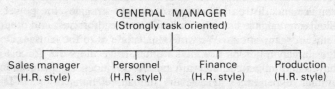

Figure 7.2 Balance in managerial styles

absorbed as individuals adapt their expectations about power. As an example, if the branch manager of a bank is task oriented, then it may be sensible for a human relations oriented accountant to be sent to that branch. Helping equilibrium by style analysis is more relevant to the effectiveness of that team than some of the other considerations used in selecting managers. Selection needs to be seen as selection to fit into a team, rather than as a search for yet another remarkable individual. Yet from my experience, selection is always preoccupied with the potential manager, while the people he is to manage are ignored.

Nor is balance simply a matter of two people. It is much more complex; often the human relator or maintenance role is dispersed and played by several people, depending on the situation. Sometimes at the top of the structure the task oriented thrust is provided by the king, while his secretary provides the warmth and becomes the listening post for all the king's subordinates. Similarly, task oriented power roles may be divided between an initiating structure role and an expert task oriented role.

Contrary to most popular beliefs, there are some inconsistencies in jobs and the assumed leadership styles adopted by job occupants. For example, we have found most personnel managers tested to be higher on the task oriented dimension than on the human relations dimension. Marketing managers are invariably task oriented. Welfare people, induction officers, etc., are more consideration or human relations oriented, which is often a cause of the criticism that they do not solve problems. First line foremen, who traditionally have been accused of insensitivity to the needs of their men, are most often human relations oriented, but have been brainwashed to believe that adopting that role in the power game is feminine and weak.

The failure to establish a balance of preferred styles within an organization is a major source of conflict. In a study of a females-only organization, we found all the top executives preferred task oriented roles. This produced a very high level of conflict and distress, because of endless struggles for power. Similar imbalance can be found in hospitals, libraries, and other female organizations. We would speculate as to the causes. Do the human relations oriented women leave the work force to have children and relate to a family? Or does the promotion system discriminate against the human relations oriented female? It is the sort of work (patient care, information retrieval,

140

etc.) which is best suited to task oriented executives? I do not have the answers but I do know that where task oriented styles dominate, imbalance does occur, and conflict resolution may require outside assistance in the form of a consultant or facilitator.

There is a higher percentage of task oriented leaders among female managers than among male managers. Certainly, the nurturing, child-rearing role does withdraw many females from work organizations, leaving the task oriented, career motivated females behind. But this is reinforced, in our male dominated society, by the male tendency to expect that a career female will be highly task oriented, career motivated, and frustrated, with the result that many women who are not strongly task oriented in their 'twenties become increasingly so in their 'thirties and 'forties, as if to live up to the males' expectation of what is an appropriate style for a leader.

Styles are not right or wrong, ideal or not ideal. Style refers to the way leaders or managers behave. What we need to study to understand organization is the *combination* of those styles into a team or role system. Hence my earlier argument, that cognitive and perceptual skills are important in identifying leaders. An effective leader can perceive what a situation needs, and have sufficient style flexibility to provide it. Experience is the best teacher of both seeing what is there *and* reacting to it. Unfortunately, we give people almost no opportunity to learn before they are promoted to lead others. Worse, we know so little about interpersonal relations that our understanding of the balance of power is embryonic.

Shifting patterns of styles

There is a noticeable shift in preferred leadership styles among the under-25 age group. For a variety of reasons, the socialization of young people is producing a much higher percentage of people who feel comfortable adopting either style. This group shows a greater willingness to be flexible, and shift from style to style depending on the situation and on the others involved. Some of these younger people are experimenting with role reversal in marriage, and are eager to equalize opportunities for men and women in organizations. As this group exerts more influence in organizations, we can expect to see less concern for hiring men or women and more concern for hiring people, regardless of sex. Women's Liberation movements are reinforcing this shift in values and in styles, but may alienate some supporters. Most 'movements' are dominated by highly task oriented people, and Women's Lib. may succeed in driving away those women who are equally oriented to people and task *or* who are more people oriented. I would prefer to see People's Liberation, rather than just Women's Liberation. But no one can deny the women's movement its case.

In the period since the end of the Second World War, the percentage of women in the labour force has grown continually. Yet the number of women in managerial positions is not consistent with these statistics. While some 11 per cent of all males in the work force are managers, less than 4 per cent of females hold such positions. Yet I have no data to support this discrimination. Women are just as intelligent, just as highly motivated, and just as effective managers as men.

The ritual of leadership

If the leader is able to reconcile his goals, his style and the situational variables with the styles and goals of his followers then he or she must sustain that common purpose. This is primarily a question of ritual and religion. It is this magic of leadership that has been the stumbling block of attempts to scientifically prescribe leadership behaviour. Some people have the capacity to perform; to recognize the importance of theatre, to provide the pomp and circumstance of office, to generate their own myths and legends, to lift the ordinary to be more than ordinary, to give excitement to repetitive activity: in short, to distinguish themselves from the rest. This is essentially a manipulative process and it is difficult to believe that those who excel at it are not conscious that they are doing it. Finding a model of this behaviour would be like finding a model for all actors who wish to play Hamlet. We can isolate the ingredients, just as we can isolate the ingredients of a play, but we cannot scientifically prescribe the performance. The best we can offer in advice to the aspiring leader is that he or she watch the performances of others. See how it is done; how it often becomes a form of religious experience rather than a rational process in an age short of religion, ritual, mythology and legends.

142

Conclusions

There have been several theoretical approaches to understanding leadership:

- Trait theory
- Style theory
- Situational theory
- Path–goal theory

All approaches have contributed to our understanding of leadership, but we need a method for linking what we have found in trait theory to style theory, to the situational approach. This link may be the perceptual skills of the leader, his capacity to read the requirements of the situation, especially the requirements of the task and of his subordinates, and his flexibility in reacting to that situation.

For this reason, the organization's appraisal schemes may remain the best predictor of leadership potential, as they use actual behaviour and performance as raw data.

Increasingly, theorists have become less concerned with identifying a god-like leader and more concerned with creating a balanced system – one in equilibrium, wherein the styles of those participating create harmony, most of the time. The structure of roles we have identified in families and groups has been found to occur in a similar manner within role sets in organizations as well. Unlike families and groups, most role sets in organizations work as a group only rarely, leading to more frequent imbalance and more and more use of team building exercises to teach the members how to avoid destructive conflict and establish consensus and balance.

We are beginning to see the separation of sex and role choices, as well as role reversals and role shifts without loss of face. Flexibility and capacity to change are needed for future organizations. People, rather than men or women, working in carefully structured systems, where sex category is secondary to the abilities and styles required in selecting leaders, would be the sort of human resources management I would prefer. Currently, it is fashionable for leadership to be superseded by structure, environment, and technology in debates on organizations. Yet it is still true that the effectiveness of any unit, branch, division, or corporation is primarily determined by the quality of its leadership. Industry has been reawakened to that truism, and millions of dollars are being invested in trying to update managers to make them more effective leaders.

For additional reading

Blake R., and J. S. Mouton, *Managerial Grid*, Gulf Publishing, Houston, Texas, 1974.

Fiedler F. E., *A Theory of Leadership Effectiveness*, McGraw-Hill, New York, 1967.

Heider F., *The Psychology of Interpersonal Relations*, John Wiley, New York, 1958.

Heller F. A., *Managerial Decision Making: A Study of Leadership Styles and Power Sharing among Senior Managers*, Tavistock, 1971.

Hunt J. G., and L. L. Larson (eds.), *Contingency Approaches to Leadership*, Southern Illinois University Press, Carbondale, Illinois, 1974.

Hunt J. W., 'Myths and realities of male/female managers', *Work and People*, October 1976.

Myers J. A., *Predicting Managerial Success*, Foundation for Research on Human Behaviour, Ann Arbor, Michigan, 1968. (For Standard Oil Study.)

Reddin W., *Managerial Effectiveness*, McGraw-Hill, New York, 1970.

Saul P., *Job Satisfaction, Performance and Tenure: A Theoretically Based Attempt to Predict Three Criteria of Organisational Effectiveness*, Ph.D. Thesis, University of New South Wales, 1975.

Vroom V., and P. Yetton, *Leadership and Decision Making*, University of Pittsburgh, 1973.

Zelditch M., 'Role differentiation in the nuclear family', in Parsons T. *et al.*, *Family, Socialization, and the Interaction Process*, Free Press, Glencoe, New York, 1955.

8 Managing organizations

Chapter 7 looked at the interpersonal nature of leadership. This chapter turns to one of the least developed areas of academic theorizing – management theory.

One of the problems of theories of management has been the confusion over the term *management*. Some writers use it to refer to the processes involved in running a business, or department, or section. In this sense, the word is synonymous with leading. Other writers use the word to refer to a professional class who have values about their status, authority, and power. Yet a third group use the term to refer to a collection of men and women who run a particular organization – 'the management wants more information' or 'management wants to thank the staff.'

This ambiguity has plagued the development of a theory of management. Indeed, there has been very little advance on the theories developed at the beginning of this century. In contrast, leadership and leading have attracted vast research funds, and there have been considerable theoretical developments. Management theory has remained the Aunt Sally of academia.

The confusion over the term is largely a British problem and has produced, in all English-speaking countries, an elitist view of managers. It is interesting, for example, that this is not so in Germany, where the British view of the managerial role is difficult to find at all. Nor have the Germans or the Japanese had 'management movements' or local management theorists. Of course, both Germans and Japanese, like all other nations, do have people who run things, but they have not dressed up management in all the Anglo-American frills.

The result of both the confusion over the term and the reluctance of many social scientists to write about management has meant that those managers who do run things might rightly feel that some academics have given them little about management. For this reason, I would like to look at the essentials of management theory and discuss what I think might be practical and useful for those running things. The last part of the chapter consists of a discussion of more recent attempts to find out what managers actually do.

I see managing as being synonymous with leading; so much of the material which could be included in this chapter had already been covered in the previous chapter or in other chapters. For this reason the treatment of the functions of managing is uneven; some functions receive more attention here than others.

Traditional theory

Management theory is some 80 years old. There were earlier writers, but most of the well known contributions have been made in the past 80 years, with the major contributions in the past 40 years. Two ideas form the foundations of the theory:

- Managing is getting things done with and through people
- The functions a manager should perform are:
  planning
  organizing
  directing
  controlling

The first idea, the so called 'definition of management', was not a particularly useful contribution to our understanding of behaviour apart from pointing out that managers get things done as opposed to 'doing'. In many ways, the British separation of managers and doers was unfortunate, as it created a 'me–them' conflict which permeates British industry.

However, it was useful to clarify a managerial role as one to coordinate the work of others, as a total effort, to achieve the objectives of the activity. He or she coordinates rather than does in the sense of doing the physical or mental work.

Fortunately, this separation is idealized – all managers become involved in performing non-managerial tasks. But the theory did legitimize the function of coordinator, or conductor, as a distinct activity, and for this reason the theory is important in understanding the Anglo-American view of managers. (A more recent separation sees managers concerned with the process rather than the content.)

In contrast, the second idea that there are managerial functions was a very useful contribution, because it provided a framework for analysing management, even if subsequent studies have questioned whether managers in fact plan, organize, direct, and control in the manner prescribed by the theory. Identifying these functions focused research, teaching, and practice, and provided the basis of management theory. Because of the importance of these functions, we will concentrate on them here.

Planning

Planning is not forecasting. We plan because we cannot foresee. Planning means foresight plus action to make things come out to our advantage. Planning allows us to design for an uncertain future with some assurance of achieving our goals. Planning is setting objectives, devising means to those ends, harnessing effort, and systematically feeding back against expectations. Planning is *not* forecasting the future and adjusting to it.

The field of planning has grown exponentially. The thrust of a world war, and the need to coordinate vast numbers of men and machines posed new planning problems. A whole new field of analysis called *Operations Research* grew out of the need to plan on a larger and more complex scale.

The second thrust for more planning came from the increasingly complex world we live in, with larger national and transnational diverse organizations and larger, more complex cities.

The third impetus for the growth in planning techniques and in planning departments in organizations and governments has been the arrival of what is known as the 'turbulent market place', where change is rapid, where inter-organizational relationships are diverse, and where change arises from the market place itself.

The fourth push has come from the computer and an unprecedented information explosion. It is now possible to test plans in seconds by using computer programs and to store and retrieve vast quantities of information.

For these and other reasons, the planning function has had a meteoric rise in work organizations. Long-range planning, corporate planning, and strategic planning positions are frequently appearing at the second level of the hierarchy in business organizations. America, France, Sweden, Japan and most Western countries have established highly technical government planning departments to reconcile the many demands for funds.

In most cases, the plans which the corporate or government planners produce will be wrong: they are designed on present data which is extrapolated to future dates. Correctness is desirable but not the objective – the major objective is to collect the data and continually review the entire organization's progress toward a blueprint that cannot remain static. It is the exercise of agreeing on objectives, collecting and analysing the relevant data, and harnessing effort that is important; only through practice can the various planning strategies be refined. The goal is not a recipe book answer – there are no such answers.

Plans fail when planners begin to believe that their neat logic is the organization. The motives and expectations of people in organizations change, leading to organizational change. This dynamic interaction in role systems cannot be tied down through neat logic, even if planners desire it. For this reason, the rationality of planning departments fits badly on the real world – mostly we muddle through, thinking laterally rather than vertically, often to the despair of the planners.

Underneath the jargon of planners, the day-to-day function for the manager remains very simple – so simple that most of us do it intuitively. Here are the steps in the process.

1 Establish clear objectives.
2 Collect data relating to the objectives. What factors have bearing on these objectives? What factors can be influenced? Which cannot? What are the organizational constraints (policies, regulations, people, technical systems, etc.)?
3 Examine alternative courses of action and evaluate these courses. (There is never only one way to achieve the objective. *Equifinality* is a characteristic of organizations; it refers to the fact that there are several means to the same ends.)
4 Select the course to be adopted, and recommend a course of action, including detailed procedures for implementing the planned course of action.

Step 1 The objectives

Corporate objectives usually fall into three categories:

- A statement of overall purpose – the product or service
- A statement of expected financial returns to owners
- A statement on social responsibility to employees, customers, and the society at large

Not all three will be included, but most companies seem to have expectations in all three areas.

Maximizing profit is not a realistic objective, because perfect knowledge of maximum profits is impossible from the accounting information. Perfect decision making is rare, and other variables and objectives (e.g., government intervention, social responsibilities, or public relations) confuse the picture.

Government organizations have similar categories of objectives; even though the profit motive is left unmentioned, it is replaced by cost, efficiency, and political criteria.

In setting objectives the following guidelines may be useful:

- The objectives should be precise
- They should be measurable (either quantitatively or qualitatively)
- There is never *one* objective; organizations have multiple objectives, even if only because the humans who manage them have multiple personal and social objectives. Hence we need to identify those multiple objectives and rank the priorities (profit, productivity, service, etc.)
- The feedback or control systems must be able to assess performance against those objectives without incredible cost in developing information systems
- Organizations will operate below the 'best' performance because of conflicting objectives – the price of one objective is another

In support of multiple objectives, Drucker suggests that there are eight key result areas vital to the continued existence of any business organization. He suggests the following should be the *key result* areas (or types of objectives) of the firm:

- Profitability
- Market position
- Productivity

149

- Product leadership
- Personal development
- Employee attitudes
- Public responsibility
- Balance between short- and long-range objectives

This list is merely a guide. Managers should devise their own lists *if* they believe people would benefit from a clearer idea of where the firm is going.

Objectives should not be assumed to be static. They change, particularly as powerful senior executives change their own objectives. Structures built to achieve the original objectives need, ideally, to be shifted to match the new objectives. Short- rather than long-term re-evaluation of objectives has become common – not because managers have recognized the need for updating but because the environmental changes require flexibility and revision of plans.

Most writers on setting objectives argue that they should be set by the members of the board. By law, the board has a primary function to protect the interests of the shareholder. However, senior managers have a much wider set of stakeholders: shareholders, employees, citizens, and customers. Not unexpectedly, it is senior managers who are increasingly setting corporate objectives and 'selling' them to the board.

In government organizations, objectives are usually established within the Act that created the department. This has many disadvantages. First, designers or legislation are usually lawyers, who, like their political masters, have little or no knowledge of the organizational consequences of the objectives they write into draft legislation. Second, this practice makes it inevitable that departmental heads modify, or even create, objectives of their own, as they were not involved in setting objectives in the Act. Third, Cabinet (which one could expect to establish departmental objectives) assumes that those established in the Act will suffice, even if many years have gone by since the legislation was passed. Royal Commissions into government departments have recommended (presumably to deaf ears) that the practice of setting objectives in an Act should be revised such that Cabinet accept responsibility for determining departmental objectives annually.

Where objectives remain vague, organizational members will

set their own, whether the organization is a business or a government agency. Unfortunately, as the objectives of an organization are the first step in organization design, the breakdowns in large private and government organizations in establishing and transmitting the objectives produce enormous problems. Objectives become secondary to a game of sticky-taping a structure together, through rules and regulations which reflect the needs of the senior and middle managers rather than those of the board (or Cabinet), the shareholders, or the majority of employees.

A second major problem with setting objectives has been the failure to transmit them to the employees. Nearly any consulting job in any organization unearths the need to clarify objectives (often a consultant need, rather than an employee need). Certainly, a lack of knowledge of overall direction is the foremost problem of people in large organizations. Nor is the problem restricted to those at the bottom of the hierarchy. Often it is the senior managers who cannot agree on the objectives of the organization they are leading. This confusion and uncertainty is then pushed down the hierarchy, causing conflict and encouraging all the worst forms of political intrigue.

Among role performers the problem of not knowing what the objectives are is so universal (even where a board or a Cabinet has specifically set them) that I wonder whether it is the naïvely simple logic (of setting objectives) tacked onto a dynamic group of people that is the cause, or whether it is the process rather than the content of the transmission which is the problem. Certainly, imposing a static, if logical, structure on a dynamic system is contradictory, but we have all seen managers who invest millions of dollars in selling an organization and its products to consumers but who spend a negligible sum of money in selling the current corporate objectives to the organization's employees – that is, to its own best public relations team.

In a society which encourages goal-directed behaviour, failure to establish precise objectives will inevitably lead to problems. I believe we need to use all the expertise of media specialists to communicate to employees the purposes and ends of *their* organization. What stops us is the potential propaganda machine this may entail, and the consequent concentration of power derived from this activity. A second constraint is the thought: Do employees really want to know the overall ends or vision of

151

senior managers? Does more data merely confuse? If so, then let us forget selling the overall objectives and ask employees in role sets to establish their own. Does it really *matter* if they do not know what senior management wants?

A third problem of setting objectives is that the objectives which motivate senior management may not motivate those further down the hierarchy. If overall objectives are to be useful, they must be translated into unit objectives and then into individual objectives. And the most effective way of letting people know what the objectives of their job or their section are is to involve them in establishing those objectives.

Step 2 Data collection

Assembling data for the plan is a time-consuming process. Inevitably, the search process needs to eliminate the less important data and identify the most relevant. The decision on choosing data will inevitably be sub-optimal, simply because all the data which may be relevant will not be available. Plans are always constructed on insufficient data – this is the price of decision making by people in an imperfect and complex market. And if the manager waits until he gets all the relevant data, the opportunities may well be gone.

Most plans concentrate on one factor to the exclusion of, or failure to recognize, others. Examining many variables in a situation at one time is still more an academic pursuit than a practised strategy. Most plans involve one variable – e.g., the purchase of new equipment is viewed to the total exclusion of its effect on structure, people, or informal groups. Similarly, industrial relations plans focus on reducing conflict to the total exclusion of structural and technological considerations. Managers (i.e., people who run things) are beginning to learn, of necessity, to consider several variables at once, if only because industrial strife and an uncertain market have forced a more intensive analysis of what they are doing. In the past, managers have argued with me that they do not have time to adopt a multi-variable analysis. It is interesting to see that now the costs of mistakes are so high, time is being found, especially in those industries with heavy investment in capital equipment.

The second step of planning requires the best available data – but not only on the factor being considered for change. Other variables should be considered. It is impossible to change one variable of a social system without changing others.

Step 3 Examining alternatives

Examining the options or alternatives requires that criteria for selection be defined. No matter how crude the criteria, some are essential if the plan is to have any more than gut feeling to support it. Ironically, it is often the gut feeling that is right, but choosing among different strategies should first be logical, where choice is against pre-determined criteria. Against these criteria, options can be evaluated. A great deal of time is lost at Step 3, simply because managers do not decide what criteria are important.

Step 4 Selecting strategies

The selection of the course of action best suited is often referred to as *decision making*. Some writers see decision making as synonymous with managing – that is, decision making involves more than just the choice among alternatives.

Kepner and Tregoe have suggested pseudo-scientific ways for assigning weightings in the selection process. Using their system, managers rank the alternatives against the objectives of the plan and weigh the alternatives against expected outcomes. Like scientific method, which dictates the process of research in universities, the K/T method does no more than force the manager to assess and reassess his/her choices. In this sense, it can be valuable.

The details for implementation of the strategy (strategies) vary from plan to plan. If the plan in question is the corporate plan, then separate plans for marketing, finance, production, personnel, etc., will be prepared from the master plan. Each plan will conclude with the action: *what is to be done, by whom, by when, and what criteria of effectiveness* will be used to assess the implementation of the plan.

Finally, in the planning function, recognize that plan and the real world are incompatible. One is static, the other dynamic – it is inevitable that the plan will have to change or the manager have to alter his expectations.

Organizing

The second function of the manager in traditional theory was to assess the tasks to be done, allocate tasks to people, and integrate the tasks into a whole work system. This activity is covered in detail in chapter 9. For the moment we will consider just the essential elements.

The ingredients of organizing are:

- The work

To achieve the objectives of the organization, some work has to be done. Work will involve activities to be performed by role performers in a role set in a role system.

- The people

Some people will need a far greater degree of definition of the work, the relationship between tasks, and the relationships between the people performing the tasks than do others. Contrary to traditional and sacrosanct views of structure, most modern designers are primarily concerned to produce a structure which will allow members to approach the organization's objectives *and* to satisfy some of their own expectations at the same time.

- The situation

What is the work to be done? What sort of external pressures will there be, what sort of technical system, what sort of buildings, what sort of factories, what interdependencies?

Designing a structure for these elements is discussed in detail in chapter 9. For the present, the essentials are:

- Establishing objectives
- Identifying and classifying tasks
- Collecting like tasks into task groups
- Allocating tasks to individuals or groups
- Integrating (coordinating) tasks into a 'whole' work system

The allocation of tasks raises questions of authority, responsibility, and accountability. What person in which position will determine if the tasks should commence? Who will decide on the allocation of the people? Who will have the positional power, be, in short, the final word, the arbiter in the event of conflicts?

While words like *authority* and *power* have emotional over-tones, the entire formal structure does depend on the allocation of authority. The smaller the work unit, the less definition of these terms is necessary, as group processes will resolve conflicts most of the time. But in large national or trans-national organizations, deciding who has the authority to do what is a vital part of designing the structure.

The term *authority* here means the right (a formal approval by superiors) of the occupant of a position to control resources, whether these resources are people, money, information, plant, equipment, or energy.

Authority (often called positional power) is allocated by members on a commonsense basis to assist coordination and control. Drawing on their own personal experiences, traditional management theorists devised a series of principles of 'organization' or structural design which showed managers how to allocate authority on a supposedly rational basis, and thereby predict and control the behaviour of all members (see chapter 9). If these principles had worked, some of the problems we have in organizations would disappear; we would be able to program role performers' behaviour and conduct organizations rationally.

Where the principles fell down was in their assumption that, having designed the structure and allocated the authority, members would passively accept that structure. In fact (as earlier chapters pointed out) members struggle, compete, hate, love, in irrational ways to acquire power. Man's striving for power – whether for protection, territory, ambition, or whatever – ensures that role systems are political systems in which authority and rationality are secondary issues. Yet, as authority affects power, the allocation of it is an important managerial task. But what authority is allocated and what power the recipient has are not the same. Indeed, some extraordinarily powerful members have very little authority.

Responsibility is another of the emotionally loaded words in managerial literature. I avoid using it because of its multitude of meanings, but if asked to adopt a view, I prefer the Barnard-ian view, that responsibility is an ethical characteristic of the manager. It is very confusing to talk of responsibility as synonymous with 'task' or 'accountability'. Ideally, managers should be ethical or responsible people.

Accountability suffers from fewer semantic difficulties. It is used widely to refer to the feedback loop of the control system. This is, individuals and groups feed back results of their performance; they are held to account. In this way deviations from plans can, in theory, be identified and corrected. As such, accountability is intimately related to both authority and power.

Managers who design structures do so to achieve certain explicit and implicit objectives. The structure describes the tasks necessary to achieve those objectives. A manager groups tasks into jobs. Job occupants are allocated authority (the limits on resource control). Individuals who control those jobs have positional power. Authority is not enough to guarantee task achievement. Managers must win more power from those working for them. All individuals who enter into the role system and who accept the exchange of rewards for effort are usually called to account for their behaviour.

Having established the objectives and planned the structure for achieving those objectives, the manager, according to management theory, is concerned with what some theorists have referred to as *directing* – 'Putting the car into gear and driving it'.

This involves fitting the person to the job – recruiting, selecting, inducting, and training staff. It also involves leading them, motivating them, communicating with them, and disciplining them – indeed, it involves the management of role performers and the entire role system. Much of this book is about just these topics, so here I will only discuss areas not discussed elsewhere. Because recruiting, selection, induction, and training are so important, some theorists separate them as a fifth managerial function – *staffing*. I will discuss staffing before analysing directing.

Staffing
Recruiting

A job has been described in the structure. The second step is to decide what sort of person would ideally fill that job. This is an essential step if you are to avoid the recurring habit of only selecting the 'best' qualified and 'best' trained person for the job. In many cases, the worst educated and least trained person would be a much better match.

Questions to be considered in recruiting are:

- Should we change the job (or fit the job to the man)?
- What sort of person do we want for what job (age, qualifications, experience)?
- Where do we look?
- Do we recruit internally and/or externally?
- How wide should the net be cast? Nationally? World wide? Or just in our city?
- How will we reach the person? Search, advertise, employment agencies, etc.? (One example of a poor recruiting technique is a block advertisement buried in a Saturday newspaper where those who may be interested are unlikely to see it. It is even worse if the job is for a specific group of people known to read *one* professional journal.)
- What are we prepared to pay to find the person?

Like all personnel procedures, recruiting can be described quite simply. But highly emotional issues arise when the procedures are implemented. For example, should the firm promote from within or recruit outside? My view is that it should not do either, but choose the best path for a specific job. It is true that recruiting outsiders may upset career paths and damage the egos of some employees. But the alternative – only promoting from within – can produce 'organizational incest', the stereotyped models of organization men and women found in some banks and government departments. Role systems need new blood. Bringing in outsiders is one way of achieving that.

Where staff turnover is high, new blood is not an issue. But there are positions in government and business where the turnover rate for middle and top management is below 5 per cent a year. In these situations, a conscious policy of injecting some outsiders is very practical and regenerative. I would suggest that a healthy turnover figure for middle management is between 15 and 20 per cent; less than that may indicate organizational incest.

Selecting
One of the least researched and least documented areas of management is the process of selecting new members for an organization. A whole range of questionable data is collected, and much of the relevant data (like motives) are largely ignored. (See the comments on this in chapter 1.)

Important questions in selection are:

● What precisely is the job?

For this we need a *job description*, or what in government organizations is often called a *duty statement*. The job description describes the objectives and gives a broad sweep of the tasks to be done. It should not, in my view, give an extensive list of duties. We have become preoccupied with specializing and splitting jobs into duties to such an extent that the objectives get lost. I would prefer to see:

– A precise statement of the (multiple) objectives of the job
– A precise statement of the criteria by which the individual will be evaluated in doing that job
– A broad description of the major tasks
– A statement of the authority (control over resources) the individual will be allocated
– A statement on where the job fits into future plans and where the occupant may fit in three to five years

As we move closer to the base of the hierarchy, individual job descriptions are usually replaced by group descriptions, which also concentrate on the ends not the means, on the objectives not the duties.

● What is the person specification?

The specification identifies the 'ideal' candidate for the job in terms of physical condition, education, experience, abilities, motives, socio-economic situations, etc. Invariably we overplay the 'ideal' and are disappointed when we do not find him or her. However, much time is wasted in selection simply because the organizational members have not stopped to identify the sort of person they want.

– What information do we need to gather?
– How best (cost and time) can we gather that information?

We need to consider interviews, group interviews, references, tests, and ballots.

Interviews. Group interviews or man-to-man interviews? Interviews are one of the least reliable methods of data collection, but are important in establishing whether the current members

158

could work with the new member. Interviews should be structured so that data on the pre-determined specification can be collected. Further, data on the organization and the job should be available for the applicant.

References. Research on the reliability of references suggests they are highly dubious pieces of evidence, since the recruit chooses his referees. Nevertheless they can be extremely useful, since they give the most important data of all – what the applicant has done so far. References by telephone (with previous employers) can be even more valuable. They should be structured to confirm data provided by the applicant (e.g., job, salary) and to gather new data on the applicant's suitability. Telephone references should not be used without an applicant's permission.

Tests. These are more reliable than interviews, but there are numerous problems with using them. For example (as discussed in chapter 2) school leavers have not established reliable motivation patterns. Some people cannot do tests at all. There is the psychological barrier for older executives. Finally, there are questions of individual privacy which must be respected.

Ballots. These are very rare – only used under pressure from unions or other external organizations. However, we should expect to see more ballots for managerial roles as a by-product of moves toward increased worker involvement.

The cost of interviewing or testing must be weighed against the importance of the job. If costs permit, all methods should be used in selection, as each gives a little more insight into the person.

The order of using the techniques is also important. Does the applicant write or phone for details? If he or she phones, the first selection criteria can be handled on the phone. If he writes, then it may be preferable to ask the applicant to complete the firm's application form, so that the forms of different applications can be compared. Isolating relevant data in a six-page letter of application is an expensive exercise.

If the applicant satisfies the criteria on the application form, then test him or her. Check references and phone previous (but not current) employers.

Finally, see the person. Interviewing time is the most expensive cost of selection.

The methods of selection vary from job to job. Obviously, if you were selecting a new managing director you would not use the methods described above. Nor would you for selecting the floor sweeper. But whatever the position, the selection process is designed to match person, and job, and team. The cost of mismatching is one of the largest, if hidden, costs in industry.

Finally, remember that it may not be necessary to select anyone at all. Training current job occupants, job redesign, and team building exercises may lead to entirely different structures, in which jobs are looser and multi-skilled, and the team finds its own new members.

Inducting

Chapter 3 discussed the process of role acquisition when an individual joins an organization. The behaviour change in the new member may be little more than that he or she is doing a job in a situation he or she was not in previously. But the change is likely to be more substantial than this. Attitudes, values, identifications, and friendship patterns are all likely to be affected by the move into a new organization.

The process of induction is designed to make the changes (or socialization) as easy and as predictable as possible. We can find excellent examples of well planned induction in many religious organizations (such as the Jesuits) and in the armed services. In these long established organizations, induction training is well designed to transform the outsider quickly into a member of the organization. In contrast, the importance of induction is only beginning to be recognized in work organizations, although numerous studies have shown that the induction method affects both the rate of turnover in the first six months and role acquisition.

Probably the most important facet of induction is the transfer of loyalties (or identifications or belongingness) to the new organization. Previous role sets (especially peers at church and school) claim loyalties of the recruit. Yet, to satisfy his or her need to belong or to identify, identification must be transferred at least in part to the role system of the work organization. This is an important process, and one we need to examine here.

Many stages of establishing one's identity have been observed

160

in children; one of these stages occurs at puberty. In all previous societies, when children reached puberty and recognized that their parents were not infallible gods, their identification was transferred from parents to religious institutions – ancestors or Christ became the parental substitutes. It was also usual then to initiate the teenager into adult life with ceremonies designed to reinforce this identification (confirmation in Christianity, initiation ceremonies in tribal worship).

In an age when this transfer from identifying oneself with parents to identifying with religious figures is occurring less and less, and attendance by teenagers at Church is falling, the need to identify, to be inducted into a new institution, has become stronger. This need to identify with someone or some institution has created a multi-million dollar market for new gods – a market which pop stars and football players have been only too willing to serve.

Many managers assume that when teenagers begin work they have resolved their identification problems, and feel secure with themselves – and particularly secure with the identification label of their job. On the contrary, most of them are still trying to find out who they are and what they want to be. Induction into the work organization is a most important occasion for these individuals. And if the induction is badly handled, they are likely to leave and search for another place to work where they will feel comfortable. Very often the search for a career identity goes on into the late twenties and early thirties. Some never discover what they want to be.

The results of this major shift in identification from church, village, and family to the work organization can be seen throughout most organizations. Ties, badges, uniforms, car stickers – all proclaim the identity of the individual. Unfortunately, work organizations were not established for the purpose of solving an individual's search for himself and, in the main, induction procedures, rituals, and use of symbolism reflect the assumption that 'belonging' or finding a work identity is learning trite, childlike rules and regulations.

Some organizations have responded to the change in social values and have produced quite amazing induction systems. Sometimes these last for months, with reinforcements applied to family and friends. Still other induction programmes raise questions of ethics: when does a super salesman's sale of the

XYZ Corporation, with all the trappings of a film première, become immoral manipulation of human beings? Some pyramid selling firms gave us glimpses of the possibilities of such highly emotive induction procedures.

I believe induction training should tell the recruit:

- What the company and/or department does
- Why the organization is different from others
- What the achievements of the organization are
- What members do here that may be different – what behaviour restrictions apply that do not apply elsewhere

The objective should be to make the individual think and feel, 'What a great place to work'. The next stage of induction is the *situational* induction, which should be handled by the boss. Here important questions are:

- What is the job?
- What is the boss to be called?
- What restrictions are applied to behaviour?
- Who are all the members of the team?
- What hygiene (heating, lighting, salary, equipment) needs have or have not been satisfied for this individual?
- How does the reward system operate?

Induction is easiest on the first day of the new member's arrival. When the new member is anxious and insecure, changing behaviour (in minor ways) is easiest. By the second day, when the peer group has told the informal story of life in the organization, the best time for induction is over.

Training
There are numerous excellent publications on training which do not need any elaboration here.

Training has four basic forms:

- Induction and skill training: inducting and training a person to do the job he or she was hired to do. Re-training where new skills are required could be included in this category
- Management education: training potential and current bosses to be 'better' managers (planning, organizing, etc.)
- Management development training – a continuous programme to enhance the individual's development. This is

162

normally restricted to executives and seen as long-term development

- Renewal or resuscitation training: re-stimulating members who are suffering from organizational fatigue

A great deal of work has been done on skill training. Similarly, management education and development are universally accepted, and the programmes offered are comparable right round the western world. Resuscitation training is only beginning to appear. *Training* is used very loosely here to refer to the fact that organizations do stifle people. Organizations are unable to cope with all the creativity their members have to offer; they are basically repetitive systems. For these reasons, human potential is killed, thwarted, not wanted, and major problems like mid-career crisis and organizational 'death' occur.

Resuscitation training may include sabbatical leave, organizational role analysis, overseas trips, or training programmes quite unrelated to the needs of the organization. There is only one objective: to maintain a self-fulfilled work force, excited, stimulated, and healthy in its adjustments to organizational realities.

Whatever the training, there are five steps:

- Identify the need for training
- Define the objectives
- Design the programme
- Conduct the programme
- Measure the effectiveness of the programme against the objectives

The simplicity of this plan is deceptive. Training, especially managerial and resuscitation training, is exceedingly difficult to evaluate. But trainers can hardly continue to ask top management to support their, often elaborate and costly, programmes on the basis that they must be 'good' for the 'system'. They probably are – even if they only make people less satisfied and more determined to improve the system – but this sort of gut feeling may not be enough to justify continued costs.

Performance review
Having selected, inducted, and trained an individual, the end of the feedback loop is to appraise performance. Appraisal schemes are one of the most controversial of the personnel

163

manager's procedures. There have been numerous studies illustrating how destructive/beneficial/useless they are. Yet, while it is easy to ridicule the use of personality traits, or the scales used, or the open-ended questions or the objectives of appraisal, it is impossible to ignore the continually cited need we all have for feedback on how we are doing.

It is not my intention here to design a review system; it is rather to suggest why appraisal systems are full of traps.

The objectives of appraisal are multiple. The first objective of appraisal is a two-way review of boss–subordinate relationships. The second objective is to feed back to the senior managers data on an employee or a group of employees' performance. Third, the appraisal is designed to tell the individual what his strengths and weaknesses are. Fourth, it is used in selecting people for promotion. Fifth, it is often used for reviewing salary and other rewards. Sixth, it attempts to identify the training needs. Seventh, it aims to provide a human inventory of talents, skills, qualifications, etc. Eighth, the review provides input for manpower planning, career path planning and numerous other devices. Given the breadth of objectives and the contradictory nature of some (feedback on self *and* salary review) it is not surprising that performance review is still handled badly in most organizations.

There are also cultural values which militate against its success. For example, it is not regarded as good form in our society to tell another person what his weaknesses are. There is also the question of individual rights and secrecy. And who will be honest with his boss if that boss controls his future – especially in a contracting or shrinking organization?

The irony of this breakdown in reviewing performance is that the very same people leave work, go home, and use a direct feedback system in which all members of the family know pretty well where they stand. Feedback in families is direct and constant. Deviations are not tolerated for long. Performance on family tasks is immediately appraised and rewards offered for good performance.

My own impression is that the size of work organizations has killed appraisal. Once it is standardized, hidden in head office files, passed surreptitiously from boss to subordinate and back again, then the most important feature of reviewing performance – i.e., a two-way analysis of boss–subordinate relations –

becomes institutionalized. Any real openness is lost, as we play out our power games under the scourge of literacy – writing and filing information until it chokes us.

Feedback can improve performance, under certain conditions:

- Open, non-documented feedback from manager to subordinate
- Objectives, rather than means, are the focus of attention
- Objectives are jointly set by manager and subordinate (not imposed from above)
- Performance review is related to future objectives, not personal appraisal
- Criticism is offered in a helpful, friendly way, not aggressively
- Honesty prevails. We should tell people openly what the chances for them are in the organization, rather than perpetuate the myth that everyone will be managing director one day
- Most important, reviews should occur where the people work. Most data discussed should remain confidential to that subordinate and his boss

Yet these are ideal conditions, requiring no documentation. The realities of organization size, human resource management, and information needs of governments, industry associations, unions, etc., force documentation upon us.

If we have to devise a formal process then my views are:

1 We should separate the objectives of performance review and use different people to collect different data. We should not attempt to appraise performance, recommend salary increases, and work out training needs from one procedure.
2 The appraisal should be restricted to the section or department in which the individual works.
3 The official documentation should be restricted to one or two pages, and should occur only if the personnel department *really* needs such documents.
4 All 'official' documents should be destroyed after three years.
5 Research on appraisal has shown that self ratings are superior to boss ratings. Better still (but costly) are self, boss, peer and subordinate ratings.

6 Rather than use documents, groups should be encouraged to use the team critique methods of team building to assess the performance of the team. Or, in other words, attempt to make the appraisal more like that which exists in a family – not a once-a-year activity, but a continuing process related to the objectives important at the time. In small organizations, this *is* how appraisal is handled.

Recruitment, selection, training and performance review are each very large fields of study. Those who want a more detailed analysis of these subjects should turn to the list at the end of this chapter, in which several excellent studies are mentioned.

Directing

The third function of managing – directing – means taking the structure which was planned and organized and bringing it alive. The process of making the structure live and become a productive role system involves leading, motivating, delegating, cooperating, disciplining, communicating, and so many other activities that only some of them can be covered here. Since separate chapters are devoted to leading, motivating, and interpersonal relations, this section will concentrate on two further aspects of directing: delegating, and disciplining.

Delegating

This refers to the transfer of authority (or positional power) down the hierarchy. The whole of the hierarchy depends on progressive, clear delegation from the top of the hierarchy down to the lowest level. In principle, few managers would dispute this. Yet, from my experience, the majority are poor delegators! And it is just this reality of organizations which produces so many of the frustrations, communication blockages, and inevitable conflicts.

There are many factors which affect delegation. Until recently, there were few opportunities to learn to delegate. The whole socialization process of the child and teenager depends on doing everything oneself. Schools do not normally permit the child who is poor at mathematics to delegate his mathematics to the child who is much better at mathematics. Everyone must do his or her own work.

Further, if the individual makes a mistake, the negative feedback is his. There is little point in kicking a friend because of one's own poor performance in physics or English. School is a *one person* performance, regardless of all the current noises about groups and team sports.

These two forces – the total accountability of the individual for his or her performance and the explicit negative feedback on poor performance – mean that by the time a person becomes a supervisor, he or she has had precious little training in delegation. Indeed, delegation holds a whole number of risks which may be easier to avoid. The risks involve the possibility of mistakes among subordinates (and negative feedback), or loss of control (and negative feedback), or attempts to take over the supervisor's job (negative feedback). Further, the principle of the absolute authority of the boss endorses the negative feedback structure.

To overcome these problems, we take managers into training rooms and tell them that times have changed and that they must delegate and forget the backlash of negative feedback. After 15 or 20 years of doing the reverse, it is not difficult to understand why this training has little or no effect, especially if the supervisor finds that, while he was at the training course, problems arose in his section and the moment he returned to his normal routine he received a broadside of negative feedback from his boss.

Delegation will only improve if the subordinates want more power, which means more control over their work. Pressure from below is becoming the most effective method for improving the supervisor's tendency to delegate, but the costs through industrial action are great. Understanding more about organizations and the changes in power relations would be a less painful way of overcoming a school system which does not teach delegation.

Sloan, who decentralized the American giant, General Motors, in the 'forties, is reported to have said:

I will not promote a man until he has got rid of what he is doing now.

That is, if the supervisor is unwilling to delegate, then he should not be promoted. This solves one of the chief executive's major problems: the knowledge that there are many, many people waiting to be promoted, but few or no vacancies at the top. If a supervisor is prepared to go on doing what he is doing now, then the chief executive has one less to worry about. But if the supervisor delegates most of his job, he will be bothering the boss for a new job.

Contrary to this view is the fact that when senior managers move up the hierarchy, they appear just as unwilling to delegate as the bosses they criticized. It is as though, having climbed up the structure, they do not want (or are unable) to change it while they are in control. So there are reinforcements for the delegation problem right at the top of the hierarchy, and much of the blame rests with the elitist views of senior managers.

Disciplining

Organizations depend on large numbers of people behaving in predictable and repetitive ways. The university expects the professor to lecture at specific pre-arranged times, and to behave in a fairly predictable way. This need for predictability has produced a multitude of formal behaviour codes, some universal, others peculiar to one organization. (See chapter 9 for a discussion of formal structure.) The codes refer to work to be done, ways in which it should be done, times of starting and finishing work, times of eating, codes on dress, and personal tidiness, etc. There are others which may be implicit rather than explicit, which refer to relationships with superiors, subordinates, or peers. There are explicit codes for resource control (money, people, materials, equipment, and information).

To ensure that these codes and expectations are followed, senior members can apply sanctions, rather than let the person's role set deal with any deviation. In extreme cases in our culture, if the codes are not followed, members place the person in gaol, or fine him, or, in organizations, expel him. But in the day-to-day life of members in role systems, the sanctions are often less explicit and more subtle. For example, we can totally ignore the person until he or she conforms; or we might not answer his memos; or we can isolate him to the extent that he is forced to leave.

All these reinforcements have been based on insecurity or the fear of expulsion, or loss of freedom. They are imposed, in the main, from above. So the boss kicks the subordinate who arrives late.

From the 'forties to the 'sixties, some managers became obsessed with what Denis Pym calls *organizational literacy*, or documented controls. For example, it was more important to be in the office at 9 a.m. than to have specific objectives for your job. The controls became more important than the objectives of the unit. Tidiness, neatness, documentation, punctuality, and obedience were more important to many supervisors than output. Signing the office attendance book was more important than what one produced. And the ritual surrounding the book and that sacred red line (drawn precisely at 9 a.m. by a clerk) became institutionalized as well. Instead of focusing on ends or tasks, the means became ends and bureaucratization or organizational literacy flourished.

The best discipline is not imposed from above by an elite called 'managers': it is self-discipline. We are at last seeing a shift in work organizations to more self-discipline and less imposed discipline. In a situation where clear goals exist, where they can be easily measured, and where the control can be given to the individual or the group, imposed discipline is outdated. You can say:

Here is the goal. Achieve it as you wish, sort out your own disciplines, and the system will evaluate your performance. Rewards will be based on results, not on dress or manners.

But such self-discipline is contrary to the Anglo-American view of the manager as a disciplinarian. Because of this self-discipline, it is not always effective. There are many older employees who have been told what to do, and when and how to do it all their lives, and the possibility of radically changing their behaviour to a new system is slight. For these people, it may be necessary to maintain imposed discipline. For the remainder, we will increasingly see self-discipline or group-discipline replacing imposed discipline. The move toward semi-autonomous work groups in government and industry shows recognition that self-regulating, smaller units, with positional power to act as a group and be rewarded as a group, is the structural forum for the 'eighties. However, as self-discipline will radically change the role of the manager, resistances are strong.

Controlling

The last function in the 'rational' manager's life ends a theoretical work cycle; he has planned his objectives, designed his structure, recruited, trained, motivated and rewarded his subordinates, and now he needs to ensure that the role system is in fact achieving what it was designed to achieve.

In traditional management theory, the control function referred to the design of feedback loops, the recording of deviations from plans, and the correction of deviations.

Deviations occur from budgets, targets, quality levels, deliveries, arrivals, machine capacity, and in members' behaviour. In a manufacturing business, we would expect to find (as a minimum) controls in the following areas:

Production
- Quality
- Quantity-time
- Cost
- Machine capacity/utilization
- Individual job performance
- Waste

Finance and accounting
- Profit and profit control
- Capital expenditure
- Sources of funds
- Liquidity
- Inventories
- Costs
- Cash flow

Personnel
- Lost time due to industrial disputes
- Turnover of employees
- Absenteeism
- Compensation and superannuation
- Sickness
- Pensions
- Wage and salary administration
- Vacations

- Levels of job satisfaction/dissatisfaction
- Safety

Marketing
- Sales volume
- Sales expenditure
- Credit
- Advertising costs
- Salesman performance
- Customer satisfaction

There are many other areas where control systems may be useful. For example, profit does not 'fall' out of organizations. There are 'profit extracting' controls to provide managers with information on progress to date and to collect often unrelated information on costs to revenue and profit. Also, there is increasing demand for evaluating a firm's contribution to society (social responsibility), and for evaluating in advance the organization's ability to adapt to a changing environment. Finally, in complex markets, there are an increasing number of attempts to predict and, if feasible, control future events.

The important considerations in any control system are:

- The feedback should be concerned with *now*

Too much data is collected on a historical basis. We need to know *before* the deviation becomes excessive.

- The feedback system should not be designed as a witch hunt among employees
- The only justification for a control is that it shows correctable deviations from what members have decided are desired ends

Much data which bears little or no relationship to the objectives is religiously collected because some individual (often many years ago) thought it would be useful to have. An army of staff specialists and consultants are responsible for this obsession with data – an obsession which makes it almost impossible for some managers to manage.

- The feedback should go to the individual(s) involved

There is little point in telling the general manager that quality

171

is poor in the plant. The employee in the plant influences quality. The controls should be documented for 'before and after' correction comparisons.

Elaborate control systems have been devised, by experts and consultants, without any real idea of the objectives of the organization. This has been particularly true of government organizations, where changes in political fortunes shift the presumed objectives with each election. The essentials of a good control system are quantifiable, precise objectives, and the realization of this basic truism has been the resurgence of Management by Objectives (MbO) as one of the fads of the 'seventies.

This brief discussion of controlling has analysed the functions of the manager as identified by traditional theorists. As mentioned at the outset, some functions are discussed in detail in other chapters and, for this reason, have received little attention in this chapter.

Let us now ask ourselves if managers *really* plan, organize, direct, and control.

What managers do

So far this chapter has concentrated on the traditional view of management – the functional approach of planning, organizing, directing, and controlling. This approach persists in schools of management, largely because it provides a framework for analysing some of the important tasks with which a manager should be concerned. I have used this approach so far simply as a framework to allow some comments on some of those tasks.

We should now turn away from the traditional theory and ask what a manager *really* does. Not what he *should* do, but what he *does* do. There have been several studies of what a manager does. The most popular method has been to ask managers to keep diaries of their activities and their durations (see Rosemary Stewart and June Carlson). A second approach uses observational techniques: the researcher observes the manager at work (see Guest, Jasinski, Ponder). Mintzberg used a structured observation method to observe five chief executives and identified managerial roles.

There are common themes in both diary and observation reports: all studies emphasize interpersonal relations, the amount of time spent on horizontal and lateral information transfer, and the erratic nature of the managerial job. These findings are in contrast to the traditional view of the manager as someone who rationally plans, organizes, directs, and controls his situation. Instead, the picture that emerges from actual studies of managers is one of fragmented activity, incomplete tasks, interruptions, variety, and unpredictable events. Little time is in fact spent on planning, or organizing, or controlling. Most time is spent on what the traditional theorists would call directing. So, despite the elitist image of the Anglo-American theory of management, most managers *do* spend their time running the show.

Minzberg's summary of his findings reflect other studies:

- Managers feel compelled to complete great volumes of work; free time is scarce and breaks are rare
- Brevity, variety, and fragmentation are preferred by the manager and characterize his job (in contrast to the repetitive nature of many other jobs)
- Managers gravitate to concrete activity tasks, rather than the conceptual or abstract. Answering mail, for example, is considered non-active and a burden. Current information (whether it is gossip, hearsay, or speculation) receives much more attention. Planning is seen as important but receives little attention compared with the activity of a stimulus–response work style
- Managers are primarily information processors. They use five media: mail (documented), telephone (verbal), unscheduled meetings (informal face-to-face), scheduled (formal face-to-face), and tours (observational). Managers favour the three verbal media
- Up to one third to one half of a manager's time is spent on external relationships and up to one third (to one half) with subordinates. Relatively little of a manager's time is spent with his boss

Mintzberg's study led him to an interesting classification of what a manager *actually appears to do*. He identified ten managerial roles by observing five chief executives.

Interpersonal roles

● Figurehead

He is the symbolic head, obliged to perform a number of routine duties of a legal or social nature.

● Leader

He is responsible for the motivation and activation of subordinates; responsible for staffing, training, and associated duties.

● Liaison

He maintains a self-developed network of outside contacts and informers who provide favours and information.

Informational roles

● Monitor

He seeks and receives a wide variety of special information (much of it current) to develop a thorough understanding of the organization and environment; he emerges as the nerve centre of internal and external information of the organization.

● Disseminator

He transmits information received from outsiders or from other subordinates to members of the organization; some information is factual, some involves interpretation and integration of diverse value positions or organizational influencers.

● Spokesman

He transmits information to outsiders about the organization's plans, policies, actions, results, etc., and serves as an expert on the organization's industry.

Decisional roles

● Entrepreneur

He searches the organization and its environment for opportunities and initiates 'improvement projects' to bring about change; he supervises design of certain projects as well.

● Disturbance handler

He is responsible for corrective action when the organization faces important, unexpected disturbances.

- Resource allocator

He is responsible for the allocation of organizational resources of all kinds – for, in effect, the making or approval of all significant organizational decisions.

- Negotiator

He is responsible for representing the organization at major negotiations.

One could argue that most of the traditional management theory's functions of a manager are covered in Mintzberg's ten roles, and that the differences are not nearly as great as he suggests. Further, he has studied overt behaviour and ignored cognitive activity – some managers plan continuously but intuitively. What is clear from observations is that managers manage *situations*; situations differ, and what will hold for one manager may not hold for another.

Like much of the material on leadership, which implies we are dealing with Nelson, Bonaparte or Roosevelt, Mintzberg's research has concentrated on chief executives. The vast majority of managers are not in that class and never will be. What does the research tell us about these men and women who manage small groups of people, often within large organizations?

It tells us that the better managers

- Clarify and get commitment to goals, targets, standards
- Communicate direction . . . company objectives, policies, plans
- Appraise and reward their subordinates regularly
- Look to the future operation of the group

Perhaps in training managers we should combine the traditional version of what should be done with what appears to be done. This would mean changing our training methods.

Alternatively, we could re-design the executive trainee scheme by creating opportunities in task force structures for experimentation with the managerial job, or we could use coaches, rather than trainers, to teach the interpersonal skills, and use role consultations to clarify role expectations. Further, the jobs could be circulated so more people get experience in running the show, rather like short-term appointments of academics as faculty chairmen in some universities. Having completed a term as leader or manager, the member returns to normal work and another member becomes manager. By loosening up our concepts of the managerial role we may allow the best managers to be managers – best in the sense both of producing results and of satisfying the expectations of members of the role set. The converse is currently true – anyone can become a manager and some are clearly not suited to the role.

What is even more ridiculous is that some of these weak managers leave important and productive jobs to move into the elitist managerial class. Ideally we should be able to do what we are best at and we should develop hierarchies in which being best at *anything* reaps high rewards – not just being best at management. But that sort of organization requires a new view of the role of the manager – a view divorced from values about importance and professional allegiances, and a view anchored on contribution to work.

Summary

For centuries we have had managers. Yet management theory is a recent development. Its two major concepts are that managing is getting things done with and through people and, second, that a manager has specific functions to perform:

- Planning
- Organizing
- Directing
- Controlling

In this chapter, each of these functions has been analysed. The section on *planning* covered setting objectives, collecting data, examining alternatives, and choosing a strategy.

The section on *organizing* referred to the work to be done, the people, and the variables affecting the role system. Traditional theorists argue that, once the organization is planned and structured, we need to staff it. In the sections on *staffing*, we discussed recruiting, selecting, inducting, training, and performance review.

The next function of managing to be examined was *directing*.

As so much of this function is covered elsewhere in this book, the material in this chapter was confined to delegating and disciplining.

The final section was on the *control* function.

Recent studies of managers have suggested that managers do *not* plan, organize, direct, and control in the way proposed by traditional theorists. These researchers hold that the manager is primarily a reactor – doing little planning or organizing, but reacting face-to-face with subordinates and external agents. What the manager actually does is probably somewhere between the traditional and the interpersonal view.

The next chapter returns to the organizing function for several reasons. First, organization design has become a major issue for managers. Second, very little practical advice is available, and I would like to try to correct that.

For additional reading

Byrt W., *People and Organisations*, McGraw-Hill, Sydney, 1971.

Crane Donald P., *Personnel Management: A Situational Approach*, Wadsworth, Belmont, California, 1974.

Cummings L. L., and D. P. Schwab, *Performance in Organisations: Determinants and Appraisal*, Scott Foreman, Glenview, Illinois, 1973.

Davies I. K., *The Organisation of Training*, McGraw-Hill, New York, 1973.

Department of Employment and Industrial Relations, *Appraisal: A Two-Sided Process*, Australian Government Publishing Service, Canberra, 1976.

Drucker P., *The Practice of Management*, Harper & Row, New York, 1961.

Fayol H., *General and Industrial Administration*, Pitmans, 1949.

French W., *The Personnel Management Process*, third edn, Houghton Mifflin & Company, Boston, 1974.

Glueck W. F., *Personnel: A Diagnostic Approach*, Business Publications Inc., Dallas, Texas, 1974.

Hague H., *Executive Self-Development*, Macmillan, 1974.

Kepner C. H., and B. B. Tregoe, *The Rational Manager*, McGraw-Hill, New York, 1965.

Koontz H. and C. O'Donnell, *Management: A Book of Readings*, McGraw-Hill, New York, 1968.

McFarland D. E. (ed.), *Personnel Management: Selected Readings*, Pengiun, 1971.

Mant A., *The Rise and Fall of the British Manager*, Macmillan, 1977.

Mintzberg H., *The Nature of Managerial Work*, Harper & Row, New York, 1973.

Perrow C., *Complex Organizations*, Scott Foreman, Glenview, Illinois, 1978.

Pugh D. (ed.), *Organisation Theory*, Penguin, 1974.

Pym D., 'In quest of post industrial man' in N. Armistead (ed.), *Reconstructing Social Psychology*, Penguin, 1974.

Pym D., 'The crisis in authority', *Journal of Association of Teachers of Management*, Vol. 6, Pt 2, 139–43, 1975.

Schein E., *Career Dynamics: Matching Individual and Organisational Needs*, Addison-Wesley, Reading, Massachusetts, 1978.

Torrington D. P., and D. F. Sutton (eds.), *Handbook of Management Development*, Gower Press, 1973.

Williams M. R., *Performance Appraisal in Management*, Heinemann, 1972.

Yuill B., and D. Steinhoff, *Developing Managers in Organisations*, Wiley, Sydney, 1975.

9 Structuring organizations

This chapter is going to discuss one of the most controversial activities of managers: the design of formal structures. It is a complex field of study, so I have concentrated on some structural types and suggested indications of these types. In fact, it is rare for examples of the types to occur in a pure form – most structures are hybrids. This chapter will concentrate on a macro view of structure; the micro view of structure at the work place is dealt with in chapter 11.

What is a formal structure? Structure is a collective noun which incorporates all those explicit and implicit decisions of members about who does what, for whom, for how long, for what rewards, for what punishments, under what conditions of work, etc. The formal structure refers to those shared values and beliefs among people about the law of the organization. Much of the structure is not documented, but parts of it are: the hierarchy, job descriptions, rules, regulations, procedures, etc., are often available for people to read. But documentation is not a necessary condition. Structure exists in the minds of people, and it refers to those values and beliefs that are shared by the majority of role performers as controlling their behaviour. What we can observe in performers' behaviour is the influence of those shared beliefs and values.

Formal structure is always out of date, because it operates on precedent. It is a major source of conflict and dissatisfaction, yet it appears to be essential for task achievement. Even very loosely structured organizations have hierarchies, behaviour codes, and reinforcements for goal achievement (see chapter 3). At the other extreme, the highly structured organization may have volumes of documented controls, rules, and regulations. The most structured organization of all is that in which those common beliefs and values which I have called the formal structure are more powerful than the role performers, where nearly every eventuality of those beliefs and values has been documented in a manual, where the manual *is* the king and where behaviour programmes permit no deviation.

Traditional views of structure

Traditional guides for designing organization structures required that one of several structural models be adopted for the whole organization. Either the firm centralized *or* decentralized, divisionalized *or* departmentalized. The most common choice was a centralized, departmentalized structure. The conditions which allowed this relaxed choice of structure were:

- A stable market
- Centralized decision making
- Employees motivated by basic life needs
- A long history of task oriented management
- A conservative and predictable government

Given these conditions, designers could select their 'chart' with some assurance that the resultant structure would work. If the choice of structure was wrong, then time would permit minor modifications on a trial-and-error basis.

Charts, job descriptions, man specifications, budgetary accounting, financial systems, and a host of other documented controls on resources were the 'bread and butter' trade of the O & M section and of the management consultants.

Long deliberations on structural change usually meant that the match between the chosen structure and the expectations of members was sufficiently close for there to be only minor modifications to either the guides or the practice. Similarly, predictability resulted in a vast body of theory, from such people as Fayol, Urwick, Koontz and O'Donnell, Newman, etc. Two major changes have altered this comfortable scenario for organization design: a new breed of employees, and a rapidly changing and unpredictable environment.

The new breed
The affluent, well clothed and well fed middle-class generation (the 'Spock' generation born in the 'fifties) has arrived in work organizations. This post-war generation has lower concern for security and basic survival. They have never been hungry or cold, and very rarely, if ever, without money. Hence, the old

control systems, based on fear, poverty and hunger, are no longer relevant for a large section of the work force.

We could philosophize about the pros and cons of this change, but my research data clearly show differences from other generations. What was satisfying and rewarding in the traditional organizations is not necessarily satisfying or rewarding for today's young, upper- and middle-class adults. On the other hand, traditional rewards and satisfactions are still important to the over forties and to the young adults from lower income families.

Older managers frequently express fear of the affluent generation, particularly that they will encourage chaos and disorder in organizations. Critics point to changes in dress, hair styles, lack of respect for such Victorian but organizationally sacrosanct behaviour codes as arriving before 9.00 a.m. in the morning, taking precisely one hour for lunch, and working industriously till 5.00 p.m. For many supervisors, these controls are more important than what an employee produces.

Where the critics err in their argument is in the assumption that the well fed, 'television' generation will not introduce a structure of its own. One fascinating characteristic of humans is their infinite capacity for structuring their perceptions and behaviour. This is just as true of the affluent generation of employees as it was for previous generations, but the parameters are different. Performance is their major criterion of effectiveness, not dress, or organizational loyalty, or hours of work, or respect for the boss. They have been measured and probed probably more than any previous generation. They respect performance, not pretensions, and they want to be measured and rewarded on performance. *Unfortunately, in most organizations there is almost no direct relationship between rewards and performance* – on a short time scale. There is certainly no tangible reward for arriving at 9.00 a.m., dressed in a navy suit, with short hair. And after all, what is more important – the performance or the appearance?

This generation has criticized the pretensions and power games of their elders. They are more anxious to work in teams, with team goals, and to participate in making decisions. They expect a share of the resultant cake. Contrary to most public outcries, they do not expect hand-outs for nothing. Certainly, if the hand-outs are there, they will take them, but their experience has been of a direct relationship between achievement

181

and reward. For thousands of them, this is the way their school system operated.

It is pointless for designers of organizations to talk of the good old days of predictability among employees. Similarly, it is rather pointless to moralize about the death of the old systems of control. These are questions which every individual in dealing with his own employees or his own children must resolve for himself. For may part, I am concerned that we are not trying to match the expectations of the bulk of the under thirties with organizational expectations. It is a little late to argue that we should belt them, psychologically or physiologically, as a learning experience.

The environment

The second major influence on organization structures has been the increased external pressures in the market place. For all Western markets, the 'seventies was an age of turbulence. Herbert Spencer, the nineteenth-century philosopher, predicted that, with increasing heterogeneity in the market place, no regulatory or government body would be able to manage the resultant complexity.

Turbulent markets are characterized by exceedingly short time spans, changing combinations of organizations, and fluid relationships. This is the market approximating the economist's idea of pure competition. Competition is never pure – there are always power lobbies, friends, takeovers, mutual arrangements, or long term contracts which prevent organizations from being exposed to purely competitive markets. But for hundreds of business organizations, the past decade has brought the first taste of a really competitive struggle. For many fat, over-protected businesses, this period has been very beneficial: costs have been cut, and finance, production, personnel, and marketing departments have been challenged on cost. Performance has become a central issue. Some businesses and individuals were unable to adapt, and this is a cost of the turbulent market. Politicians will continue to debate the cost of organizational death; when does the cost of survival warrant government protection?

Rapid change is only one characteristic of this market. A second characteristic is the market forces themselves. We can no longer assume that there is a lethargic but responsive market out there, encouraging the self-indulgence and arrogance of the marketing concept. There is a dynamic, errupting, changing, living force, external to the organization, and this force has become the major determinant of what happens inside the organization in terms of size (number of employees) and formal structure.

The degree of environmental uncertainty varies from one organization to another. Some government agencies and some monopolistic firms ride above the pressures of the market place; they change slowly, and are structurally little different from what they were ten years ago. In contrast, other government departments and some firms – like brokers – are subject to continual external pressures, and their structures reflect those pressures. Between these extremes lie the majority of organizations. But even for those less vulnerable, cost rises are increasingly a source of externally derived pressures which are forcing internal change. Cost of living adjustments, devaluations, tariff changes, political changes, and inflation are making us all subject to uncertainty. And for many, many people, uncertainty is terrifying, even if, in a very short time in man's history, we have learned to live with it.

Symptoms of the twin forces hitting the organization

The symptoms of environmental uncertainty and the new expectations of employees are:

- Hierarchical instability; vertical authority relationships break down
- Complaints from older staff that they cannot predict people's behaviour
- Loss of business because of extended delays and time-consuming controls
- Customer dissatisfaction and brand fickleness
- Exponential growth of internal and informal lateral information flows
- Vertical communication blockages
- Demands from work units for more resources to cope with the market uncertainty

- Distrust of old performance measures because they are seen as unrealistic
- Increased union activity, reflecting increasing employee dissatisfaction
- Increased staff turnover, absenteeism, sickness
- A multitude of structural 'props' designed to save the system (manuals, charts, rules, controls)

Organizations, especially large ones, can be very resilient. Even faced with all these symptoms, many systems survive, especially if there has been sufficient capital invested to guarantee financial momentum or if large numbers of people are employed. What has stunned the market place in the last decade is that financial momentum or numbers of employees are not necessarily the life jackets they were. We have been forced to accept that even large organizations can and do collapse.

The degree of external turbulence or pressure *and* the sorts of people working in an organization are two primary determinants of the structure. For example, it is no accident that highly uncertain businesses (e.g., real estate, life assurance sales, management consultants, advertising, or entrepreneurial businesses) attract people who place safety low among their priorities. Nor is it an accident that most of these businesses have loose structures. Conversely, it is not surprising to find that prisons attract warders with high security needs into a highly structured organization on which environmental pressures have little effect.

Our previous experience as designers of structures has been with predictable markets, longer time spans, clearer objectives, and employees who did as they were told. Given these ingredients, it was possible to preach 'principles of organization design' which reflected the similarities observed by management writers in different organizations in the 'twenties, 'thirties, and 'forties. These guides for 'good' structural design persist even today. Many managers in our society still regard them as law. I will discuss them briefly, before moving on to more realistic guides.

Because times and conditions have changed, we need to change our approach to designing structures. Unfortunately, as most of today's managers were brought up in schools, families, and churches where these concepts prevailed, it is difficult for them to imagine any other set of guidelines. This restricted vision is reflected in our national obsession with either/or thinking: *either* we enforce the traditional guidelines *or* we accept chaos. In practice, role systems are rarely as simple as either/or thinking suggests.

The traditional guidelines for design

The Conference Board in New York restated the guidelines in the early 'sixties.

- There must be clear lines of authority running from the top to the bottom of the organization

Clarity is achieved through delegation by steps or levels from the leader to the working level – from the highest executive to the employee who has least accountability in the organization. It should be possible to trace such a line from the chief executive to every employee. From military language, this vertical line is often referred to as 'the chain of command' and the principle is known as the 'scalar' principle.

- No one in the organization should report to more than *one* line supervisor. Everyone in the organization should know to whom he reports and who reports to him

This is usually referred to as the 'unity of command' principle. Put bluntly it means that everyone should have one boss.

- The accountability and authority of each supervisor should be clearly defined, in *writing*

Putting accountabilities in writing enables the supervisor to know both what is expected of him and the limits of his authority; it prevents overlapping of tasks and authorities.

- Responsibility should always be coupled with corresponding authority
- The responsibility of higher authority for the acts of his subordinates is absolute

Although a supervisor delegates authority, he still remains responsible for what is done by those to whom he has delegated it. The executive cannot dissociate himself from the acts of his subordinates. He is as accountable as they are for what they do or neglect to do.

- Authority should be delegated as far down the line as possible

Permitting decisions to be made on as low a level as possible releases the energies of those on the higher levels for matters to which only they can attend.

- The number of levels of authority should be kept at a minimum

The greater the number of levels, the longer is the chain of command and the longer it takes for instructions to travel down and for information to travel up and down within the organization.

- The work of every person in the organization should be confined as far as it can be to the performance of a single leading function

This is the economists' concept of specialization. It applies to departments and divisions as well as to individuals.

- Whenever possible, line functions should be separated from *staff* functions, and adequate emphasis should be placed on important staff activities

Line functions are those which accomplish the main goals or objectives of the organization – e.g., the production line departments are often called 'operating' departments. *Staff* functions are those which aid in, or are auxiliary to, the line functions. Members of staff departments provide service, advice, and integration for line or operating departments.

- There is a limit to the number of positions that can be coordinated by the single executive

This principle was known as the 'span of control'. What determines its width?

1 The similarity or dissimilarity of the subordinate positions and how interdependent they are: the more positions interlock, the greater the work of coordination.
2 How far apart, geographically, the people's activities are.
3 The complexity of the duties of each of the positions to be coordinated.
4 The stability of the business.

5 The frequency with which new types of problems arise

- The organization should be flexible, so that it can be adjusted to changing conditions
- The organization should be kept as simple as possible

By the 'sixties, the traditional principles of design had been watered down considerably, but the Conference Board's survey confirmed their importance to managers designing structures.

Quite independent of this American approach to structural design was the work of the German sociologist Max Weber in the early years of this century. His analysis of bureaucracies found structural similarities which read rather like some of the management theorists' principles. Weber was *not* advocating bureaucracy, as so many writers have contended. He warned of the consequences of adopting this form of structure. However, he did believe (as many sociologists do today) that it is the most efficient way to achieve production. Where he differed from early management theorists was in his superb analysis of authority and his theoretical support for these guidelines of bureaucracies.

Weber's views of bureaucratic structures
Weber's analysis found bureaucracies had the common characteristics noted below.

- Official business is conducted on a continuous basis
- It is conducted in accordance with stipulated rules, in an administrative agency characterized by three interrelated attributes:
  - The duty of each official to do certain types of work is delimited in terms of impersonal criteria
  - The official is given the authority necessary to carry out his assigned functions
  - The means of compulsion at his disposal are strictly limited and the conditions under which their employment is legitimate are clearly defined
- Every official's responsibility and authority are part of a hierarchy of authority. Higher offices are assigned the duty of supervision; lower offices the duty to obey. However, the extent of supervision and the conditions of legitimate appeal may vary.

- Officials and other administrative employees do not own the resources necessary for the performance of their assigned functions, but are accountable for their use of these resources. Official business and private affairs, and official revenue and private income are strictly separated
- Offices cannot be appropriated by their incumbents like private property that can be sold and inherited. (This does not preclude various rights, such as pension claims, regulated conditions of discipline and dismissal, etc., but such rights serve – in principle, at least – as incentives for the better performance of duties. They are not property rights)
- Official business is conducted on the basis of written documents

Weber's insightful analysis led to a multitude of sociological studies of bureaucracy. His work has become a major reference in any course in design, whether in business or government. Yet he is blamed for promoting 'bureaucratization', which, for some people in the field of organizational behaviour, is like promoting cancer. It is difficult to know what some people, who use this word very loosely, mean. But worse, it shows very little reading of Weber by his critics. A second error of many writers is to assume that bureaucratic structures exist only in government organizations. Bureaucracy is a form which can and does exist in any organization, business, government, educational, or religious. For example, the conditions isolated by Weber hold for most employees in the larger, publicly listed, companies on our stock exchange.

Structural reactions to turbulent environments

Apart from theories of bureaucracy and what have been called 'traditional' management theories, the design of structures received very little attention from organization researchers until the late 'sixties (e.g., the Aston Studies in the UK). However, since then there has been a resurgence of interest among practitioners and academics.

Design is no longer a simple process of applying 'laws' and drawing charts, but a process of combining a group of variables to create a best fit. And, increasingly, the resultant contingent design looks messy, temporary, 'people-centred' rather than 'rational', and preoccupied with adaptability rather than stability. To traditional design theorists, the results are disturbing. But for those in the 'real' world, structural design theory has finally become realistic.

Contingency theory

Contingency theory refers to attempts to understand the multivariate relationships between the components of organizations and to designing structures piece-by-piece, as best fits the components. This approach rejects earlier theories of universal models for designing formal structures, and argues that each situation must be analysed separately. Contingency means: 'it depends'. Moreover, choosing a design for the whole is seen by contingency theorists to be restrictive: units of structure may be adopted from all along a design continuum, depending on the situation. Contingency implies that within the same organization there may be units of bureaucracy, units operating in a matrix structure, and units which are divisionalized. Single design types, neatness, symmetry, and permanance are not indicative of 'good' design. The only criteria for good design are task performance and individual/group satisfaction.

The important part of designing structures is collecting relevant data. A would-be designer should first ask the people involved for their views on design, what they do as tasks, and how the many tasks fit together into a product or service. Second, to prevent 'instant' solutions to design questions, he or she should draw a simple task analysis matrix (see Figure 9.1), with the tasks on one axis and the design variables (objectives, differentiation, people, external pressures, technical system, integration, managerial style, size, number of people involved) on the other. Each task can be rated on a pre-determined scale against these design criteria. Then and only then they can refer to possible structural typologies and to the pool of possible integrative mechanisms, because by then the situational variables will have been analysed and a choice of a structural design can be made. Contrary to this, most designs are chosen because someone at or near the top of the hierarchy reads or hears about a structural type which he or she finds attractive. Too little time is spent analysing the needs of the people and the situation.

	Task 1	Task 2	Task 3	Task 4	Task 5, etc.
Objectives					
Time					
Differentiation					
Ext. press					
People					
Technical system					
Size					

Figure 9.1 Task analysis matrix

The resultant design may look messy but it is likely to be functional, as it is based on data from those involved and on an objective analysis of the tasks to be performed in that situation.

Similar combinations of the variables in the task analysis may result in those tasks being grouped together. But if the task profiles are not similar or interdependent, there is no real justification for combining those tasks in a department or section or division. Nor should past experience be considered sacrosanct. Many previous combinations of tasks reflect organizational politics rather than objective analysis.

Integrating tasks into an efficient and satisfying whole is one of the most pressing issues in design. The need for integration and the techniques employed vary with the external market pressures and the expectations of those employed.

If we adopt a contingency approach, what variables should we analyse? They are:

- Objectives
- Time orientation
- Task/differentiation
- People involved (including experience, motives, numbers)
- Market (or external) pressures
- Technical system
- Possible integrators
- Managerial style

Only after an exhaustive analysis should we consider a design for the structure. Let us examine these variables in more detail.

The objectives. Are senior managerial objectives clear, unclear, partly clear? How precisely do other employees know the ends? Vague objectives make structural design more tentative. Conversely, the clearer the ends, the easier to structure.

Time orientation. How much time is necessary for task completion – long time (over 12 months), medium time (6 months), or short time (day-to-day, week-to-week, or shift-to-shift)? The longer the time, the more complex the structure.

The differentiation of tasks. How different are the tasks essential for reaching the objectives? (This is traditionally referred to as the *division of work.*) The greater the differentiation of tasks, the more complex the integrative mechanisms.

Tasks may be differentiated (like or unlike) by:

- Product (e.g., cars, soap)
- Skill (e.g., surgeon, anaesthetist)
- Territory (e.g., Sydney, Melbourne)
- Process (e.g., polishing, packaging)
- Customer (e.g., retail, wholesale)
- Technology (e.g., batch production, mass production)
- Time (shift or non-shift workers)

The people. Different sorts of motivations and skills attract people to different organizations and occupations. Traditionally, design of structure meant *ignoring* the people. What sort of people? What experience? What qualifications and skills? How many? What motivation profiles? High security goals, low tolerance of ambiguity, age, experience, all lead to more structure. Low security goals, etc., lead to looser structure. High social needs may indicate a group structure. High power needs may indicate centralized control, etc.

Technical system. What plant and equipment? Is the influence of the technical system on behaviour very high, medium, or negligible? What restrictions does the technology place on design? A £23 million paper-making machine places extraordinary restrictions on structural design. One typewriter places very little restriction on the overall organizational design. The more complex the technical system, the more specialization of skills and functions – and subsequently, the greater pressure on integrative mechanisms.

External pressure. Market uncertainty has become *the* major influence on design. We need to know if the market pressures are high or not, and how far the pressures penetrate the organization. For example, sales departments are very exposed to uncertain markets, while a production department may be less exposed. We should look at the following dimensions of the environment:

● Complexity

How many different activities are there for us to deal with in the environment? How diverse are they? How many markets?

● Certainty

How predictable is the direction of change in the market? How predictable is the rate of change? How predictable is the tone (friendly or hostile) of the market place?

● Relations with other organizations

What are the relations between our organization and others? Are requests from others predictable? If so, we can use routine responses to those requests. Are our relations direct or indirect? If indirect, then it is much more difficult to plan a structural response. How much do we depend on other organizations? The more dependent we are, the more tasks will be devoted to maintaining relationships. How much power (size, control of resources, financial links, capital invested, sales, number of employees) have we, compared with other organizations?

Integration. Having examined the objectives, the major tasks, the people, the technology, and the market, we need to know what tasks need to be integrated. Some will need close integration, others may have no bearing on one another at all. Integrative mechanisms are many and varied – from accounting systems to task forces, from liaison officers to industrial spies. Table 9.1 lists a range of integrative mechanisms used as either external uncertainty and/or peoples expectations change.

TABLE 7.1 Methods of integration as affected by uncertainty and expectations

External Certainty →					→ External Uncertainty
Vertical Information System					
• Centralized hierarchy • Rules • Sanctions • Resource controls	• Centralized line and staff hierarchy • Rules • Sanctions • Planning • Resource controls • Assistant to • Executive assistants	• Centralized hierarchy • Functional authority • Sanctions • Planning • Resource control • Training • Cost reduction programme • Electronic data processing • Centralized records (personnel, inventory)	• Divisionalized hierarchy • Planning • Resource controls • Training • Management by Objectives • Management information system • Market research • Decentralization of personnel, purchasing, etc.	• Conglomerate hierarchy • Training • MbO • Changed goals • Surplus resources • Management information system • Consolidation of divisions	• Dual authority hierarchy • Planning • Reduced HQ staff • Financial resource control • Training • Short-term end results only • Management information system • Subsidiary companies • Participative consultation
Lateral Information System					
• Committees	• Committees • Direct informal contact	• Committees • Direct contact • Liaison officers	• Executive committee • Task forces • Liaison officers • MbO assist. • Corporate planning department • Management consultants	• Head office task forces • Liaison officers • Corporate planning dept. • Management consultants	• Semi-autonomous groups/project teams • Functional teams • Resources management • Project managers, team leaders • Functional internal consulting service
People Expectations					
Imposed control High safety needs Medium achievement needs					Self-control Low safety needs High social needs High achievement needs

Managerial style. What sort of management style best suits the combination of objectives, tasks, markets and people?

Having analysed objectives, tasks, people, technology, and environment, using a simple *task analysis matrix*, we can select the formal structure and integrative mechanisms best suited to these variables in specific situations. For example, because the variables will be different, it is likely that in the accounting section we will see one organizational form, and another entirely different from in the sales section. Linking these units together will be integrative mechanisms, of which the most important is the hierarchy. And it will remain the most important in the future, simply because authority and power form the basis of hierarchy. We may flatten hierarchies, carve them up into small units, even overthrow them, but they always reappear. Every overthrow of the establishment (or power elite) creates another – whether it is the informal leader of a semi-autonomous work group, the prince of a realm, or the shop steward.

The hierarchy is the most important characteristic of structure. There are numerous hierarchical types and even more hybrids. To make my argument easier to follow, I have selected six well-known examples of hierarchies. They are presented in Figure 9.2, where these types are shown on a continuum from market certainty to market uncertainty. That is, the relevant type alters with market uncertainty. However, one should remember that there will be examples of different types in one

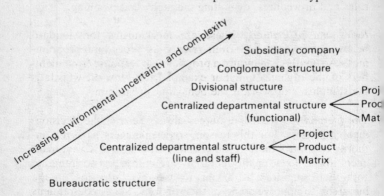

Figure 9.2 A continuum of hierarchical types

organization. Table 9.1 has added a second continuum: the changing needs of people. Using both variables of certainty/uncertainty and changing expectations, Table 9.1 lists the increasing use of integrative mechanisms as these two important variables change. While the six examples of hierarchical types on Figure 9.2 are similar to the six columns of Table 9.1, they are not intended to be identical.

The integrating mechanisms are the second important characteristic of structure; some are intended to hold the structure together *laterally*, whereas others (hierarchy and controls) attempt to hold it together *vertically*. Table 9.1 also shows a major redistribution of power from the centralized bureaucratic structure to the team-based structure. However, as I have suggested already, whether power devolves or not is highly contentious. Table 9.1 is not meant to indicate exclusive categories. It is very possible some of the integrative mechanisms will occur in structural forms where I have not included them. What the table aims to show is the increasingly complex design issues as size, uncertainty and complexity increase.

Methods of integration

While much has been written on the division of work into groups, departments, functions, or divisions, less attention has been given to coordinating or integrating those units. There are many techniques for integration. Among the most common are rules and procedures, exploiting hierarchy and planning.

Rules and procedures. These are mechanisms for standard behaviour – what some writers refer to as 'procedural programmes'. A stimulus can induce a programmed response from members of the organization. For example, the blow-off whistle is the stimulus, stop work is the behaviour programme.

The hierarchy. Limited resources always restrict the decision-making process. For this reason, some managers have the authority to control more resources than others. In this way, managers lower down in the hierarchy are compelled to integrate with their superiors by having to ask their superiors in the hierarchy to approve some of their actions. Such requirements result in managerial control.

Planning. By developing standardized plans as behaviour pro-grammes, the integration is made easier. Hence, the railway produces a schedule of train departures to integrate its services and the numerous trains at its disposal. The Second World War gave a great impetus to highly intricate methods of assisting the planning process, and the increased complexity of our society has added to these techniques.

Increased market uncertainty means more processing of infor-mation through the hierarchy. There will be more requests from the subordinate to his boss for guidance, and the traditional exception rule becomes less operative. There are numerous tac-tics we can adopt to meet this. They fall into two major cate-gories, and the tactics of both categories are integrative.

Delegation. This means trying to do the following:

- Refer fewer decisions upwards for approval
- Divisionalize or regionalize by product
- Allocate resources to the units so that they will not be found wanting – give more people, money, materials than are required immediately, to allow the unit to handle the highs in demand (so management has to approve slack resources during low demand)
- Employ more independent managers who will make decisions on their own

Devise mechanisms for handling more information. It may be possible to introduce the following:

- Management information systems, to improve the vertical flow of information
- Lateral mechanisms to improve the flow of information across the different skills, products, etc., in the firm. Liaison officers, task forces, royal commissions (in government), temporary committees
- New structures to formalize the vertical and lateral information flows
- Matrix structures, project teams or *ad hoc* organizations

The increasing complexity and size of our work organizations, corporations, hospitals, government businesses, government departments, municipal councils, etc., has compelled us to search for new, mechanically based methods of encoding, storing, and retrieving information. In a relatively short period, man has devised intricate methods for doing this – yet in organizations the problem remains: information flows just are not as good as they were in the 'good old days' when there were 30 people, all of whom knew each other by name, and talked to one another. Perhaps one solution to organizational integration is to consider one effect of greater external pressures, *size*, as a major determinant of the shape and structure of each unit.

Research into size, or number of employees in the organization and in *one* location, has produced varied results. As a consultant, it is easy to see both the positive and the adverse effects of increasing size, especially after 1000 employees. However, while the research on size has clearly supported the positive advantages in production capacity, it has not supported the consultant's gut feelings about behavioural disadvantages. Some studies show that administrative and behavioural problems increase as the size increases, while other studies do not. What is clear is that it is *not* size alone which causes problems. Size plus lack of group identity may be the vital variables. Because of these two variables we are witnessing a worldwide tendency to attempt to reduce size – by divisionalizing, if not into product groups, then into production or work groups within the larger structure. One irony of this so called decentralization is that it invariably leads to greater centralization, but it can lead to greater group identification by role performers. 'Small is beautiful', as Schumacher's book tells us, but small can lead to great pressures for integration between interdependent parts.

Table 9.1 illustrates the different structural forms as size and market pressures lead to decentralized operating units. While the table is not exhaustive, it tries to illustrate the shift in and expansion of integrative mechanisms.

Using some of the hierarchical types and some of the integrative mechanisms, Tables 9.2 to 9.6 show how the design variables combine to suggest specific hierarchies and specific integrative mechanisms.

197

Combinations of the design variables

Tables 9.2 to 9.6 consider, for each structural form, the following design variables: the nature of objectives, time orientation, task differentiation, people, technical system, and external pressures. They also suggest the integrative mechanisms appropriate to each form, and the managerial style likely to prevail. They suggest a macro-view and a one structure form which I have already said rarely occurs but the tables do allow us to look at the different combinations of the variables.

Bureaucratic structure
Table 9.2 outlines the conditions which lead logically to a bureaucratic structure. If any of the following conditions change the structure, the other variables will get out of kilter:

Table 9.2 Bureaucratic structure

Objectives	Clear only to the power elite. For the majority of members, unclear. Functions or duties override objectives as ends
Time orientation	Long term, even infinite
Task differentiation	Low. All tasks are distinct subsets of the primary task – e.g., collect taxes, provide health care, supply water and sewerage, administer life assurance
People	Attracts people with strong needs for safety and predictability. The highly prescribed rules, regulations, and authorities are reinforced and extended by the very people who work there, because they want prescription, definition, etc. This makes it very difficult to change the structure. High achievers are attracted, but risk taking is low because of the effect on security needs, and because the large size (in terms of numbers of people) makes change difficult
Technical system	Traditionally, low influence from plant, equipment, and physical constraints. The computer is changing this and affecting the control systems. It is feasible that the computer (cf. duty statements) will become the major control on behaviour

External pressure	Low. This is one of the important conditions for this structural form. A second condition is a monopolistic position, or at least only two or three suppliers in the market. A third condition is large size. Structural devices (such as complaints departments, inaccessibility of people, form completion techniques, etc.) are used to 'ricochet' off complaints or threats. The influence of the market is therefore minimized in terms of its penetration into the role system. (One interesting result of this defensive system has been the increasing tendency of frustrated customers to bypass the official complaints channels and contact the managing director, minister, or chairman of the board. The result is the emergence of a new appendage for protection, around the king's office, duplicating the skills of the customer relations department much lower down the hierarchy)
Managerial style	Highly centralized and task oriented
Integration	• The hierarchy collects vertical information
	• Committees collect lateral information
	• Job descriptions, rules, regulations and formalized procedures ensure that people stick to their prescribed roles. Sanctions may be used to reinforce the rules. Justice is handled through appeals tribunals. Impersonal controls are vital to this structural form. Very stereotyped workforce

• The objectives change
• External pressures increase and penetrate the system
• People with lower safety needs are employed
• The computer changes the control system

Signs of breakdown in the structure are seen first in a hasty attempt by those in positions of power to reinforce the legitimacy of the structure as it was – e.g., universities bringing in police to stop student riots in the 'sixties and early 'seventies. A second sign is a search for new integrative mechanisms to hold together what will no longer stay together. (An excellent example is the love affair of senior executives with management information systems, which promised a return to total predictability.) A third sign of structural problems is continual cost reduction campaigns.

Table 9.3 Central functional structure

Objectives	Much clearer and certain
Time orientation	Medium-term time orientation
Task differentiation	Increasing task differentiation, leading to all the traditional functions of a business
People	Safety needs still strong for the majority of employees, but more achievers prepared to take risks. The number of people may be very large, and for this reason the organization is seen as bureaucratic
Technical system	May be exceedingly complex, but is programmable and repetitive – as in mass production, oil refining, or large-scale batch production
External pressures	Medium to high
Managerial style	Task oriented – but more dependent on the style of the king than the climate of the organization
Integration	• The hierarchy remains the major vertical integrator • Standardized controls over people, materials, money, and equipment, *but* managers may interpret them for local consumption • Complex computer-based management information systems have largely replaced hand-written forms • The increasing breakdowns in lateral information flows have led to more head office task forces and integrators who visit different locations of the firm

The first positive sign that those in power recognize that the structure must be altered is when they begin structural experiments with task forces or project teams. A second sign is when managers realize the market can be influenced and the marketing function emerges – initially with logos, tentative advertising, and amateurish public relations efforts, but eventually with a fully-fledged department called *Marketing* (c.f. *Enquiries*, or *PR* or *Complaints*). But by the time this happens, the formal structure is being moved from a bureaucratic form – it has acquired the characteristics of a centralized departmental structure, in which departmental positions show a greater degree of specialization and differentiation. If pressures for change continue, then the line and staff departmental hierarchy shifts to a functional authority structure.

Central functional structure
In this form, functional specialization (finance, marketing, personnel, production, etc.) had led to an increase in functional delegation, laterally and vertically. By 'functional' I mean authority is based on the function (e.g. line and staff where line executives have authority to make decisions and staff advise). In a functional authority structure those with authority for a function can *tell* others what to do in that function.

Characteristics of the centralized functional structure are

- Very high degree of centralized decision making
- Positions are defined but are more influenced by who occupies them – the structure is less sacrosanct
- The major structural question is whether the structure is a line and staff structure or a functional authority structure – i.e., can the head of personnel tell the head of production what to do on personnel matters (functional) or can he only advise him (line and staff)?
- The major difference from the bureaucratic structure is the serious questioning of a whole range of rules, controls, and pieces of paper. This is a period when structural consultants may be invited to comment on, but not change, the structure

Figure 9.3 gives a section of a centralized, highly task differentiated hierarchy found in most large business organizations (functions, not positions, are named).

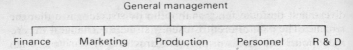

Figure 9.3 Task differentiation in a centralized functional structure

Functions which are likely to be differentiated as third-level functions or departments are:

- Managerial accounting
- Data processing
- Industrial relations
- Corporate relations (with governments)

If external pressures increase further (clearer objectives but shorter time spans), the functional model of a hierarchy undergoes periods of breakdown, while members attempt to meet the increased uncertainty through a highly centralized structure. Signs of the increasing inability of the people or inadequacy of the structure to meet the information requirements are:

- The planning of even more elaborate management information systems
- Increasing use of liaison (integrator) positions (assistants to, deputy managers, personal secretaries, task forces, teams)
- Increasing demands for more vertical information *in addition* to that required by the management information system (and invariably an inability by those in power to understand why subordinates have not got the data)
- A contraction (centralization) of authority, which worsens the situation as it breaks communication channels and annoys subordinates
- Recognition that *lateral* information flows need attention
- Use of project teams, management committees, and a sharp rise in time spent in meetings
- Increasing evidence of employee dissatisfaction, which is often blamed on the management training courses

The first sign of an offensive attack on a threatening market place (as opposed to a defensive stand) is a regrouping of tasks on a product or market basis. Diversification often follows as the only alternative option. However, if the firm is large and

202

diversified, then the functional authority structure is no longer tenable. The painful result is usually structural change – maybe a divisional structure, or a project structure, or a matrix structure. More likely, it is a messy-looking hybrid of many structural forms. As a divisional structure is increasingly common, we will look at that form first.

Divisional structure

The appearance of this type arises from four major changes in the highly centralized structures:

1 Objectives are clearer, quantifiable, and directly related to suvival.
2 Tasks are clearly differentiated – most frequently by products (see Figure 9.4).
3 There are much higher levels of environmental uncertainty.
4 Different needs and expectations of people.

Given these changes, highly centralized structures are not workable.

The divisional form of structure is seductively attractive, in that it reduces large size to manageable terms. It was first developed in the US and subsequently spread to Europe and Australia. Yet it is not a panacea – there are many problems with this form.

- Divisionalization is inevitably divisive, thereby increasing the need for integrative mechanisms
- Inter-divisional competition, especially over allocation of funds, is also inevitable, often leading to major political conflicts
- Employees' identification with the overall organization is likely to decrease because of identification with a division
- Divisions themselves grow too large and diversified, and no longer have a logical base for grouping products
- Head office – division conflicts may run rampant in a system in which divisional general managers are told to 'run their own shows' yet are subject to a whole range of head office guidelines, even if those guidelines are 'suggestions rather than commands'. (As head office controls the future careers of divisional managers, it is inevitable that head office executives have considerable influence on the divisions.)

Table 9.4 Divisional structure

Objectives	Clear, but multiple and product based
Time orientation	Much shorter time dimension, with rapid changes occurring because of innovations of many competitors. Products have 'lives' – birth and death sometimes in months
Task differentiation	High, usually (but not always) on a product base. Each division is quite different in product, manufacture, market, and usage from others (e.g., soap compared with cars, compared with property). Diversification is now a permanent search for growth. Co-ordination will become a central issue in this structural form, but products provide logical units to break up the structure (see Figure 9.4)
People	Much lower concern for structure, safety, and security, and more willing to take risks. The higher achievement needs are stronger among senior executives, the demands for involvement greater. The necessity for structural innovation is greater. Psychologically, size has been reduced by collecting people into product groups
Technical system	High technological component, ideally product based (this condition is often the major stumbling-block in choosing a divisional form). By product based, I mean the equipment used for property development is not used in soap manufacture, etc. Divisions *ideally* have their own separate technical systems
External pressure	High, variable, uncertain. The shift to more decentralized day-to-day control in the divisions comes initially as a response to the increasing vertical information needs of the separate product groups. Decentralization of day-to-day issues is essential, but, in fact, centralization of information usually increases

Managerial style	Difficult to generalize, as we now have several different structures. But there is a noticeable increase in concern for people, and people or human relations oriented styles are encouraged
Integration	Separate divisions operating as cost (or profit) centres lead to the rapid emergence of new devices for more reliable vertical information flows. This is the period of complex Management by Objectives, head office task forces, and central training programmes, all of which are designed to facilitate the increasing need for both vertical and even more lateral information flows

If large size within a division makes the divisional form unworkable, it is difficult to return to a purely functional authority structure. Most frequently, the structure becomes a hybrid or mixed structure, and the neat logic of the divisional structure becomes blurred. Divisions may be retained as profit centres, but head office departments are given functional authority within divisions. Another possibility is a matrix structure (see pp. 213–214), whereby a second logic for grouping activities is superimposed on the divisional structure. But before looking at these hybrids I want to look at a particular form of the divisional structure, the conglomerate.

The conglomerate
A conglomerate is a fairly rare type. Basically it is a very large transnational divisional structure. It is characterized by:

- Size – large and diversified
- Multi-divisional – unrelated products
- Involved in five or six industry categories
- Grows usually through acquisitions or mergers
- Sales of several hundred million dollars
- Simple divisional integrating devices

The conglomerate consists of many product divisions, which each sell products to their own markets rather than to each

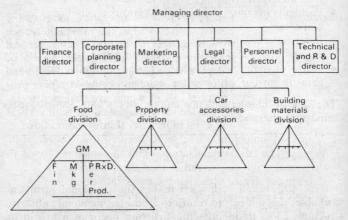

Figure 9.4 Task differentiation in a divisional structure

Notes

(a) The head office functions are given the title director, or general manager, or vice-president.

(b) The major functional differentiation is repeated in each division (see the food division, for example).

(c) Each division can be run and evaluated as a unit.

(d) Once operating, divisional structures can divide again – e.g., food division can divisionalize into non-frozen packaged foods division and frozen foods division, etc.

(e) The most important prerequisite for a divisional structure is a standardized information system, so that divisions can be compared.

(f) Most fights between divisional managers and head office occur because of
  - Allocation of head office overheads
  - Head office interference in the day-to-day running of the division
  - Failure to specify quite clearly, exactly the authorities of the head office directors compared with local functional heads. Controversial areas must be defined clearly if conflict is to be minimized.

(g) Market size is a major problem. The cost of duplicating head office functions in each division may be prohibitive. A second problem may be the spread of consumers over a vast area.

(h) Banks, government departments, and insurance companies prefer to call geographic divisions *regions*.

other, although there will be internal sales and transfers. The consequences of the diverse activities are:

- A small, highly professional head office group (compared with an expansive, large group in the divisional form)
- Problems in comprehending the various technologies and markets
- Independence among the groups, which allows one group to expand operations in its area without affecting other groups
- A loss of some overall benefits from cooperative effort, but gains in smaller, competitive, manageable units

The lack of interdependence among major units leads to three important characteristics.

1 Major sub-units tend to be self-contained to a considerable degree. The basic organizational unit in conglomerates is the divisional profit centre rather than the functional department. Thus, although the corporate office may provide certain staff services, each product division has nearly all the operating and control functions necessary to do business in its particular industry.

2 The main area of interdependence is between the product divisions and the corporate headquarters. Subject to the constraints posed by overall corporate goals and resources, most divisions in a conglomerate can operate independently of their sister divisions. Thus, comparatively little direct inter-divisional coordination is required.

3 Product divisions enjoy considerable autonomy from the corporate headquarters. Because of the number of broad-range industries encompassed by its product divisions, the corporation is obliged to permit them considerable autonomy in both strategy and operations. Corporate control tends to be exercised through evaluation of the economic aspects of divisional plans, budgets, and requests, and through allocation of funds rather than through direct participation in formulating the divisions' product–market strategies, unless production occurs only at the head office or in a few locations. In this case, autonomy on products is lost and a product-location matrix is used.

There have been many critics of the conglomerate form, most claiming that it is as unworkable as uncontrollable. And the experience of Litton industries in the 'sixties in America supported this argument. My own view is it should be workable, provided that the vertical information system is reliable. But this does assume divisional managers and their own subdivisional managers are honest and will provide reliable data. Often this is assuming too much, and it may be preferable to break the massive conglomerate into separate or subsidiary companies or to re-centralize the controls even further such that the man-on-the-spot is little more than an ambassador enforcing (usually at great cost in terms of personal rewards) the centrally determined decisions. This second choice is only sensible if product groups are similar, e.g., computers and calculators.

The subsidiary company

If we go to the end of our structural continuum, the subsidiary company has achieved far more independence from the central office, with the exception of financial reporting through a modified management information system. Here, the objectives are multiple within subsidiaries; markets are quite different and of diverse complexities, functions are duplicated without concern for overall costs, different sorts of people work in the subsidiaries, and any generalizations for the whole company are so general as to be useless. As the units become more autonomous, the variety and number of integrative mechanisms between units declines. There is no need to elaborate lateral information flows – the units operate best on their own, doing their own thing, unrelated to the other parts except in a consolidated Balance Sheet. Heterogeneity and diversity have replaced the predictability and homogeneity of the bureaucratic form.

In this analysis I have concentrated on the three most common forms of hierarchy: bureaucratic, centralized functional, and divisional. Yet increasing market pressures are compelling even the most centralized structures (e.g., banks, insurance companies, or government departments) to find alternative forms.

Figure 9.2 suggested three variations of centralized structures:

- Project teams
- Product management
- Matrix structures

Most frequently, these are three variations of a centralized departmental structure, but they also occur in divisional structures and most transnationals. They are all 'project' or task centred and are increasingly common; they are sometimes referred to as *mixed structures*. I will look briefly at the project team structure and the matrix structure. Product management structures (which are a subclass of project teams) occur in organizations with centralized marketing, finance, personnel and production functions where a need exists to integrate product marketing laterally. The product manager is the integrator, taking a product as his function but integrating functional inputs to that product. Product management is usually a precursor to divisional management.

The common characteristic of the mixed structures is a lateral grid which is superimposed on the vertical hierarchy. In this sense, teams, workshops, and semi-autonomous work groups are also variations of the centralized departmental or functional structure. Production groups or work groups or semi-autonomous groups are discussed in the last chapter.

Project team structure

A project team structure consists of a group of specialists drawn laterally from diverse disciplines, working under a single manager to accomplish a fixed objective. It is an organizational form which allows efficient performance of interdependent activities that cross functional and/or the firm's boundaries.

The members of the team are often part-time members, belonging to a functional department (or an external organization), accountable to both the functional head and to a project manager (who may also be called a product manager, an integrator, or a coordinator).

The manager and his team operate independently of the company's normal chain of command. The manager is accountable for the project's success or failure, although not always accountable for the people assigned to the project tasks. Figure 9.5 shows a project structure. This form of project management structure – where the project manager has complete accountability for the task and all resources – is used only on very large projects.

A more common form is the functional alignment structure illustrated in Figure 9.6. The functional alignment project manager is usually not assigned complete accountability for resources. Instead, he shares them with the rest of the

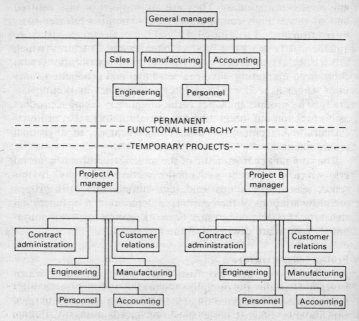

Figure 9.5 Typical project organization in the aerospace and construction industries

organization. He may have a project organization consisting of a handful of men on temporary assignment from the regular functional organization. The functional managers, however, retain their direct line authority, monitor their staff contributions to the project, and continue to make all major personnel decisions. This 'two boss' design is not without problems, and a resource allocation manager is usually introduced to resolve potential conflicts between project managers and functional heads.

A project team structure is indicated in a large, centralized organization, when the structural design variables are different for a specific project. The conditions are set out in Table 9.5. The project may last three months or three years, but its life cycle is finite. The objectives require the diverse skills of experts and the client needs a responsive group with which to deal. Initially, the centralized system tries to cope but, after successive

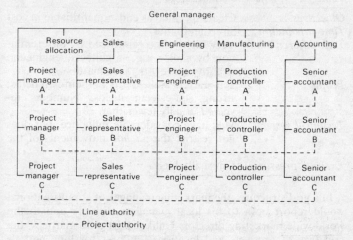

Figure 9.6 Project organization in general industry

breakdowns in the functionally organized departments, and after considerable client pressure for results, this laterally derived task force is created. The project manager is primarily a 'team builder' whose expertise, I believe, should include group dynamics.

Matrix structure

A matrix is a special kind of structure, created for *short periods* of time to solve a problem or to link a multitude of products to geographically widespread markets. Usually the matrix is introduced after many traditional structural attempts to solve the problem have failed.

In its simplest form, a matrix structure formalizes lateral, informal communications by bringing together different functional experts to concentrate on a problem. It is used both at a sub-unit level and for the organization as a whole. Where superimposed on the whole, as in some transnationals, the structure is usually called a *grid*.

At the sub-unit level, a matrix means a task force – a problem-solving group or a buzz group. However, it has its roots in a departmental, functional, authority structure.

Table 9.5 Project team structure

Objectives	Clear, specified as ends, quantifiable in cost
Time orientation	Short and finite
Task differentiation	Very high, often reinforced by differentiation by skill – e.g., architects, engineers, quantity surveyors, accountants
People	Self-starters and experts in their own fields; strong self-esteem needs. Numbers involved usually fewer than 20
Technical system	May have considerable influence, but does not restrict the *ad hoc* movements of the term
External pressures	Unusually high

In a grid structure, the marketing manager of a multi-national would report both to his local managing director and to the world-wide marketing director. Unlike short time matrices, the grid (say of products and locations) endures for long periods and is used to coordinate sales production and territories usually in companies with many foreign subsidiaries.

As in the project team structure, members of the matrix, plus their machines, procedures, and techniques, are collected together because of the need for immediate attention to a complex problem. Often selecting a matrix form is a response to exceedingly high external pressures. The traditional departmental structure which derives solutions by moving the problem up and down functional departments, is unable to respond fast enough. Hence the problem or product becomes the focus, and the necessary skills, services, or machines are brought to the product, service, or problem.

The major difference between this structural form and the project team is time; matrices are very short term. A second difference is the degree of definition of contributions to the problem. The project team may define quite clearly the contribution of the architect, the engineer, the quantity surveyor, etc. The matrix structure is often unable to define clearly the roles people will play or how they will play them. The lack of structure of the problem or of the roles to be played means very few people can tolerate the uncertainty.

Shull and others have identified several forms of matrix on a continuum. At one end is the *routine* matrix, at the other end the *heuristic* matrix.

The routine matrix is closest to the project team. It is contained within an overall hierarchy, is specific in choosing personnel, devises integrative mechanisms, and stipulates methods of solution, etc. It is different from the project team, in that it occurs for hours rather than weeks, or months, or years.

The heuristic matrix has more autonomy. The problem has first to be defined, personnel are chosen as needed, controls are problem-related, and *ad hocracy* allows problems of extreme complexity to be solved by people with creative, professional skills. It is usually seen in research work, where the integrator is the major researcher. Concern for positional power is secondary. Power is given to those who have the expertise to solve the problem.

Matrix structure projects are most frequently seen in task force exercises. The American Polaris and Apollo projects are two of the best-documented uses of this structure. Medical or surgical teams, new product groups, research and development teams, and creative buzz groups in advertising agencies, are the most frequent users of the matrix form.

The configuration of design variables which would indicate a matrix structure is shown in Table 9.6. There are many writers who believe the heuristic matrix is not a structure at all. Certainly, it is little more than an informal group. Yet it can be effective in solving highly uncertain, complex problems *if* the necessary professional skills are available. The major difficulty with this structure is finding people who can endure the endless change, from one group to another, the uncertainty and unpredictability of their working day. Placing individuals with high social needs or high safety needs in such a structure can cause major psychological problems.

Further out on the uncertainty continuum is the self-designing organization. Here uncertainty, irrationality and 'muddling through' are dominant characteristics. Other features are ambiguous authority structures, unclear objectives, contradictory assignments of accountability, unclear statuses, overlapping

Table 9.6 Matrix structure

Objectives	Complex but clear
Time orientation	Very, very short
Task differentiation	High, differentiated by skill
People	Low concern for safety, low social, high self-realization, few people. High tolerance of uncertainty and ambiguity
Technical system	Highly variable, usually transportable to the problem
External pressures	Very high or highly uncertain, complex, often hostile
Integration	Immediate, by having all 'skills' working on the problem together

jobs, volatile rules, unstable behaviour patterns, vague communication channels, and trial-and-error methods of analysis. Under conditions of great uncertainty, this sort of organization produces conflicts, collisions, and interactions which generate answers. Yet to those obsessed with neatness and so called rationality, this 'mess' is unendurable. Nevertheless, muddling through in messes is under certain conditions an entirely viable organizational form.

Conclusions

Structuring organizations has been a relatively unrewarding part of managing. Everyone is an expert on what should be done to fix the current structure. This chapter has only touched on some overall issues in design. There are areas not even mentioned here: job design, documentation of manuals, charts, and a multitude of accounting, marketing, production, and personnel controls, ranging from petty cash to annual appraisals. Most of these have been well documented elsewhere, and some references for further reading are given at the end of the chapter.

I would like to finish with some general guides for those who structure organizations.

- Begin with an open mind and analyse the important variables. Too often we choose the sort of hierarchy and the integrative mechanisms without first analysing the situation.

214

- The important variables are the objectives, time scale, differentiation of the tasks necessary for achieving the objectives, what people are involved, what technical systems, and what external pressures.
- Having analysed these variables, decide what hierarchical type approximates the combination and what integrative mechanisms might link the tasks together laterally.
- Contingency means searching for the best fit. The result is likely to be untidy and violate some traditional theories of design, but the important consideration in designing structure is that structure is the cause of many organizational problems, and neatness or adherence to time-honoured concepts does not help solve those problems. If the structure works, leave it alone. If it begins to break down, begin your analysis again.
- Whatever structural configuration you adopt, do not set it in concrete. Structural change should be something we are all able to accept and plan for. Many of our problems in organizations today arise simply because the structure has been sanctified. Structural rigor mortis may satisfy our desire for security, but its effects on creativity, job enrichment, and challenge are often destructive.
- Finally, as designers of structures, we should remember that neatness and logic do not guarantee results. Irrational, messy organizations are often very successful.

The next chapter looks at what comes out of the structured role system – its outputs.

For additional reading

Byrt W., *Management and People*, McGraw-Hill, Sydney, 1972.

Child J., *Organisation – A Guide to Problems and Practice*, Harper & Row, 1977.

Clark P., *Organisational Design: Theory and Practice*, Tavistock, 1972.

Crozier M., *The Bureaucratic Phenomenon*, Chicago University Press, Chicago, 1964.

Galbraith J., *Designing Complex Organisations*, Addison-Wesley, Reading, Massachusetts, 1973.

Kingdom D. R., *Matrix Organisation*, Tavistock, 1973.

Klein L., *New Forms of Work Organisation*, Routledge & Kegan Paul, 1976.

Litterer J. A., *Organizations – Structure and Behaviour*, Vol. I, Wiley, New York, 1969.

Lorsch J., and P. Lawrence, *Organization Planning: Cases and Concepts*, Richard D. Irwin, Homewood, Illinois, 1973.

Mintzberg H., *The Structuring of Organisations*, In Press, Montreal, 1977.

Mouzelis N. P., *Organisation and Bureaucracy*, Routledge & Kegan Paul, 1967.

Pugh D., *Organization Theory* (Parts 1 and 2), Penguin, 1974.

Shull F. A., A. L. Delberg, and L. L. Cummings, *Organisational Decision Making*, McGraw-Hill, New York, 1970.

Tannenbaum A., *Hierarchy in Organizations*, Jossey-Bass, New York, 1974.

Weber M., *The Theory of Social and Economic Organisations*, Oxford University Press, 1946.

Yuill B., and D. Steinhoff, *Developing Managers in Organisations*, Wiley, Sydney, 1975.

10 Outputs from organizations

All the chapters in this book have been concerned with factors or variables that influence people at work: power, motives, abilities, perceptions, groups, leaders, structures, environments. Now I want to look at how all these influences are interrelated, how they can be measured, and the outputs of role systems.

Unfortunately, simple, straightforward relationships between all the variables discussed in earlier chapters are not found in organizations. We cannot even successfully predict that a technical system capable of producing 1000 units an hour will result in 1000 units of production an hour. Structural, personality, environmental, interpersonal, and managerial variables affect those potentially simple relationships and produce complex sets of relationships between the variables.

First, I will split all the variables (or influences) into those that cause outputs and those that moderate output, and then I will discuss the outputs themselves. I will try to show how vastly different organizations are from one another, and then how they differ within themselves. Second, I want to talk about measuring these variables and concentrate on some intervening variables not discussed in previous chapters (satisfaction, conflict, and cooperation). Third, I want to discuss possible end results or output variables, like profit, productivity, etc.

Likert has suggested that we should view the relationships between the variables from three perspectives: variables which are *causal*, variables which are *intervening* and variables which are *outputs* (or *end results*). Here are examples of each sort of variable, taken from the previous chapters of this book, and then related to one another.

Causal variables
Chapter 6 identified five causal variables:

- Organizational variables

formal structure
informal structure
individual (personality) variable
technical system
external environment

Intervening variables
Chapters 3, 4, 7, and 8 mentioned some intervening variables:

- Role system variables
    power
    leadership style
    decision making
    communication
    cooperation
    satisfaction

End results variables
This chapter will elaborate on some common end result (or output) variables:

- Performance variables of the role system
    productivity
    market share
    profitability

Between the causal variables (organizational) and the end result variables there are many behavioural variables, which are called intervening variables. If we are to understand how organizations function, we need to analyse all three groups of variables.

(A detailed analysis of inter-variable relationships is made in Part 2 of my earlier book *The Restless Organisation*.)

Different combinations of variables

What is becoming clear in my research is that the combinations of the variables are specific rather than general – each manager needs to work out his/her combination of variables and sort out the relevant relationships between them if he/she wishes to solve problems (e.g., low output). Universal solutions are not available. What will be effective in one organization will not necessarily be effective in another. Yet we spend hours investigating other people's solutions, in a hope that a magnificent recipe will become available for us all. Once found, the recipe is deified, and we expect our problems to disappear. Problems never disappear: they are modified or redefined, and by that process become 'new' problems.

There is no universal recipe because organizations are constantly changing, no matter how imperceptibly. They reflect the constant changes in the needs and perceptions of individuals. Managing is dealing with a constantly changing phenomenon. Today's fad will be superseded by tomorrow's, and tomorrow's, and tommorow's. Universal solutions to problems such as productivity, satisfaction, absenteeism, or industrial disputes are not and cannot be available; all we can hope for are temporary configurations of the variables which *may* be more effective than other configurations now. And even then, we must recognize that the configuration which works now is unlikely to be effective in two years time. Nor will the configurations be the same.

The development of organization theory reflects the search for universal solutions. Traditional management theory preached structure and programming of behaviour through routinized solutions, and managers liked it because it told them how to do their jobs. Subsequent theoretical developments have had to grapple with the fact that organizations are coordinated groups of individuals cooperating to achieve ends. Managers have been less impressed with this social theory because it did not tell them how to manage. What it gave them was the opportunity to understand a social system and to identify the variables which affect people's behaviour – it did not and could not give them answers for specific situations. Yet the moment a new fad appears, whether it is MbO, work groups, OD, cybernetics, transactional analysis, or the quality of work-life, we see a multitude of managers drinking up the latest fad because perhaps this will be *the* answer. There is no *one* answer.

More recently, the literature on managing talks of styles, contingencies, combinations, configurations, rather than solutions. What the theorist can provide is a framework or model for analysis. By using models we can reduce conceptual ambiguity and uncertainty to tolerable levels. What models or theories cannot do is provide answers for specific problems: only managers or leaders can select specific solutions.

Even more frustrating for the manager is the realization that there are many possible answers, and organizational realities (like power, influence, cost, availability and time) will dictate the solutions used to change the configuration of the organizational, intervening, and end result variables. The change may be complex and messy, and uncertainty of the longer-term implications of the change has to be accepted as a condition. No wonder studies of managers find them reactive, not proactive: much of the manager's job is reacting (often on a gut feeling) to his/her perception of the situation.

Most data on organizations are collected either by interviews or surveys. I use both in analysing problems in organizations. Interviews are probably one of the least reliable ways of collecting data, yet they give insights into individuals and relationships which are almost impossible to collect using surveys. Interviews also provide data on past events on the formation and evolution of the company, department, or section, and on the nature of the interpersonal relationships that have occurred.

Surveys present problems too but they do provide a yardstick against which organizations can be compared. It is little use finding that 40 per cent of the respondents to a survey feel dissatisfied unless results from many other organizations have been collected. Perhaps 40 per cent of a work force are always dissatisfied.

Differences between organizations

To illustrate different perceptions of the variables in my model of an organization, Table 10.1 shows three configurations from a study of 80 branches of a bank. All three branches were rated by their superiors as *equal* in overall effectiveness. Scores for people working in each branch are given on a scale from 1 to 100. A score of 10 means that a branch is perceived by those working there to be *very low* on that variable, while a score of 90 means that that variable is *very high* (or is perceived to be important by the employees in that branch). Responses are taken from the Organisation Attitude Survey devised by Hunt and Saul. All the causal variables were surveyed, some of the intervening, and one end result variable.

These three branches are structurally and technically almost identical. They are from the same geographic area and employ the same number of people. Yet there are significant differences if we look at them as 'configurations' of organizational, intervening, and end result variables.

Case 1. Here we have a branch in which people rank their career or achievement goals as less important (relatively) than other needs. Physiological needs are important to them (score 93), safety (96), and relationship (92) needs, rather than the power-recognition (31) and fulfilment (32) needs. The formal structure (65) of a bank is perceived to be above average. Informal relationships are average.

The dominant organizational variable is the technical system (which is computer-based). External pressures are perceived by respondents to be above average for this industry.

These organizational variables have an influence on the intervening and end result variables, but they do not explain them. Effectiveness is very high, cooperation is seen to be low (33), satisfaction with intrinsic factors (recognition, challenge, etc.) is average, and dissatisfaction (or non-satisfaction with extrinsic factors – pay, working conditions, supervision, etc.) is above average to high.

Case 2. Here is an almost identical branch – same number of employees, similar market and very similar view of organizational variables – with the exception that external pressures are perceived by the employees to be much less than in Case 1.

This branch is rated by the manager's superiors as very effective. Notice, however, that the intervening variables are perceived to differ significantly from those in Case 1. Cooperation is higher, satisfaction is higher, and dissatisfaction with extrinsic factors is very much lower. Overall, this is a much more contented group of people than Case 1, yet both branches are comparable in terms of assessed effectiveness.

Case 3. This is a comparable branch – same sort of market, same number of employees, and very similar organizational variable scores to Case 2, but some significant differences, especially for perceived cooperation and informal structure. Like the other two cases, the level of satisfaction with intrinsic factors is average. In this case, dissatisfaction with extrinsic factors is

221

Table 10.1 Comparative study of employee perceptions of their branch on causal, intervening, and end result variables

	Case 1	Case 2	Case 3
Causal	Percentiles	Percentiles	Percentiles
Formal structure	65	75	78
Informal structure	58	58	74
Technical system	88	80	85
External pressures	65	38	38
Individual variables			
physiological	93	98	97
safety, security	96	96	96
relationships	92	96	92
power recognition	31	42	31
fulfilment	32	25	32
Intervening			
Cooperation	33	42	60
Satisfaction (intrinsic factors)	46	66	55
Dissatisfaction (extrinsic factors)	79	25	71
End result			
Overall effectiveness of the branch	90	90	90

much higher than Case 2 and comparable with Case 1. Motives in all cases are ranked such that physiological and social needs, rather than career achievement needs, get preference. In this sense, the recruiting system in the bank is able to standardize a 'branch motives profile'.

This discussion of the three branches does not claim to show any more than that there is variability in employee perceptions between organizations, even when major variables (such as size, structure, technology, and recruitment) are highly controlled. The three branches show a high degree of similarity on three variables – formal structure, technical system, and profiles of employee motives. These are the three variables that can be programmed. Notice that the employees' perceptions of the uncontrollables – informal structure and external pressures – do differ between the branches and may explain the differences in levels of cooperation and satisfaction.

The data missing from this study concerns managerial style. Subsequent studies in banking have shown that the vital intervening variable is the style of the manager, especially in small branches. However, data on managerial style do not entirely explain the differences in the effectiveness (end result) of the other branches. Further, predicting effectiveness from one branch to another involves different variables for different branches.

Just as causal (or organizational) variables and intervening variables are interdependent, so too are end result variables. We may attempt to maximize productivity and in fact have an adverse effect on profitability. Similarly, improving intervening variables does not necessarily improve end result variables. For example, we may attempt to maximize cooperation and what actually happens is a fall in productivity. It is possible to produce a 'love in', where people are highly integrated and cooperative, where conflict is minimal, and where productivity falls.

Differences within the same organization

So far this chapter has linked organizational, intervening, and end result variables for whole branches. I have been trying to show that different variables have different relevance in different organizations. But even this is an over-simplification of what I find in my research. Rather than one configuration of the variables in an organization, there are, in fact, many different perceptions of configurations *within* the one organization, and sometimes within the same department. For example, at a departmental level of analysis, the configuration of variables will be seen to be very different in the accounting department from the marketing department.

Inter-departmental differences

To illustrate this, compare two small departments of the same organization – the key punch department and the accounting department of a computer bureau. The results are, again, perceptions of employees expressed as scores out of 100, and are available for causal and intervening variables. There were no relevant comparative data for end result variables (Table 10.2).

These two departments in the bureau are in close proximity to one another. They share floor space and service facilities. Yet the perceptions of respondents of their *own organization* (the bureau) are very different.

If the results from the systems analysts are added, we see even more marked differences within the *very same* relatively small organization. The important differences for systems analysts are:

• Much higher ranking for the importance of power recognition and fulfilment goals
• Lower ranking of the formal structure – i.e., seen to be looser
• Lower perceived informal relationships – i.e., less time given to informal relationships
• Higher ranking or awareness of the external pressures

Table 10.2 Inter-departmental differences

	Key punch N = 15		Accounting N = 7
Individual variables			
physiological	76	*	44
safety	65		60
relationships	60		73
power-recognition	40	*	69
fulfilment	27	*	60
Formal structure	44	*	61
Informal structure	51	*	38
Technical system	83	*	50
External pressures	13		10
Intervening variables			
Cooperation	26		28
Satisfaction (intrinsic)	29	*	40
Dissatisfaction (extrinsic)	54	*	5

* Significantly different responses

The intervening variables for the systems analysts also reflect these differences:

- Cooperation perceived by respondents to be higher
- Satisfaction much higher on intrinsic factors
- Dissatisfaction (extrinsic factors) similar to the key punch group (i.e., about average)

What these differences between departments mean is that overall organizational survey results used to compare *different* organizations should be viewed with some suspicion. The differences between departments within one organization are often so great as to make me question research using group or departmental mean scores for computing organization means. We should analyse data at the unit level first, and then see what are their overall trends. Then we can compare overall trends between different organizations.

Intra-departmental differences
The survey results in Table 10.3 are from three employees working in the *same* jobs in the *same* department of a retail organization. All the results are expressed as scores out of 100. Certainly, the Table shows extreme examples, but this divergence of perceptions of the retail organization must be explained, and the only way to do that is to interview the respondents.

One easy explanation is that the questionnaire is unreliable. Of the 13 people surveyed, the results were consistent on both causal and intervening variables except for these three cases. The questionnaire was probably not the answer. As we know from studying perception (see chapter 3), people have very different perceptions of the same situation, and when I examined the responses of each of the above three cases I found quite simple explanations.

Case 1 is a married woman with three children. She has returned to work in the retail store to satisfy her sense of isolation. She is strongly involved, informally, and would seek even greater involvement. She is not interested in people other than those in her immediate work group, and sees other groups as uncooperative. Her dissatisfaction is primarily caused by her salary.

225

Table 10.3 Intra-departmental differences

Employee	1	2	3
Causal variables			
Individual variables			
physiological	38	100	88
safety	22	77	81
relationships	83	61	73
power/recognition	35	5	60
fulfilment	34	4	62
Formal structure	34	19	27
Informal structure	97	50	77
Technical system	100	100	53
Intervening variables			
Cooperation	28	24	81
Satisfaction	14	25	18
Dissatisfaction	84	61	70
End result variable			
Productivity (as assessed by average weekly sales)	60	40	70

The reported lack of job satisfaction reflects the lack of challenge in her job. But she seeks and finds high levels of interpersonal relationships.

Case 2 is unmarried, 30 years of age, and female. Her career needs are unimportant compared with her need to establish a permanent, secure relationship. When interviewed, she appeared depressed and very dissatisfied with the organization. Satisfaction with her job is secondary to her own personal problems.

Case 3 is an excellent case of bad recruiting. She is motivated to pursue a career, has good clerical ability, and is locked into a processing job which she does not find challenging. Her dissatisfaction is general rather than specific – it includes the boss, working conditions, salary, and job security. Her productivity is the highest of the three, but not of the group. She sees opportunities outside her section as much more attractive and spends a great deal of her time relating to other sections, and discussing her lack of satisfaction. Yet she sees cooperation as very high in her group.

What we need to recognize is that a person's motives and expectations affect his/her responses in surveys and interviews. Using the arithmetic mean for departmental scores does eliminate the 'odd' respondents, but it also clouds reality: Case 3 in those cited above is one of the most ardent public critics of the retail store and is herself an intervening variable, one who is vital in understanding the relationships within her section.

Identifying and measuring the variables

Very few managers of organizations attempt to assess either the causal or the intervening variables. Most concentrate on one or two end result variables. Those managers who do try to assess the whole system use surveys, and rely on the accounting department to provide the end result variables.

Not all variables will be important in predicting outcomes. For example, Peter Saul's research showed that it is feasible to identify which of the causal variables are most important in situation A, which of the intervening variables are important, and, by elimination, find the best combination of variables for predicting the end result variables.

For example, we may find that the best predictors of outputs in situation A are high safety needs, high informal relationships, and high external pressures. In this case, we can drop other variables and concentrate on these – at least until we think the configuration or the relative significance of the outputs has changed.

The next section discusses all variables, although it is not likely we would need them all if we wanted to predict outcomes in a specific instance. However, I will concentrate on intervening variables and particularly on satisfaction, cooperation, and conflict. My objective is to include research data on these variables since they have not been discussed elsewhere.

227

Causal

Chapter 6 listed the variables I feel are important in describing an organization. They were repeated at the beginning of this chapter. Most theorists use similar variables, so I will not labour this further. Data about these variables (formal structure, technical system, etc.) can be collected by survey, by interview or by observation. Surveys have the advantages of speed and low cost, and there are many commercial surveys available for those who wish to find out which variables are most important in explaining variations in output in their organization.

Intervening

Intervening variables, as their name suggests, intervene, minute to minute, day to day, week to week. They are characterized by immediacy, and occur within the role system. Until recently, organization theorists tended to ignore these variables, but most of the recent organization change and development movement has been concerned with intervening variables.

Researchers have identified three major classes of intervening variables:

- Managerial style (role, power, decisions, communications, etc.)
- Employee satisfaction
- Cooperation (conflict, teamwork, cohesiveness, openness, etc.)

As managers are concerned primarily with these intervening variables, the organization change and development consultants found a responsive audience. Consistent with the practical orientation of the OD consultants has been their disregard for validated testing devices. To measure the intervening variables, most have devised their own instant measures (instruments), using brief questionnaires, interviews, group discussions, or observation to assess the state of the intervening variables. For the academic purists, most of the OD consultant's instruments are extremely dubious documents. But to the manager these instruments have been like a breath of fresh air.

My research has led me into all three groups of intervening variables – style, satisfaction, cooperation. Chapter 7 discussed managerial style in some detail, so I will not repeat myself here. Related to style is power, discussed in chapter 4. Style is a most significant intervening variable, and in some organizations it is the best predictor of end result variables. Style data can readily be collected using self-administered tests.

Employee satisfaction

The second category of intervening variables is less easy to deal with. Employee satisfaction (also called need or job satisfaction) is one of the most controversial areas of behavioural research.

Job satisfaction relates to how an individual feels overall about his or her job. Satisfied individuals like their job more than they dislike them.

The components which produce this overall feeling of contentment or satisfaction represent one of the most hotly debated fields of organizational behaviour.

There are currently some six schools of thought on satisfaction at work. This might imply that satisfaction is a uniquely personal experience and that general theories of occupational satisfaction are doomed to be less than universal.

One approach to satisfaction is the *psychological needs* theory. Argyris, Maslow, Herzberg, and Likert have been the high priests of this approach. The theory argues that you and I have psychological needs which we wish to satisfy at work. If we do not satisfy these needs, we will not have job satisfaction. The needs that they have found to be important in satisfaction are the relationships, self-esteem, and self-fulfilment needs, and they are indicated by requests for jobs with opportunities for recognition, cooperation, status, achievement, responsibility, challenge, and growth.

Herzberg takes this argument further, and suggests that the needs which will give satisfaction are different from those that cause dissatisfaction. The needs that cause dissatisfaction are the physiological, safety, and relationship needs, and the factors which are significant in influencing levels of dissatisfaction are the company structure, the boss, working conditions, salary, the people with whom one has to work, etc.

Herzberg argues that satisfaction (happiness) and non-satisfaction (non-happiness) represent one scale of needs (see Figure 10.3) and dissatisfaction (being upset) and non-dissatisfaction (not being upset) represents a separate and distinctly different facet of an employee's feelings. Hence, he argues, we should assess two separate dimensions for everyone.

The second school of satisfaction theories is the *style–leadership* school. Blake and Mouton and Fiedler argue that the climate of the work environment is the important determinant of satisfaction. There is an 'overall' feeling that things are going great, which is the product of the managerial style of the boss.

The third school, represented by motivation theorists like Vroom and Lawler, approach satisfaction from a very different angle. They look at the *relationship between effort and reward*. This leads them to consider what the individual expects from working and the relationship between those expectations and the actual reward. The Manchester theorists (e.g., Lupton) include an analysis of how wages and salaries of particular groups are constructed and how overtime and economic conditions affect attitudes about pay. People have subjective perceptions of what is a fair day's pay, and if they do not feel they are receiving a fair day's pay for a fair day's work then their satisfaction will be low.

A fourth group of behavioural scientists distinguish between the *extrinsic and intrinsic factors* of job satisfaction and argue – not unlike Herzberg, but without some of the Herzbergian assumptions – that the extrinsic factors (like bosses, rewards, and situational factors) are secondary to the work itself. The design of jobs and control over jobs are the clues to increasing satisfaction. This group includes Thorsrud, Davis, and some of the consultants at the Tavistock Institute in London.

Yet a fifth group argues that the *managerial philosophy* of the senior executives is the clue to satisfaction, because of the climate they create. Crozier, Gouldner, and Likert all argue that

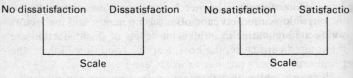

No dissatisfaction	Dissatisfaction	No satisfaction	Satisfactio
Scale		Scale	

The lack of hygiene or environment factors causes dissatisfaction. Needs that are physiological, safety, and relationships.

The presence of challenge, recog nition, growth cause satisfaction Important needs are self-esteem self-fulfilment.

Figure 10.1

the managerial style and values of senior executives create climates and attitudes which encourage an overall feeling of satisfaction.

Finally, there is the so-called argument that warm *interpersonal relationships* lead to satisfaction at lower levels of the hierarchy. My research supports this argument, but only for people at the bottom of the hierarchy.

What is clear in analysing satisfaction with work is that it is the result of many factors rather than one dominant one. The job, the boss, the climate, the work group, the external environment, the expectations of the individual, the formal structure, the rewards, and the technology all appear to have an effect on satisfaction, depending on the situation being analysed. Satisfaction seems to be a complex result produced by a host of personality and situational factors.

Satisfaction and the influence of the organization

Satisfaction has been found to be related to all the variables in our model of an organization. For example, levels of satisfaction are affected by:

- Formal structure
    job design
    controls
    rules
    hierarchy
    span of control
    rewards
- Informal structure
    peer group relationships
    informal leaders
    group norms and controls
- Individual variables
    intelligence
    sex
    needs and expectations
    age
    abilities
    education
    marital status
    number of dependants

231

- External pressures
    - socio-economic
    - community size
    - culture
- Technical system
    - mass production
    - autonomy of operators
- Leadership style
    - task oriented
    - human relations oriented

In addition to these factors, there is a vast literature on how to measure job satisfaction. As this chapter is concerned with measuring and relating causal, intervening, and end result variables, let us look at some of the issues of measuring satisfaction.

Is there a single attitude or feeling which the individual has against which we can measure job satisfaction as a unitary concept? Much of the Herzbergian literature rejects the unitary concept for a multiple group of intrinsic and extrinsic factors, many of which are quite unrelated.

Even if we accept the overall feeling someone has about his/her job as the important indicator, then there are some nine definitions currently of what *overall* means. For example, is it the difference between what I want and what I get? Or is overall satisfaction an attitude which can be expressed along an attitude scale?

The last complication of what, on the surface, seems such a simple issue, occurs when we look at different samples used in studies of job satisfaction. Unskilled manual workers have been found to show lower levels of job satisfaction than semi-skilled workers. Similarly, professional and managerial workers show the highest levels of both overall satisfaction and satisfaction with specific organizational factors (pay, job, boss, etc.).

These problems in analysing job satisfaction show again the complexity of both the concept and its measurement.

Satisfaction in work organizations
Should we be concerned about levels of work satisfaction? The vast majority of employees I have interviewed and/or tested are satisfied with their jobs. There is very little hard data from any

of the many surveys conducted in this country or other industrialized economies which suggest that employees are highly
unsatisfied with their jobs. On the Hunt and Saul Organisation
Attitude Questionnaire, from a sample of several thousand, the
percentage of employees who are dissatisfied, overall, with their
jobs is 14.5 per cent. The HEW report on American workers
reported between 10 to 20 per cent dissatisfied. In a survey by
Jarvis and Hunt of 5800 men and women in one large government department, we found nationally that 18.2 per cent of
respondents found their work fairly or extremely uninteresting.
Emery and Phillips, in their survey of urban workers, found 12.5
per cent dissatisfied or unexcited by their jobs.

In all these studies, the expressed level of non-satisfaction is
less than 20 per cent, which suggests satisfaction is normally
distributed. However it raises the question, *'Is there a group of
employees in all organizations who are permanently not satisfied
with their lot?'* Certainly, the consistent findings at or below the
20 per cent level in all sorts of organizations, from banks to
entrepreneurial ventures to government departments, could suggest that there are pockets of non-satisfaction. However, it is
difficult to conclude that the pockets are entirely job determined. That is, a wide dispersion of satisfaction occurs for all
people and these are distributed in most occupations. Does this
mean, as some writers have argued, that we are identifying
personality problems rather than organizational factors. In other
words are some people 'happy' being unhappy?

On the other hand, we tend to forget that some 80 per cent
are mostly satisfied, and in my own research some 65 per cent
of respondents from all sorts of organizations are highly to very
highly satisfied.

Academic research often becomes preoccupied with the bad
news and totally ignores the good. Similarly, behavioural scientists are adept at interpreting other workers' levels of satisfaction
by asking 'How would I like to do that job?' The shocked
responses to this question point to one of the major problems
of research on job satisfaction – researchers all relate *their* goals,
motives, and expectations to others. My experience has been
that there are many people who like highly programmed repetitive jobs, because such work satisfies their high expectations
for security and predictability.

The prospect that work can be self-fulfilling for everybody, or for almost everybody, in circumstances of necessity, hierarchy, specialization, and hard physical and mental effort is utopian, and even deceptive. The very concept of self-fulfilment is insatiable and is characterized by needing more and more goal achievement, often in organizations based on repetition and compromise.

However, despite the lack of hard data to indicate a miserable work force, what data are available have been used for highly political ends, and the reported disaffection with industrial work cannot be ignored in a country so dependent on industrial workers. When people have a choice, they do move from the industrial organization to a tertiary industry. Whether surveys show it or not, industrial conflict has risen sharply, and staff turnover has continued to run high in many industries, even when the economic climate has been depressed. In short, while the attitude surveys may not indicate there is widespread dissatisfaction here or overseas in Western economies, other indicators are that 12 to 20 per cent of dissatisfied people have a great deal of political clout, often to the detriment of the satisfied people. For this reason, we all need to understand what the research data means and to question that data. For example, lack of satisfaction may be more about loss of control, freedom, and power than about challenge, or pay, or supervision.

Let me summarize the research findings.

Things that make people satisfied with their jobs are:

- Challenge
- Recognition
- Freedom
- Control over one's own work, power, status
- A complete job
- Knowing what the goals are
- Individual growth
- Working with compatible people
- Developing 'satisfying' relationships with those people belonging to a worth-while organization
- Being rewarded at a level commensurate with expectations
- Succeeding

Things that make people dissatisfied with their jobs are:

- The formal structure – control, rewards, rules
- Bosses
- Salary and wages
- Working conditions
- The people we work with
- Boring work
- No contact with users of our products or services
- Poor communications within the hierarchy
- Limited opportunities for promotion
- Loss of control over one's life (i.e., power)
- Failing

You will notice that the lists are similar but not identical to those proposed by Herzberg. Herzberg has been criticized for over-simplifying the causes (motivators and hygiene for dissatis-fiers) into two independent sets of factors. Various research studies, including my own, have not supported this two-factor theory. There is not a neat separation; so many of the factors overlap. For example, if monetary rewards are dissatisfiers, then they are also motivational if seen as recognition of a job well done.

The practical approach to understanding satisfaction is to keep our minds open. Recognize that the causes of dissatisfaction will never disappear. The very nature of work means that some dissatisfaction is inevitable – and desirable. Dissatisfaction leads to conflict, which can have an energizing and constructive effect in social systems. Certainly, there are times when the level of dissatisfaction becomes intolerable and the conflict which results is costly and destructive. But it would be foolish to try to elim-inate conflict and dissatisfaction from organizations, even if it were possible. Some irritation and overt conflict energizes role systems.

Cooperation and conflict

The third group of intervening variables I use in research refers to interpersonal relations – specifically the level of cooperation, or its converse, the level of conflict. In earlier work, I separated these two factors, but a consistently high, negative correlation between them meant we could concentrate on either one or the other.

In several chapters (especially chapter 5) I argued that organizational conflict is inevitable, if only because organizations involve more than one person and when two people interact, their different goals, expectations, hopes, etc., ensure conflict. Similarly, conflict is inevitable between different levels of the hierarchy, between management and unions, between different ethnic groups. We need to recognize the inevitability of conflict and use it constructively to bring issues to the surface. So much of the literature on organizations is promoted by a neo-industrial human relations movement – we will 'save' organizations from conflict by using various organizational development interventions. As many writers have noted, 'We solve one problem and by that process create another'. Conflict is with us; it will not go away. Where we are making progress is in recognizing it and resolving destructive conflict.

A second assumption of much management literature is that conflict is bad for organizations. Conflict need not be destructive, however. Much of it is exceedingly healthy, productive, cathartic, and creative. If we could eliminate conflict from social systems, we might destroy them. Conflict may energize, excite, rejunvenate, whether it occurs in families, groups, or organizations. Probably one of the most distressing family situations occurs when conflict has been so destructive for so long that members no longer even care enough to fight.

Destructive conflict is that interpersonal confrontation in organizations which has detrimental effects for the organization and its members. Its manifestations include white-anting, ridicule, strikes, inter-group fights, win–lose power struggles, unresolved interpersonal conflicts, etc. It inhibits openness, stimulates excessive political game playing, and can destroy groups and individuals.

Destructive conflict may arise from internal or external organisational causes. The most frequent cause is the formal structure.

Internal causes of conflict
Interpersonal conflict. Different perceptions, motives, goals, temperaments, ambitions, physical characteristics, capacities, psychological conditions, backgrounds, etc. make interpersonal conflicts inevitable. Some of these become totally destructive – e.g. radical conflict, the conflicting power needs of union leader and manager, etc.

236

Inter-group conflict. Organizational variables appear to stimulate inter-group conflict. The structure, the size of the units, the communication channels, the technical systems, or unresolved external pressures can all lead to conflict. Group members' perceptions of each other, power struggles, degrees of dependency, jurisdictional boundaries, territory, conflicting interests and even the physical obstacles to communication lead to destructive conflicts between groups.

Causes of conflict may also be found in inter-variable incompatibilities: technical systems which upset informal relationships, external pressures with which the operators of the technical system are unable to cope, formal structures which restrict and constrain the individual. This area of study – the inter-variable relationships within the organization – is still one of the most neglected areas of research.

External causes of conflict
Organizations exist in environments with other organizations, individuals, and groups. External pressures can lead to internal conflicts. Often that conflict is resolved rapidly, and a substantial increase in cooperation occurs. External threats thereby increase internal cohesiveness through the process of resolution *if* the external threat can be handled. If it cannot, internal cooperation may decline and conflict become destructive.

In a turbulent market place, where inter-organizational relationships are vital, members of organizations are themselves acted upon by the dynamic processes arising from the market place itself. Causes of conflict arising in this sort of market may be exceedingly difficult to isolate and resolve, simply because of our limited understanding of dynamic markets. That level of analysis is only now being attempted by social scientists – in the meantime, Schumacher tells us, we should build smaller, decentralized units rather than emulate the problems of turbulent markets like New York, London or Tokyo.

I mentioned when I began my analysis of the intervening variables that I would classify them into leadership style, satisfaction, and cooperation categories. I have preferred fairly narrow interpretations of these variables, as my research takes me from one organization to another, and the variables I use have to be generalizable. In specific organizations there will be other intervening variables which are more relevant. For example, time constraints, resource suppliers, energy source, openness, participation, or interpersonal skills may be more precise and relevant intervening variables.

End result variables

The first question we have to ask is what end result variables we should measure. The answer to this question depends entirely on the organization and its objectives. If the objectives include making profits, then some measure of profitability seems warranted. If the objectives include making sick people better, then some measure of the number who recover their health would seem appropriate.

The second consideration in selecting output or end result variables is that members of organizations are only rarely concerned with a single objective. Hence, multiple measures of the results are more common than a single measure. For example, the organization that manufactures paper aims to make a profit to return rewards or dividends to those who invested money in the venture, and to those employees who made the product. However, profit is rarely the only objective. If it were, then a whole host of other costs incurred to make staff and customers satisfied and boost the company's corporate image as a good citizen could be eliminated.

The third characteristic of end result variables is the longer time span. They are what their name suggests: *ends*, assessed at the conclusion of a sequence of events, or at the conclusion of a specified time period, or when resources have been exhausted. In business organizations, the time span is 12 months; similarly, in government departments, most accounting and efficiency measures are based on a 12-month time span. However, in some organizations (e.g., construction) the time span may be 5 years or more, while in others (matrix organizations) the time span may be much shorter than 12 months.

These three considerations make it difficult to generalize about end result variables for all organizations. Government organizations will have different objectives from businesses, which will have different ones from a religious organization, which will be different from an educational organization. However, as business organizations have spent more effort measuring effectiveness than other organizations, it is not surprising to see a group of end result variables emerging which are held by their exponents to be transferable.

Drucker has suggested that the end result variables of a business are:

- Market standing
- Innovation
- Productivity
- Physical and financial resources
- Profitability
- Manager performance and development
- Worker performance and attitude
- Public responsibility

Government organizations using this approach to identifying end result variables use cost efficiency data rather than profitability, but are able to use productivity measures and asset management (people, customers, finance, materials, equipment, information), as well as public responsibility indicators.

The process of identifying specific, preferably quantifiable, end result variables is one step in what has been called *Management by Objectives* and, provided the employees are from a goal-directed, high achieving culture, this method can be very successful. However, like many other management techniques (or recipes), it has been elevated into a gospel – with the result that it has also been spectacularly unsuccessful in many organizations here and abroad, particularly where it was thrust on people by top management.

While I can be critical of methods of setting end result variables (see chapter 9), I would be dishonest if I did not admit that from my experience the greatest single need in large bureaucracies is for the clarification of organizational objectives and, subsequently, of the end result variables. Lack of knowledge of clear objectives is the most frequent complaint of members of organizations. For this reason, let us examine the types of 'ends' available for end result variables.

Economic measures

Profitability. This can be expressed in terms of profits, return on investment, earnings per share, or profit to sales ratios, among others. It is the central measure of performance in a business, and in this sense the business has a much easier task in relating organizational and intervening variables with end result variables than does a government department, where there is no single and universally recognized measure of performance. Profit has the further advantage that it is readily understood even by the least gifted employees – it may not mean very much in terms of motivation, but they do understand roughly what profit means, even if they do not know for what it is used. Even non-profit organizations resort to profit (euphemistically described as 'surplus') as a viable end result variable.

As profit is expressed numerically, it is possible in establishing objectives to express this end result specifically: for example, 'To increase the return on invested capital by 12 per cent after taxes within five years'.

Market share. This end result variable may be expressed as dollars or unit volume, or market standing. Whatever its name, it has the advantage that it is also understood. If we have 49 per cent of the market, then we know a great deal more about our potential, our relative competitive position, than if we have no idea of market share at all.

Where industry associations can provide this data, or where market researchers can establish a figure for a company, this information is invaluable. However, much of it is speculative, whether presented nationally or by state. What the manager of a unit would like to know is what share he has of the market he is working in, and often that is a much smaller segment than national or state figures provide. In government departments, which are monopolies, market share is not a relevant measure. Customer opinion may be more relevant.

Productivity. This is probably the most controversial measure of results because of the emotional overtones it has for management and employees. Where units are produced in short time spans, the motivational advantage of this end result data is clear – feedback is available. People need to know where they are and what they have produced. However, one of the problems of moving into a managerial group is the loss of productivity measures. If the factory manager works hard all day, he is not necessarily very productive in terms of units – indeed, actual productivity figures may increase when he is not there.

Where possible, productivity should be expressed as a ratio of inputs to outputs – for example, 30 units per worker per 8 hour day. However, with cross-cultural data available from overseas, this unit productivity measure is often used as a 'union-bashing' mechanism. With different markets and technological under-utilization, such international comparisons do not stand statistical scrutiny.

Productivity measures are appearing more and more in government departments, where they are most relevant, but there are many civil servants for whom productivity measures are difficult to establish.

Physical and financial resources. Financial results may be expressed in a variety of ways, depending on the company – such as capital structure, new issues of shares, cash flow, working capital, dividend payments, debtors, creditors, etc.

Physical resources may be described in terms of sq‸ are metres, fixed costs, units of production, etc.

Human and environmental results. There is a multitude of human results measures. Most of these are never presented in the annual reports of companies or reports to Parliament, so we have no indication of the condition of the major resources – people. However, this is changing. Several major companies are preparing reports to *staff*, which is a rather condescending way of saying 'You are important.' There is also increasing interest in human assets among those who want to measure everything in the hope that organizations can be programmed and conducted scientifically.

Worker performance and attitude. Traditionally, data collected on the adjustment of individuals to the system have been 'after-the-event' data (staff turnover, absenteeism, sickness). In this sense, the data are very end-result oriented, but they point to the need for shorter time scales in measuring individual and group adjustment as intervening variables (such as satisfaction, conflict, cooperation), and holding the traditional measures strictly for the end of a period.

The end results might include absenteeism, turnover of staff, sickness, number of grievances, and industrial disputes, etc.

Public responsibility. This result has also been measured with after-the-event data – financial donations per year, scholarships awarded, number of public activities, etc. The assumption is invariably made that the more spent the better. The last 10 years has seen a rapid increase in attempts to measure this area of business, especially where it relates to corporate image or customer satisfaction. In both these instances, ongoing intervening measures have been used rather than end result variables. A similar concern for impact on clients is occurring in government agencies. At an even more general level, there has been a rapid increase in research on *social accounting* – the attempt to assess an organization's contribution to society.

Of necessity, this look at end result variables has been oversimplified. It is important that managers of organizations not only decide what their objectives are but also what quantifiable or qualifiable data they are seeking. In most organizations, economic measures are used and others are assumed. Free-forming, modular or self-designing organizations do not fit easily into end result categories. Muddling through, experiencing, and concentrating on now rather than tomorrow's end results characterize these organizations. Entirely different and certainly 'new' assessments would be necessary to establish the relevance of output. But I have ignored this type of organization in my analysis simply because this book is for managers, most of whom work in structured role systems.

Conclusions on outputs from organizations

Analysing outputs involves looking at three levels of variables:

- Organizational or causal
- Intervening or operational
- End result

Analysing the total performance of the organization means understanding the relationships between these variables. This is not easy. Not only is there a multitude of possible combinations of the variables in organizations, but there are also configurations within configurations. That is, departments within organizations may differ widely because individuals' perceptions within those departments differ widely.

242

Outputs are increasingly being identified in terms of the MbO concept of *key result areas*. Obviously, they are dependent upon the organization being analysed. For example, the most important end result variable for an advertising agency may be creativity; for a hospital, patient care, for a business, return on investment, for a university, quality of research. Yet, although managers in each organization must identify their own result variables, they tend to fall into two categories:

- Economic
- Human and environmental

Working out the relationships between these end result variables, the intervening variables, and the causal variables is what managing is all about. And we are just beginning to devise the tools to manage more effectively by monitoring a system as an ongoing social system.

The next chapter looks at current attempts to change the combination of the variables into new configurations.

For additional reading

Drucker P., *The Practice of Management*, Mercury Books, 1963.

Drucker P., *Management: Tasks, Responsibilities and Practices*, Harper & Row, New York, 1974.

Emery F., and C. Phillips, *Living at Work*, Australian Government Publishing, Canberra, 1976.

Follett M. P., 'The giving of orders', in H. G. Metcalf, and L. F. Urwick (eds.), *Dynamic Administration*, Harper, New York, 1941.

H.E.W., *Work in America*, MIT Press, Cambridge, Massachusetts, 1963.

Hunt J. W., and P. Saul, *Organisation Attitude Questionnaire*, University of New South Wales, Sydney, 1973.

Kast F. E., and J. E. Rosenweig, *Contingency Views of Organization and Management*, Science Research Association, New York, 1973.

Likert R., *New Patterns of Management*, McGraw-Hill, 1961.

Nadler D. A., *Feedback and Organization Developments Using Data Based Methods*, Addison-Wesley, Reading, Massachusetts, 1977.

Robbins S. P., *The Administrative Process*, Prentice Hall, Englewood Cliffs, New Jersey, 1976.

Schumacher E. F., *Small is Beautiful*, Blond and Briggs, 1973.

Srivastra S., P. Salipante, T. G. Cummings, W. Hotz, J. D. Bigelow, and J. A. Waters, *Job Satisfaction and Productivity*, Kent State University Press, Cleveland, 1977.

Warmington A., *et al.*, *Organisational Behaviour and Performance*, Macmillan, 1977.

11 Participating in organizations

Much of the discussion in earlier chapters has emphasized a truism: organizations change and adapt to changing environments, expectations of employees, customers, shareholders, etc. In the past, smaller, less complex organizations, in less complex environments, adapted relatively easily to changes in the environment. With larger, more complex organizations, in complex and uncertain environments, the content and process of change have become major issues for managers and behavioural scientists.

We can no longer assume that organizations will adapt. In fact, we have to accept that what we want from our institutions and work organizations and what we, in fact, find are drifting further and further apart. And the consequences of several contradictions in our society are more significant than ever before. Rather than increased harmony, we find increased conflict. Rather than the elimination of poverty, we find poverty in the middle of affluence. Rather than control over one's lifestyle, we find innumerable restrictions on personal freedom. Rather than satisfying work lives, we find more people questioning the meaning of work.

These inconsistencies have led to a wave of attacks on power centres of our society – corporations, government departments, institutions, universities, etc. People appear to be unwilling to accept that the ideal and the reality have to be so very different, and some are asking what purpose a democratic society has unless the individual has some influence. Part of the blame must clearly be put on educational systems which do not teach people the skills necessary for participating in a democratic society. However, most of the blame must rest with the structures of the institutions of that society.

The literature on the potential (if not real) changes in attitudes and values is extensive. My interest in this chapter is not to re-work that well trodden ground, but to itemize the variety of techniques currently in vogue as a means of changing or adapting our organizations to the needs of our times. Most of these techniques attempt to increase the participation of those involved in reducing the gap between the ideal and the reality. However, not all techniques derive from the same premise.

One major stumbling block has been the terms used. Some are inclusive (industrial democracy, worker participation, organizational development), while others are more exclusive (job enrichment, job re-design, work groups). Unfortunately, no two behavioural scientists agree on how the various approaches to adapting organizations should be classified. There are theoretical classifications, relating to content and process; there are shopping lists of unrelated techniques; there are time scales; there are scales for a redistribution of power; there are legislative as opposed to non-legislative classifications; there are 'real' compared with 'felt' participation scales; there are scales of industrial democracy which present continuums of power devolution; there are scales which use managerial strategies to illustrate degrees of worker manipulation; there are scales of 'depth' of participation; there are scales which suggest an individual, organizational, societal rearrangement of power and influence. Because of the generality of most terms, none of them has been very clear to the practitioner.

The origin of this confusion is our obsession with labelling our adaptive tactics. Any movement suffers from having originated in a problem (the gap between what we want from organizations and what we get) and from attempts to reify solutions for that problem into theory. Problems are not static, but exist in different societies in different ways. Their very dynamism means that, while theorists attempt to hold the problem steady, the problem has already changed. Theory and problem drift apart, so we devise a new label and hope it will be the new theory to solve the new problem. The more rapidly the problem changes, the more rapid is the generation of the latest fad for solving it. In the 'fifties, when there was clear evidence of a failure of some organizations to adapt, communication and human relations training courses were offered to practitioners as *the* answer. In the 'sixties, the organization change strategies dominated the literature as *the* answer. By the 'seventies, organization development, worker participation, and the quality of work life

246

superseded change theorists. And in the 'eighties new labels, new theories, and new potential recipes will be marketed.

At each stage of this evolutionary process, adherents to the solution surround themselves with seductive symbols, emotional rhetoric, over-simplified logic and theory, and clutch to themselves the gospel according to whoever is current. And when salvation is not forthcoming, they turn disillusioned to another god who has updated the symbolism, redefined the problem and offered another set of answers. Meanwhile, back in the organizational world, life goes on relatively unaffected by the fragility of movements and their adherents. And the same basic organizational variables are still there, being moved by members into a new configuration to meet a new set of constraints.

Nevertheless, the apparent indifference of members to movements is deceptive. Changing organizations can be a slow and painful business. There are few short cuts for renewing and revitalizing them. There are no simple answers to changing relationships between workers, managers, and tasks. However, compared with even 10 years ago, the rate of change has accelerated almost imperceptibly in our organizations. Not because of the gimmicks or the current fervently exploited solutions (although a myriad of interpersonal and inter-group techniques have become part of our organizational life), but because of a deeper conviction that organizations must change, there must be a better way of reconciling what we want and what we get. Whereas a decade ago, pressure for change came primarily from top management, pressure is now coming from all over – from workers on the shop floor, from disillusioned middle managers, from top managers who may foresee a post-industrial society when economic issues are secondary to social issues, from customers impatient with corporate products, from families with absent breadwinners, and from groups concerned for the social milieu.

Yet whatever the current theory, long-term reconciliation of what we want and what we get is impossible. Organizations are not designed for individuals, and an individual's goals can never be completely satisfied in an organization. And the whole history of our answers to problems, including industrial democracy, reflects a basic conflict of individual and organization goals, of the individual and the collective. That conflict is as old as man, and continues even where power is more equitably shared. There are gains and losses for us all when we join an organization.

Yet explaining the dilemma for the manager is of little comfort in his day-to-day attempts to adapt and manage. Telling the manager of a factory which has been plagued with industrial problems that he must work out solutions with his own people is obviously not much help to a person preoccupied with 'how to' techniques. The inevitable response is: 'I want to change the place, I don't like it either. But where do I start?'

There are two basic classifications for most current attempts to renew organizations,

- Representative redistribution of power
- Direct participation

This chapter concentrates on these two approaches. Of necessity, this method of classification is excessively simple and it suggests a dichotomy which is false. However, because of the variety of theories and techniques and the limits of space, we will stick to this classification.

Representative participation

Representative participation in work organizations is primarily concerned with reforming corporate law. It includes co-determination, worker directors, works councils, joint consultative committees, shop floor committees, safety committees, production committees, etc. In these forms, representative democracy is a formally structured attempt to involve people in the decision making. This approach is found in most European countries, especially West Germany and Yugoslavia. Representative participation is concerned with the collective interests of employees, and has its origins in a class struggle between the powerful and the not so powerful. More recently the class struggle has been superseded by a search for 'real' democracy rather than the overthrow of one powerful class. For some unionists and managers, the end result of this approach is worker control.

While I believe that some form of representative democracy is inevitable, I seriously question some of the expected outcomes. Having my elected representative sitting on the works council, or the board of directors, does little to improve the job

I perform or my feelings of being non-involved in the decisions which affect me day to day. Probably the most fallacious argument of the supporters of a formal system is that democratic processes lead to power equalization. Democracy, whether at state, national, or local government level, is no longer participation of the people, for the people. It has become participation of the power-seeking few for the preservation of the bureaucracy which dictates to a powerless, non-involved majority. And in both the local and national spheres, even 'our' elected representatives appear overawed, overpowered by the massive structure and power of the bureaucratic government departments.

The important formally structured sorts of representative democracy are

- Representation at senior policy level
- Representation at plant or departmental level
- Collective determination of conditions of employment
- Collective ownership

Representation at senior levels

This usually refers to worker directors on a board, or worker representatives on an executive or supervisory committee of top management. The objective is to involve employees, through their representatives, in the overall direction of the enterprise.

There are many European precedents to draw on for this structural form. In West Germany, half the boards of companies with more than 2000 employees are worker directors. In Yugoslavia's State-owned enterprises, the State owns the assets and directs major policy, but worker representatives direct local operations of the firm, including the appointment of managers. In Britian, the ill-fated Bullock Report recommended worker directors for firms employing 2000 or more employees. In the US and Australia there are very few examples of this form of representation, although some companies (both private and public) have a diluted form of representation at the senior management committee level. Conversely, the wide co-operative movement and the credit union movement do provide excellent examples of representation.

Impetus for a representative democracy has come from the European Economic Community's socialist political parties and academics rather than from employees. The debate on whether legislation is the way to achieve this or not has been continuous. As most other structural reforms in private enterprise have required legislative 'clout', I expect we will see legislation in the near future. This form of representation really means changing company law.

However, if senior managers were caught unprepared for this possibility, no less so were union organizers. There has been a flurry of huddlings, both among managers and unionists (unfortunately rarely together), to adopt 'postures' on the possibility of worker directors. For the unions, representation raises many vital issues. For example, will worker representatives handle terms of employment rather than union representatives? Will the corporation negotiate with its own representatives at senior management boards, or will the worker representatives not become involved in discussion about the firm's major cost, salaries, and wages? Who will be the representatives – union or non-union delegates? How will they be elected? For how long? From what number of people? There are also, as Pritchard has documented, numerous legal constraints on this form of representation. His excellent summary identifies restrictions on representation in three areas of the law: industrial law, company and equity law, and constitutional law. For example, would a worker director be compromised if, by law, he is required to exercise judgement for the benefit of all the stakeholders of a company and not solely for the interests of employees?

These are but a few of the issues involved with representation at the top level of the hierarchy. Yet, to place the scene in its context, these legal restrictions are used too frequently by managers to defend their own positions of power. There *can* be supervisory boards which do not run into the same legal problems, nor the same union–management problems.

Moreover, anyone working in the field of industrial relations or organization development could not help but be impressed by the sanity and common sense of most people. We too often design strategies on the basis of one paranoid, dishonest individual who caused a major fracas 10 years previously. All people, given the opportunity, can adopt a sensible approach in coping with governmental or legal restrictions on their behaviour. Supervisory boards that do exist have not had the problems American, British, and Australian company directors love to quote.

My reservation about this form of participation is that it is, again, participation by the few for the many, and it assumes the few will give the many more control over their work life. And while the many report, in research surveys, that they want to be represented, they show considerable lack of interest where representation does exist. Perhaps the problem of lack of interest has nothing to do with representation but is caused by the size of the organization. Or is it a reflection of disillusionment and lack of interest in the democratic processes at the local, state, or national level? Or, as Crombie has suggested, does representation at board level run counter to localized involvement in one's own affairs? Certainly, representation alone is not enough. Much more would have to occur at the job level for representation to have significance.

Representation at plant or department level
A modification of representation at the top of the hierarchy, this form exists where representatives sit on councils or safety committees or planning committees, which integrate functions across the hierarchy and involve more than one section or group. The advantage of this level of representation is that members become involved in issues much closer to their own work – e.g., job design, environmental factors (safety, heating, facilities), and technical systems.

There are numerous examples of this form of participation. In Europe, it was introduced in the 'fifties. Since then, it has been given legislative support and representatives can use their power to protect their electors, safeguard justice in promotion, and, if necessary, in some countries, veto the decisions of senior managers on new technology if the safety of members is threatened.

One of the major criticisms of this form of participation has been the tendency of managers to use plant or departmental committees for cosmetic or 'felt' participation rather than real participation. And because the common sense of employees tells them that this is cosmetic, they have regarded the safety committee or the consultative committee with some cynicism. If this form is to be valuable both for the employees and for managers, clear guidelines, a genuine desire to share power, and the release of information are needed. The clear guidelines involve the following principles.

- Voting rights must be defined
- Decision making areas must be defined
- The implementation of decisions must involve accountability of members of the committee
- Committee members must feed back the results of their deliberations at meetings to their electors
- Organizational communication channels, including journals, pictures, intercoms, etc., should be available to 'sell' or communicate what is happening through the plant or department

These representative meetings have considerable value if given teeth. But, because they have been primarily concerned with important but not central issues (such as safety), they will require considerable support from managers in selling representation to the work force. Learning to participate in decision making is time consuming and often depressing, and the structural arrangements are only part of the job. Situations must be provided in which learning can take place. We must accept that the values and attitudes of managers are radically different from those of most other employees and that negotiating compromises will be time consuming and sometimes painful. Participative decision making is, therefore, slower than most other forms, but the pay-off is the much faster rate of implementation. Of all representative systems, works councils offer the greatest chance for involvement, especially if work design is included in the council's charter.

Collective determination of conditions
This approach is based on the premise that worker's interests are best advanced through their own separate organizations (unions) negotiating with employers. A third participant in this system is a supposedly neutral, legal court (or commission), which uses industrial law to solve irreconcilable conflicts between the parties. Theoretically, this simple system is beautifully logical. In practice, it is difficult to imagine a more complex way of solving disputes. Structuring the conflict simply reinforces it – just as, in the past, marital breakdown was invariably made worse by the employment of conciliators, called solicitors, who structured the problem. Emotional issues are rarely improved

by structural devices. Structural devices assume the status quo; militant leaders have no such reverence for status quo.

This system works best where:

- There are few large unions
- There is agreement between the parties about their contractual obligations
- Negotiation rather than confrontation has been the pattern of union management relations

In the US, Italy, Norway, Denmark, Sweden, and the UK, where collective bargaining is common, it covers a wide range of issues, from wages to negotiating on managerial decisions. The trend has been for continuous bargaining of a joint consultative nature rather than the previous, specific arrangement of annual or bi-annual or tri-annual bargaining sessions.

As a form of real participation, collective bargaining is yet another case of participation of the few for the many. It does little to involve employees in decisions affecting their lives.

Collective ownership
By participating in the ownership of the organization, workers participate in the rewards flowing from their investment and work. An alternative form of 'ownership' is to own a percentage of the production.

Share issues to employees of companies have not been common outside the US. This is not to suggest that the stock exchanges have not encouraged a wide dispersion of shareholdings and a wide involvement of small investors in public companies. We have seen, especially in times of economic abundance, a dispersion of equity holdings. But there has not been a comparable dispersion of shares among employees of private companies. Those companies which do issue shares tend to restrict the issues to senior executives, who either receive shares as 'rewards' for performance or buy shares at below market prices. There are three forms of ownership:

- Employees hold shares as individuals
- Employees own the corporation as citizens
- Employees are the producers who collectively own the company

Ownership in any of these forms does increase the commitment of members to the outcomes of the organization. But ownership does little to change day-to-day facts of work, or to involve non-managerial employees in the decisions which affect them. Sharing in productivity gains is a much more realistic approach to increased participation, because increases are current and often visible. Conversely, annual shares or bonuses are relatively useless rewards, because they are spread over long time periods. More important, I have great difficulty in believing that in the future in our culture, people will agree to be transferred inter-state or even intra-state for 'the good of the corporation' without wanting a greater share of the cake. It is difficult to believe that employees can be induced to strive for higher levels of productivity without sharing in the rewards of that productivity. Rewards will not necessarily be financial, but they will be costs against increases in productivity, e.g., more leisure time, social activities, etc.

For the past 20 years, the number of firms using productivity sharing as a way of rewarding increased activity by workers has been very few. However, problems of absenteeism, motivation, sickness, and industrial disputes have given new relevance to sharing as a possible solution to problems.

Like ownership, shared productivity has short-term interest only. It does not really tackle the problems confronted by employees in their jobs, but it can restore a link between performance and reward which is exceedingly important in motivating some people. And if the pay-outs are enough, productivity can be increased.

I have discussed the major forms of representation and ownership. There are numerous hybrid versions of these formalized schemes for participation. They are more than adequately covered elsewhere; for further information, readers should consult the references at the end of the chapter.

Direct participation

Also referred to as shop floor or office participation, direct participation has its origins in making the day-to-day work experience of employees more satisfying, involving, and challenging. I will consider the major techniques used, and conclude with the all-embracing field called *organization development*.

Direct participation is the process of decentralizing decisions on tactics to where they belong – with those doing the work – rather than holding them in a central power centre. The major techniques for achieving this have been labelled as

- Work restructuring
- Job enrichment
- Socio-technical approaches

As there are extensive surveys of this literature, I will briefly discuss each approach and give my own experiences with it. My basic premise is that direct participation is only democratic if those involved decide whether or not they want change. Much of the literature tells us (as employees) what we want, and how we are going to get it. It would be nice to think someone had asked us first.

Work restructuring

Philips Industries has been one of the exponents of this largely European method of increasing participation. That company describes the underlying hypothesis as follows:

The organization of work, the work situation, and the conditions of labour in such a way that, while maintaining or improving efficiency, job content accords as closely as possible with the capacities and ambitions of the individual employee.

There are three distinct phases in the restructuring process.

- The work environment phase

Managers decide to improve the attractiveness of the work environment as a forerunner to further change. This is sometimes called a 'curtain raiser', and may involve new amenities, re-painting, etc.

- The work phase

The actual work individuals do is analysed and re-designed using the theories of job re-design, job enrichment, or enlargement or rotation. This is an industrial design phase, as opposed to the 'unfreeze' phase of, say, the organization development consultant. Having re-designed jobs, the industrial engineers present the possibilities to the work groups for their comments and criticisms, and together designer and group work out solutions.

- The departmental structure phase

Once the jobs have been re-designed, accountability is delegated to the group. This leads to a demand from employees for changes in the hierarchical controls, and a 'bottom up' re-design of relationships, accountabilities, and power within the department occurs.

Probably the most interesting factor in this approach is that it is usually the industrial engineer, rather than the behavioural scientist, who is the catalyst. And for this reason the literature has a distinctly different tone to it – more results-oriented, less preoccupied with job satisfaction, more management controlled.

We have tended to separate behavioural scientists and engineers far too often in our organisations. It is very easy for the behavioural scientist to opt out by saying, 'We will let employees re-design their own work', but this often places enormous demands on what has previously been a neglected group. Not surprisingly, their response may be, 'Re-design is the job of management', 'We are not paid to think'. After all, design is a specialist function, especially in plants with huge capital investment in technology.

The work restructuring engineer plans for the intended changes and his 'unfreeze' is to show the employees the possibilities. In this way, he can save a great deal of time and expensive group huddles in motels or training rooms. Conversely, the criticism of the approach is that it originates above and that a solution is forced on the group.

In many situations, I believe this method has merit, especially with older employees in highly complex technical systems. Its success depends on the competence of the engineer in offering possibilities rather than thrusting solutions upon the group. However, if the group does not see the choice of the final design as its own, then participation is negligible.

Job enrichment
This approach relies on the theory that the 'motivators' are the factors that meet man's need for psychological growth, especially achievement, recognition, responsibility, advancement, and challenge. The 'hygiene' factors are concerned with the job environment and have little influence on productivity.

From this Herzbergian assumption direct changes in the work

itself are planned to permit the motivators to emerge. The ingredients of the change are direct feedback to the employee, a client relationship, a learning function, individual control over scheduling, unique expertise, control over resources, direct communication, and personal accountability.

Sceptics about the theory of job enrichment are strengthened in their disbelief by the absence of solid and detailed material which states in numbered paragraphs the processes by which jobs are enriched. Most material is vague and some is tantalizingly so. No better examples exist of this than some of the often quoted American experiments. There are two explanations for this lack of data. First, the uncertainty about whether or not job enrichment is really occurring in a situation, as opposed to a research induced euphoria. Second is the difficulty in obtaining economic data on job enrichment experiments.

Herzberg sees the advantages of job enrichment as:

- Possibility of providing lasting growth and competence
- Speed of implementation
- The way it minimizes the new hygiene problems

He does concede that the major disadvantages are the reported inability of older employees to adapt, the increased employee defensiveness for incompetence, the role ambiguity of supervisors, and the fact that an assumed lack of motivators can become alibis for low productivity.

My own view is that job enrichment exercises have provided some of the most dramatic and rewarding changes in organizations. On a job level, direct re-design of jobs through employee participation in that re-design may be the only practical, and therefore plausible, way to change jobs. For example, West German experiments concentrate on enriching individual jobs.

My concern about job enrichment programmes is caused by the following problems:

- It is dictated from above, using managerial values and motivations
- There is the disturbing suggestion that each and every employee has exactly the same motivation profile and organizational expectations – a fallacy which my own collection of motivation profiles (chapters 1 and 2) would question

- The raging controversy about the Herzbergian two-factor theory is not something that a person concerned with reliability of empirical research data can ignore. The theory stands poorly when the research method is changed. What satisfies and what does not satisfy people in work organizations is not adequately explained by the motivator–hygiene theory, and changes based on this theory will inevitably face this problem.
- Workers may gain satisfaction through demonstrations of power – a fact which Herzberg ignores

Nor is the problem of job satisfaction simply confined to extrinsic and intrinsic factors. Numerous papers have suggested that the relationship between the motivators and hygiene factors appears to differ with location, age, sex, occupation, degree of independence, and education level.

Socio-technical approaches

This approach relies on the argument that the technological system (see Figure 11.1) determines the characteristics of the social (or people) system through the allocation of work roles and the technologically given dependence relations between tasks. The performance of the organization is seen to be a function of the interface of the social and technical subsystems. The functional consequences of the social system are not easily modified because of the requirements of the technical system.

In practical terms, socio-technical consultants see as essential a change in work design from adapting humans to technology, to adapting technology to humans; from single, prescribed, rigid structures, to structures where responsibility is allocated to hierarchical self-organizing groups, commonly called *semi-autonomous work groups*. Job enlargement or rotation within groups is feasible if members want it.

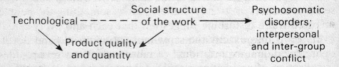

Figure 11.1   A socio-technical approach

The major argument for this approach is that the employee is participating in the decisions of his group and can attain a sense of personal worth and achievement from the achievements of the group and the social relationships within it. And, as the most important secondary need of some 60 per cent of the work force is social rather than achievement, participating in one's group's decisions is a way of satisfying social needs.

In an age where identity appears lost, where people seek relationships which have been shattered by major socio-economic movements, the provision of a work group as a source of growth, interpersonal satisfaction, and participation seems good psychology. Furthermore, over the past 25 years we have had more than enough literature (from England, Sweden and Norway) to know that this approach is viable – it comes closest to reconciling the individual to the organization.

The major advantage of semi-autonomous or autonomous work groups is the logic of relating task, technology, employees, and environment in a multivariate analysis. My own research has adopted a similar scheme for analysing organizations. The resultant concern for job design, the environment, the technology, interpersonal relationships, power, and participation can lead to group goal setting, group control of resources, group quality control, group discipline, and group reward allocation. Probably more than any other method, this approach recognizes the common sense of individuals who for decades have been treated as morons by managers of large organizations.

My first reservation for this approach lies not with the method but with the almost tyrannical fervour of some of its exponents. Not everyone wants to be in a work group; it is important that we recognize this and allow for choice. To suggest that this is *the* answer is just as erroneous as every previous suggestion. West Germany's industrial experiments do not, for example, concentrate on groups, but on individuals.

My second reservation is that work groups become ends in themselves. That is, having them in an organization is seen by senior managers as 'trendy' rather than as something the people involved want.

My third reservation is that, where groups have been developed, the degree of individual commitment to the group fades – sometimes after a few months, sometimes later, depending on the opportunities for change in that work situation. As group cohesion fades, there is a feeling of disappointment among members and requests for change, more control, more fun. Unfortunately, many of the jobs that have to be done in our industrial society are very limited in opportunities for change and re-design.

Finally, we should not minimize the behavioural problems. Inter-group rivalry, competitiveness, failure, preservation of 'face', and protection of territory are all human problems of this method (and of others concentrating on groups). We are in danger of reifying the group into a structural form and using it most inappropriately. Chapter 4 discussed the problems of groups – autonomous work groups suffer from just those same human problems as well.

For the past 100 years we have seen centralization and accumulations of power, in capital resources, people, and information. Organizations have expanded in numbers, often to an unmanageable size. The world-wide shift to decentralize, first to the division or region and then to the smallest viable unit (the work group), is a reaction against that concentration of power. Maybe we have learnt that big is not necessarily best, at least for those working in the system. In an industrial society, where cutting organizations up into divisions or subsidiaries is technically and economically not always possible, the semi-autonomous work group provides experience with participation within the larger, economically viable units.

I have separated these three approaches (enrichment, re-structuring, and work groups) into discrete sections. In fact, they overlap, and the current state of development is a mishmash of all approaches. Inevitably, this merger of previously separate approaches has been labelled: *organization development*. Like earlier approaches, it has achieved the two signs of respectability – a jargon of its own, and an association of OD professionals. Like previous methods, it concentrates on techniques rather than ends, and as a 'bag of tricks' it suffers from a lack of empirical support. Yet, in a stumbling way, OD attempts to carry on from the change theories of the 'sixties in developing a theoretical understanding of the content and process of organizational renewal, revitalization, growth, survival. We have yet to develop an adequate theory of social change, but the glimpses of a theory of organization renewal are visible.

Organization development

One journal has described the goals of organization development as:

. . . to release human creativity and potential, contribute to
self-fulfilment and improve communication between
individuals and groups; thus making society as a whole a more
desirable place in which to live.

Such definitions may do more harm than good. At a practical
level OD relates to changing organizations in a planned way for
the better.

The techniques of the OD practitioner are much more specific, and include personality, structural, technological, and interpersonal variables. The end result variables of the OD
programme include both economic measures (productivity,
profit, cost efficiency) and human, environmental measures (satisfaction, cooperation, creativity).

All attempts to change organizations assume that there must
be a better way. However, it does not follow that there is one
best way.

In searching for the 'better way', or better configuration of
the multivariate system, OD practitioners are looking for a
management initiated increase in organizational effectiveness
through a series of planned interventions into the processes or
intervariable relationships. They recognize the truism that any
change must involve the ideas, effort, and contributions of the
people who will be affected by the change. In this sense, OD is
often grouped as a subset of participatory strategies. Conversely,
as OD has the *imprimatur* of top management, it is seen by
others as 'felt' participation, or the use of behavioural sciences
to increase management's manipulation of its employees. Yet a
third group consciously avoid the OD label as being too short-
sighted, preoccupied with economic ends, and unrelated to a
genuine, society-wide devolution of power.

My own view of OD is that it is a collection of techniques
rather than a theory of change. I have described it elsewhere as
a 'bag of tricks', which as a consultant I am pleased to use for
the short-term, adaptive ends of change programmes. Like other
adaptive tactics, OD does not deliver nirvana. My concern is
that our theoretical understanding of change and adaptation in

organizations is in its infancy; we still do not understand empirically the process of organizational renewal, nor have we developed sufficiently sensitive techniques for initiating change on the level some members of organizations may want. Systemic change, or changing whole systems is still the preoccupation of academics rather than practitioners, whether the system is a society, a city, a town, an organization, a group, or a family.

What is OD?

OD acquired all the mystique of the latest fad in the late 'sixties. Since then, managers have been disillusioned by the mystique and are tired of asking what it is. OD is not one technique, but a collection of often unrelated and radically different techniques, some of which have been evolving since the 'thirties. OD practitioners tied these unlikely techniques together and convinced themselves they had a new way to change organizations. Their conviction was documented in planned, logical programmes, called OD programmes. But if we examine their programmes, they have the same processes as any other consultant might use.

Steps associated with this process are:

- Recognizing a problem (disequilibrium or threat of disequilibrium)
- Awareness of the need for change
- Collection of valid information
- Developing a change strategy
- Intervening (e.g., team building, structural change, technical change)
- Monitoring and reviewing the intervention

Where OD practitioners differed from previous consultants was in their reliance on behavioural techniques and on understanding of the interrelationships of variables in models of organizations. Previous consulting strategies had relied on over-simplified models of problems which adopted micro rather than macro views of what was happening. Of course, there was a very simple reason for this: it has only been in the last decade that we have had good data relating individuals and structure; individuals and technical systems; environments and structures, individuals and teams, etc.

A second influence on the emergence of the OD cult was the economic conditions of the 'seventies. Previously, there was no urgency to achieve flexibility and renewal in organizations, and the education of managers (and of society as a whole) excluded the basics of individual and group psychology, let alone organizational psychology. Falling markets, organizational malaise, disintegration and structural rigor mortis changed all this.

Because of their reliance on the behavioural sciences, OD practitioners were most frequently from that discipline. However, this initially led to a preoccupation with behavioural, rather than structural and/or technical, changes. This has since changed, and the resultant mix in both internal and external consultations reflects a shift from a preoccupation with behavioural solutions to an absorption of them into general consulting skills. A knowledge of the behavioural sciences is as important as a knowledge of plant design, control systems, computers, etc. For this reason, OD skills are already being absorbed into the general consulting business. A second interesting change has been the increasing use of internal as opposed to external consultants.

For those interested in the specific techniques of OD, there is considerable literature available; references are given at the end of this chapter. I am more concerned with what we know of the change process in organizations, regardless of which of the participative techniques are used.

Perspectives for change

The perspective one has of an organization will affect the way one chooses interventions for change. Most of the work on organizations can be divided into four very distinctive approaches. If a manager adopts one of these perspectives in preference to another, he is likely to prefer certain methods of change over others.

The dominant perspective has been the *traditional view*, which assumes that organizations can be scientifically conducted. The major belief of exponents of this view is that by structuring the behaviour of people, behaviour can be made predictable and controllable. Hence structure, job descriptions, controls, Management by Objectives, management information systems, which reduce uncertainty to tolerable levels, are the preferred interventions of the holders of this view.

A second view is that organizations cannot be conducted

scientifically because they are full of individuals striving to satisfy their needs. I will call this the *needs view*. From this North American perspective, the manager should be more concerned about self-fulfilment and satisfaction through job re-design, work structuring, career planning, and training.

A third view, developed initially in Britain (but exported all over the world) is the *systems view*. From this perspective, the manager intending to introduce change should be concerned about the behaviour of the total system, the interdependence of the subsystem, and the relationship between the whole and the rest of society. Equilibrium, balance, and harmony through self-regulating work groups, would be a sensible strategy if this view were adopted.

The fourth and mostly European view is the pluralist view. From this view, the unitary or total team approach which underlies the other three views is seen to be too simple. Pluralist theorists see organizations as the loose couplings of different groups and different individuals struggling for resources. Harmony is short-lived, power is the important variable, and power sharing, negotiating, conflict resolution, and confrontation are the strategies recommended. The unitary concept is somewhat at odds with this view.

I do not intend to discuss all the interventions available to the manager here. There are numerous publications which do this, some of which are listed at the end of this chapter. What I do want to stress is that, depending on how one sees an organization, so too will one choose the relevant way to change that organization.

Traditionalists will argue for structural, 'rational' change; needs theorists for satisfaction; systems theorists for equilibrium; pluralists for a balance of power.

It is true that two factors have affected a manager's perspective. There is an underlying time dimension in this classification. Traditional theories developed in the earlier part of this century, especially after the Second World War; needs theories in the 'fifties and 'sixties; systems theories in the 'sixties and 'seventies; pluralist theories have been developing for centuries but became popular in the 'seventies because of industrial relations disputes and the consequent participation movement.

A second qualification on this classification of perspectives is that some parts of an organization will show preferences for one perspective over another, which makes an organizational view difficult. For example if the personnel in the industrial relations department adopt a pluralist view, then they might well regard the needs theories, taught on management training programmes, as a waste of time. Similarly, the stop steward might well regard the needs theories as another managerial attempt to squeeze more out of his union members. The accounting department's personnel may well regard their new management information system as a major development, and be disturbed to find that the marketing people regard the new controls as restrictive and childish.

In other words, all perspectives will be found in the same organization, and while they may not be labelled as I (and others) have labelled them, they nevertheless influence strategies for change. For example, the following fairly common statements from a range of managers do represent specific views of man and his organizations:

'Workers should be paid only on performance.'
'Unless we give our staff the opportunity to grow and develop, they will leave.'
'Human beings are the same everywhere. They are only out for what they can screw from the system.'
'We operate in such an uncertain market that half our time is spent rearranging our priorities.'
'A satisfied staff is a productive staff.'
'All shop stewards are communists.'
'We must design the technology to match the social requirements of our employees.'
'We need to clarify our objectives and rewrite the job descriptions.'
'There is a latent creativity in employees waiting to be released.'

Each of these statements might be seen to favour one perspective rather than another. And this must affect the sorts of changes managers are prepared to introduce.

The certainty–uncertainty factor
Schon has argued that differences mentioned above are related to learning and to our economic stages of development. For example, he argued that he could identify several preoccupations

265

of American firms from the pre-'twenties to the present time. He saw organizations as being concerned with basic questions depending on the time.

First World War to Second World War:
'Is the firm well organized?'

Second World War to the late 'fifties:
'Does the organization foster individual creativity and, with it, invention and discovery?'

Late 'fifties to mid 'sixties:
'Is the organization innovative?'

Mid 'sixties to present:
'Is the organization able to manage change?'

Similar preoccupations (usually occurring a little later) could be seen in most Western economies.

Between the wars, our preoccupation was with a safe, predictable, formal structure in organizations. Our current preoccupation with managing change is neither safe nor predictable, yet we are learning to live with that uncertainty, to manage it or to block it. And while concern for uncertainty has become a national pastime, we should remember that, within uncertainty, there is much that is certain; in most organizations members have been waiting patiently for changes in the structure or technical system for many years.

Learning to deal with new organizational questions transcends the 'bag of tricks', and brings any discussion of organizational renewal or development into the field of learning theory.

Learning to cope
Individuals learn; groups learn; organizations of individuals learn. The important issues of organization development are questions about learning, not about whether or not we should use the ABC team building package or the XYZ package, or neither of them. Organization change is a learning process whereby situations are devised for solving problems, coping with change and uncertainty, and understanding the multivariate nature of organizations.

Inevitably, members of some organizations are far better prepared for this learning than are others. There are many members (including managers) who cannot conceptualize at the organizational or even the departmental level. The macro picture is impossible to retain, the overall exercise is beyond their comprehension. This leads to a preoccupation with techniques and means rather than ends. However, if the change programme is difficult to comprehend, then conceptualizing a change in the power structure of our society is totally disturbing for those who have not had the learning to face that change.

The development of conceptual skills and learning to understand organizational change are the two pressing needs for organizational renewal. Unfortunately, developing conceptual skills and providing a framework for comprehending change in organizations are not learning experiences which can be rushed. Even a three-year MBA programme is no guarantee of acquiring either the skills or a theoretical understanding of the process.

For these reasons, the rate at which members can learn is affected by the developmental experience.

A second moderating effect stems from the phases of the learning process. These phases were identified very early in the organization change literature. They appear under various names but the most widespread are

- The unfreeze phase – relaxing people into a 'ready to learn' state stage
- The value and attitude change phase – the learning state stage
- The re-freeze phase – the consolidation state stage

We can represent these on a learning curve, like the one shown in Figure 11.2.

The techniques for hastening people into a learning experience have received an incredible amount of attention all over the world. There has been a veritable wave of creativity in designing manuals, exercises, games, etc., to assist the learning process. As I said earlier, too many managers believe that the techniques are the ends of change programmes – content assumes more relevance that the process of organizational change or development or renewal.

If we relate stages in learning and the preparation of members for learning, then we can explain why some organizations use certain techniques and others use different ones. There is clearly no one 'package' for everyone. For example, where conceptual skills are well developed and where experiential learning is

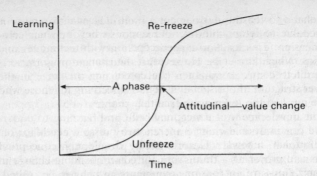

Figure 11.2 The learning curve

understood, problem-solving discussions, which cut across functions as well as encourage highly personal and open exchanges of feelings, are possible. In highly centralized, economically protected organizations, where conceptual skills and the understanding of organizations as social systems have not been encouraged, the unfreeze phase may require highly structured, safe 'management development' programmes, which approach but do not reach experiental learning techniques. After participating in such a 'safe' programme, a second programme may move the same participants further towards dealing with complex but uncertain issues. Two or three different training situations may be necessary before sufficient learning has taken place so that real issues are tackled openly.

Because of individual and organizational differences, commercial change 'packages' are fraught with problems. Not unexpectedly, they have had very little success outside America, for they assume that all members are at a similar stage of development. Where they have been used, modifications have been necessary.

The continuum along which the change programme moves is a 'learning to cope with uncertainty' continuum, and members' readiness (preparedness to entertain difference, ambiguity, and uncertainty) is the major determinant of effectiveness. This means, as I have implied throughout this discussion, that the people involved is *the* important variable of change. Are they ready? Are they familiar with the concepts? Have they developed problem-solving skills? Can they design technical systems which utilize human potential? Can they endure uncertainty?

Related to these questions are a multitude of differences in attitudes, motives, abilities, perceptions, and, particularly, learning preferences. For example, in large, structured organizations, which attract people seeking security and prescription, the preferred style of change is likely to be non-threatening and prescriptive. At the other end of the scale, in small, rapidly changing organizations, experiental, problem-solving, open-ended approaches to learning may be appropriate.

We can analyse learning preferences by using a classification developed in attitude research. Some people prefer *cognitive* learning experiences – that is, structured, vertically linked techniques. This is often true of accountants and engineers. Other people like to learn through behaving (*behavioural* learning) – they prefer experiential learning exercises. Still others like to learn through feelings, emotions, and lateral thinking (*affective* learning). This last group are often found in creative organizations. Rarely are we limited to one mode of learning, but there are combinations which each of us prefers. For example, many of those preferring cognitive experiences become most frustrated with training officers who conduct experiental courses because they (the training officers) prefer emotive, experiental learning experiences. Not unexpectedly, the accountant, whose job concentrates on vertical interaction, may regard the training officer's antics as games for budding behavioural scientists. Conversely, the highly structured approach of such techniques as Management by Objectives may be seen to be almost irrelevant to those preferring affective or behavioural learning experiences.

These are just a few of the individual differences which affect the outcomes of change interventions. Too rarely, in my experience, do people introducing change stop to think of those individual differences. Packages of experiental exercises are thrust on people preferring cognitive, vertical exercises. It is little wonder that so many of the packages have been unsuccessful – they were designed with little regard for individual differences or member readiness.

Environmental certainty

If members' readiness is an important factor in change, then so, too, is the degree of environmental complexity and uncertainty. Readiness can be increased by environmental uncertainty and

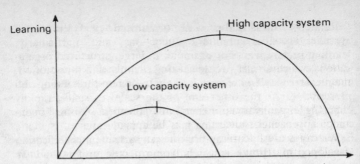

Figure 11.3 Learning in organizations related to environment. Capacity for learning is affected by conceptual skills and previous learning. If complexity and uncertainty are too great, learning declines

complexity – that is, if the market place is unpredictable, then member's learning increases to cope with that lack of predictability. However, if the uncertainty is too great, learning decreases, as Figure 11.3 shows. There appears to be a U-shaped relationship between learning and complexity/uncertainty. Similarly, as learning increases among members, a more complex/uncertain environment is necessary to optimize learning and thus to further raise members' capacity. Conversely, where environmental uncertainty is less, more manipulative behavioural techniques will be used among members to initiate changes top managers deem desirable. Most of these techniques fabricate high levels of internal uncertainty (e.g., T-groups, grid programmes).

This raises another important variable in changing organizations – the role of the consultant.

Consultants

Consultants (internal and external) give advice and/or transfer their own skills to the system. We might divide them into four broad groups:

Experts, who use their abilities for the organization – e.g., in management development, where the expert is the 'star performer', the major participant.

Advisors, who advise and recommend, rather than participate in the programme. This is seen in the external consultant's role.

Trainers, who transfer their skills to others. They lift the expertise level through experiental learning.

Observers, who are non-participant, unless requested by members.

Expert roles are least appropriate if conceptual skills are high, complexity is high, uncertainty is high, and capacity is high. Expert roles are best played by the consultant (internal or external) confronted by a conservative, protected environment, in which members have not learnt to conceptualize or to deal with complexity, but who are preoccupied with techniques rather than ends.

Just as some children learn best with certain teaching methods, depending on their capacity and independence, so too do members of organizations learn by engaging different consultants. Further, the consultant, who may be superb in the expert role, may be much less effective as the trainer, transferring conceptual skills in a non-structured, experiental learning situation. If his reputation and power depend on his expertise, then the apparent lack of opportunity to lecture in the unstructured training role may disturb him.

The strength of the 'expert' consultant is his capacity to entice, to enchant a previously sceptical group and to awaken them to organizational possibilities in a non-threatening way.

The strength of the advisor role is to point to possible answers, and even to design the process through which those answers will be found. The strength of the trainer role is the capacity to engineer an environment in which those involved find their own group answers to capacity, complexity and uncertainty. The strength of the observer is silence.

To present those different roles another way, the expert may conduct sessions on motivation, group behaviour, etc. The consultant presents a verbal or written report on the basis of this analysis. The trainer presents a problem, does not teach theory, shows members how, through their own learning, they will solve issues. The observer contributes only those inputs required by those learning. The observer role can be the most difficult to play, because it requires unspecified expertise and therefore raises doubts as to the consultant's expertise. Power relies not on qualifications but on expertise and social skills. The observer literally observes, and comments only if members of the organization ask for comment. He is neutral, passive, self-sufficient, observing in the way an artist might visit an art gallery to observe. His major contribution is to provide, if asked, his neutral assessment of the content and process of the learning occurring in the organization as members handle increased complexity and uncertainty. Unlike the expert role, which tends to be a full-time job, the observer role may occur once a year or less, as the learning of those involved will have given them the skills to plan their own interventions without help.

Harrison has argued that not only is the role to be played by the consultant important, but so too is the depth of his or her intervention into the system. In the expert role, the depth of intervention is determined unilaterally by the expert. He determines what will be tested in terms of, say, motivation. In the advisor phase, the depth is suggested by the consultant: 'The senior group should spend a weekend away together and open up with each other.' In the trainer role, the depth is determined by the members involved and their perceptions of the depth required. In the observer role, the consultant has no say in the depth of intervention, unless asked.

The capacity of members, the environmental uncertainty and complexity, and the OD consultant role are major determinants of successful change. But there are a host of other variables as well, such as the number of people involved, the formal structure, the technical system, the distribution of power, etc. There are numerous works on these influences on organization development and learning, some of which are listed at the end of this chapter.

Changing a social system like an organization occurs in a piecemeal way. Not only does members' learning differ between organizations, but it differs within organizations. What may be used in one department may not be relevant to another. A further complication is the different rates of change in role systems: some move very quickly in reaction to complexity, others are incapable of moving, and dissolve. Structure and technology change at much slower rates than do members' attitudes and perceptions. Informal relationships, in contrast, can shift substantially within hours. We are only beginning to understand the rates and direction of changes between the variables of an organization. If we add to those rates of change differences in individual learning and conceptual skills, plus environmental complexity and uncertainty, then the difficulty in planning simple models of OD is clear. Let me summarize what we know about change.

What do we know about change in organizations?

1 Change is a learning experience for individuals.
2 Change occurs after, rather than in advance of, the need for it.
3 Change is discontinuous.
4 Change is the sum of little changes experienced by individuals and groups.
5 Individuals and groups learn at different rates depending on their 'readiness', their preferred learning style (affective, cognitive, behavioural), and personality dimensions (power–influence, radical–conservative, high achiever–low achiever, etc.).
6 Effective change is initiated most frequently from the top.
7 Bottom-up change can occur, but does so rarely.
8 Planned change is a long term activity – years rather than weeks are involved.
9 Antecedents to change may be cooperation, fear, love, hate, conflict, anticipation, etc.
10 Change is easiest with successful and highly motivated individuals. (Conversely it is more difficult to introduce with the less successful and the less highly motivated.)
11 Change needs to be reinforced by (or consolidated through) structural change.
12 Interventions (structural, technical, social) may be used (by those with power) to hasten the introduction of change. Especially where size reduces the external pressures.
13 Use of interventions should be discontinuous, as learning overload is possible.
14 Planning is lacking in most official changes.
15 External consultants should be seen as planning and initiating change rather than implementing it.
16 Members and internal change agents should implement desired changes.

273

17 Technical systems and external environments introduce limitations on change.
18 Change within one group will affect others. Interdependencies are endemic to role systems.
19 Change leads to positive and negative outcomes.
20 Resistance to change is usually to the *method* of introducing change (rather than to the change itself).
21 Overcoming resistance is a process of 'selling' the intended change to those who will be affected.
22 The easiest way to introduce change is to involve those affected in designing the change (i.e., their own learning).

Conclusions

An affluent, educated work force is demanding more say in what affects its day-to-day life. The predictable outcome must be a devolution of power, such that those affected by the decision are involved in making those decisions. This does not mean the end of bureaucracy or of highly centralized structures. What it does mean is that, within these structures, most of the day-to-day decisions will be decentralized, and large congregations of individuals will be divisionalized into smaller units. Within those smaller units, work groups will gain autonomy over their work, the selection of their supervisors, and the distribution of their rewards. This sociological movement has been given the catch-all title of *industrial democracy*.

Within this broad classification we can detect two different strategies:

- The formal legal representative strategy, whereby workers are given seats on boards, supervisory councils, shop floor committees, etc.
- Direct participation at the work place in the decisions affecting one's group. Job enrichment, semi-autonomous work groups, and OD are the related strategies.

Of the two approaches, I favour the second for reasons outlined in this chapter. Unfortunately, the representative strategy does not meet the problems individuals have in their jobs; these problems may be relatively unaffected by a representative structure. Direct participation in a peer-group-centred learning experience, is the most effective way to minimize issues relating

274

to the job. As a 'catch-all' of techniques, organization development offers promise.

Yet we are just scratching the surface in understanding change in organizations. Creating a climate in which learning can occur, recognizing new power distributions, being able to handle complexity, and understanding the rates of change of variables and their interdependencies are the beginnings of a theory of change in organizations.

For additional reading

David L., and J. C. Taylor, *Design of Jobs*, Penguin, 1972.

Elliot J., *Conflict or Cooperation: The Growth of Industrial Democracy*, Kogan Page, 1978.

Emery F. E., and E. Thorsrud, *Democracy at Work – The Report of the Norwegian Industrial Democracy Program*, CCE Australian National University, Canberra, 1975.

French W. L., and C. H. Bell, *Organisation Development: Behavioural Science Interventions for Organisation Improvement*, second edn, Prentice Hall, Englewood Cliffs, New Jersey, 1978.

Hackman J. R., and J. L. Suttle (eds.), *Improving Life at Work: Behavioural Science Approaches to Organisational Change*, Goodyear, Santa Monica, California, 1977.

Harrison R., 'Choosing the depth of organisational intervention', *Journal of Applied Behavioural Science*, Vol. 6, 1970, pp. 181–202.

Harvey D. F., and D. R. Brown, *An Experimental Approach to Organizational Development*, Prentice Hall, Englewood Cliffs, New Jersey, 1976.

Herbst P. G., *Socio-Technical Design: Strategies in Multidisciplinary Research*, Tavistock, 1974.

Hunt J. W., *The Restless Organisation*, Wiley, Sydney, 1972.

Jenkins D., *Job Power*, Penguin, 1974.

Klein L., *New Forms of Work Organisation*, Cambridge University Press, 1976.

Lievegoed B. E., *The Developing Organisation*, Tavistock, 1973.

Pateman C., *Participation and Democratic Theory*, Cambridge University Press, 1970.

Poole M., *Workers' Participation in Industry*, Routledge & Kegan Paul, 1975.

Pritchard R. L., *Industrial Democracy in Australia*, CCH, Sydney, 1976.

Proceedings of International Conference on Industrial Democracy, Adelaide, CCH, Sydney, 1978.

Schon D., 'Duetero-learning in organisations: learning for increased effectiveness', *Organisation Dynamics*, Summer 1975, pp. 2–16.

Work Restructuring, TEO Department, Philips Gleoilampen Fabriken, Eindhoven, Holland.

Index

John Adair
Effective Leadership £5.99

a modern guide to developing leadership skills

The art of leadership demands a keen ability to appraise, understand and inspire both colleagues and subordinates. In this unique guide, John Adair, Britain's foremost expert on leadership training, shows how every manager can learn to lead. He draws upon numerous illustrations on leadership in action — commercial, historical and military — to pinpoint the essential requirements.

John Adair
Effective Decision-Making £4.99

Few managers devote enough attention to the *thinking* processes they should apply to their jobs. Yet long, energetic hours at work are wasted if business decisions are not logical, clear and correct. *Effective Decision-Making* is the definitive guide to the crucial managerial skill of creative *thinking*. John Adair draws on examples and case studies from business, recent history, sport and entertainment in showing how to sharpen analytical management skills.

Rosemary Stewart
The Reality of Management £5.99

This book is addressed to all managers who want to improve their effectiveness. It is also a definitive student's guide to management theory and practice. The emphasis is firmly on the areas of greatest current importance in management:

* decision-making
* leadership and development
* management and social climate
* managers and change

The whole work is updated to strengthen the advice it supplies to the managers of the eighties, and is complemented by the author's other book, *The Reality of Organizations*. Together they represent the ideal introduction to a vitally important profession.

All these books are available at your local bookshop or newsagent, or can be ordered direct from the publisher. Indicate the number of copies required and fill in the form below.

Send to: **CS Department, Pan Books Ltd., P.O. Box 40, Basingstoke, Hants.   RG21 2YT.**

or phone: 0256 469551 (Ansaphone), quoting title, author and Credit Card number.

Please enclose a remittance* to the value of the cover price plus: 60p for the first book plus 30p per copy for each additional book ordered to a maximum charge of £2.40 to cover postage and packing.

*Payment may be made in sterling by UK personal cheque, postal order, sterling draft or international money order, made payable to Pan Books Ltd.

Alternatively by Barclaycard/Access:

Card No.   ☐☐☐☐☐☐☐☐☐☐☐☐☐☐☐☐☐☐

Signature:

Applicable only in the UK and Republic of Ireland.

While every effort is made to keep prices low, it is sometimes necessary to increase prices at short notice. Pan Books reserve the right to show on covers and charge new retail prices which may differ from those advertised in the text or elsewhere.

NAME AND ADDRESS IN BLOCK LETTERS PLEASE:

....

Name ——————————————————————————

Address ——————————————————————————

——————————————————————————————

——————————————————————————————

——————————————————————————————

3/87